Nuclear World

Defence and Politics
of
Major Power

Attention Authors

Nuclear World

Defence and Politics of Major Power

Jyotirmoy Banerjee
Professor of International Relations
Jadavpur University
Kolkata

Manas Publications
(We Convert Fighters into Writers)
New Delhi-110002 (INDIA)

MANAS PUBLICATIONS
(Publishers, Distributors, Importers & Exporters)
4402/5-A, Ansari Road (Opp. HDFC Bank)
Darya Ganj, New Delhi-110 002 (INDIA)
Off. ✆ 23260783, 23265523, Res. ✆ 23842660
Fax: 011-23272766
E-mail: manaspublications@vsnl.com
www.manaspublications.in

Second Impression 2010
Rs 495/-

ISBN 81-7049-139-8

Typeset at
Manas Publications

earlier
Printed in India at
R. K. Offset Works, Delhi
and published by Mrs Suman Lata for
Manas Publications, 4402/5-A, Ansari Road
(Opp. HDFC Bank),
Darya Ganj, New Delhi-110 002 (INDIA)

Dedicated to

I dedicate this modest effort to my Ma, Didi, Pishe, friends and all my mentors.

My special gratitude to my teachers Rev.Frs. Schneider and Huart, SJ, Dr. Georg Lechner, Sri J.N.Choudhury and Prof. J.Bandyopadhyaya.

My Students over the past three decades also deserve my thanks for the enthusiasm they have often showed for International Relations, the questions they raised and the discussions they held which gave me fresh insights into a number of issues.

Inexpressible is perhaps an understatement for my wife Shyamali's infinite patience with the idiosyncracies of the scholar immersed in his work, and son Arjun's sacrifice of his precious free time to prop up the manuscript.

Senator William J.Fulbright, and the universalistic scholars Alexander Humboldt and Johann Wolfgang von Goethe forever changed my life. The prestigious Scholarships awarded in their names have directly benefited all my creative effort, including this book. I salute them all.

‹ Preface ›

The intelligent layman curious about world affairs and the issues that shaped the last half-a-century will also find it a profitable read. After all, there are better ways of nourishing the mind than watch the latest soap on the boob tube!

This book is based on a compulsory paper called *Major Powers* which I have been teaching at the M.A. and M.Phil levels in my department at Jadavpur University. The beauty of such a contemporary `paper' is that it needs constant updating. I have been doing that out of pleasure rather than a sense of mere duty. This is because otherwise the topics get stale and the enthusiasm for lecturing on them also takes a nosedive.

Nuclear World is distilled from my last thirty years of teaching and researching . I have scoured the libraries of three continents to enrich those activities. Among the various sources of help that I have received are the Fulbright Scholarship of the USA, the Alexander von Humboldt Fellowship of Germany, each of these several times, the Rockefeller Foundation of the USA, the Goethe Institute and Inter Nationes of Germany, and the University Grants Commission (UGC) of India. Among my numerous host institutions are Universities of California-Berkeley, Pennsylvania, Hawaii, Massachusetts, St.Francis college, Fort Wayne, all located with their fine libraries and experts in the USA; the German Society for Foreign Affairs and the University in Bonn; the Humboldt University in Berlin, the

Gesamtdeutsches Institut in Bonn, and the Indian Institute of Advanced Study in Shimla. A whole array of American, German and European Union agencies as well as Indian sources have been dumping tonnes of materials on me over the decades which have high research value. Add to all this the power of the Internet, and you with your 5 feet 10 inches simply disappear among the research materials which keep piling up exponentially.

My Style in this book I have tried to give wide berth to unnecessary scholasticism. In the early phase of a scholar's life sometimes the proclivity to show off with bombastic words and long-winded sentences gets the better of him. Later, maturity and experience teach the cardinal principle that a book is for reading and understanding. Better still, if the reader enjoys reading it! Why unnecessarily complicate those processes? The easier the communication flow, the more successful is the effort of the author. I have tried to keep this in view, although it's up my readers to say whether I have succeeded.

Tips to Examinees and Budding Authors Keep your language simple. Write short sentences. Use the active voice rather that the passive. Come quickly to the point. Remember the mental gymnastics in school with all those precis-writing, summary, gist and comprehension? Well, reactivate them! They are really useful for communication, especially if examiners are where your efforts is going! For new authors of articles and books, my advice would be to add a dash of humor or a personal touch here and there. That livens up an otherwise dry text and generates interest in the reader. I have recounted a few personal observations (\`eyewitness') in this book with that object in view.

My Homework But simple writing in this book does not mean less homework. As I said, thirty years of intellectual endeavor has backed up the effort. Besides English and Bengali, I use the German and Russian languages as research tools. The end-user can peek into the Notes at the end of the book to get an idea of the type of sources I have used. I must also mention Google as the most fantastic Internet search engine and strongly recommend it to the reader in case he is not yet aware of it. I have enjoyed using it, and the Net in general, for backing up my research.

Hi-tech Study Last but not least, a great companion to this book is the website I have built for students. It's called JBONLINE. According to a charming lady student of mine, it simply "carpet bombs" its users with info and links to other famous and highly respected specialied sites, worldwide, on International Relations, Strategic Studies and the German language! Well, see for youself at **http://clix.to/joyban OR http://quicksitebuilder.cnet.com/joyban/jbonline.**

I wish you, dear Reader, a thrilling and profitable read as well as surfing!

Jyotirmoy Banerjee

‹ Contents ›

‹ Glossary ›

ABM	Anti-Ballistic Missile
AEC	Atomic Energy Commission
AEGIS	Advanced Electronic Guided Interceptor System; *also* Greek for 'shield'
Agni	Short-range Indian ballistic missile
ALCM	Air-Launched Cruise Missile
Alliance 90/Greens	Alliance of East German civil rights activists and Green Party
APEC	Asia-Pacific Economic Council
APR	Asia-Pacific Region
ASBM	Air-to-Surface Ballistic Missile
ASEAN	Association of Southeast Asian Nations
ASLV	Augmented Satellite Launch Vehicle
BAM	Baikal-Amur Mainline
BARC	Bhaba Atomic Research Center
BM/C^3	Battle Management C^3
BMD	Ballistic Missile Defense
BSTS	Boost Surveillance and Tracking System
C^4	Command, Control, Communications and Computer
C^3I	Command, Control, Communications and Intelligence
C^3ICM	Command, Control, Communications and Intelligenc Counter-Measures
CBM	Confidence-Building Measure
CDU/CSU	Christlich-Demokratische Union/Christlich-Soziale Union (Christian DemocraticUnion/ Christian Social Union)

CET	Central European Time
CFSP	Common Foreign and Security Policy
CIS	Commonwealth of Independent States
CPSU	Communist Party of the Soviet Union
	Cruise Missile Subsonic, pilotless, highly accurate endo-atmospheric missile
CSCE	Conference on Security and Cooperation in Europe
CTBT	Comprehensive Test Ban Treaty
DAE	Department of Atomic Energy
Domino Theory	From Domino cards; if one state fell to communism, its neighbors would fall too, like a pushed row of upright dominoes.
Double Global Zero	No INF's for US or USSR
DRDO	Defense Research and Development Organization
DSE	(Operation) Desert Storm Equivalent
Entities List	US Commerce Dept. blacklist
ERIS	Exoatmospheric Reentry-vehicle Interceptor Subsystem
EU	European Union
F-22	F-22 'Raptor', latest hi-tech US air superiority jet fighter
FDP	Freie Demokratische Partei Deutschlands (Free Democratic Party)
FMCT	Fissile Material Cutoff Treaty
Forward-Based Systems	US forces deployed outside US, especially Europe.
FRG	Federal Republic of Germany
FSB	Federal'naya Sluzhba Bezopasnosti (Federal Security Service)
G-8	Group of Eight
GDR	German Democratic Republic
Ghauri	Pakistani ballistic missile
Ghaznavi	Pakistani ballistic missile
Glavkosmos	Soviet/Russian space agency

GLCM	Ground-Launched Cruise Missile
Google	Internet search engine
GPALS	Global Protection Against Limited Strikes
GSLV	Geosynchronous Satellite Launch Vehicle
GSQR	General Staff Qualifying Requirements
GSTS	Ground-based Surveillance and Tracking System
GUC	Gas-Ultracentrifuge
Gun barrel method	A method of exploding a N-bomb
Hatf	Pakistani ballistic missile
HEU	Highly Enriched Uranium
IAEA	International Atomic Energy Agency
ICBM	Intercontinental Ballistic Missile
IGMDP	Integrated Guided Missile Development Program
Implosion	A subcritical hollow ball involving plutonium turned critical to achieve supercompression; used for tactical nukes and as initial trigger for H-bomb.
INF	Intermediate-range Nuclear Force
IRBM	Intermediate-range Ballistic Missile
ISRO	Indian Space Research Organization
IST	Indian Standard Time
IT	Information Technology
KMT	Kuomintang
Launcher	Silo, e.g.
LIC	Low-Intensity Conflict
LRINF	Long-Range INF
M-11	Chinese ballistic missile
MAD	Mutual Assured Destruction
MEADS	Medium Extended Air Defense System
MIRV	Multiple Independently-targetable Reentry Vehicle
MRBM	Medium-Range Ballistic Missile

MTCR	Missile Technology Control Regime
Nadong	North Korean ballistic missile
NATO	North Atlantic Treaty Organization
NFC	Nuclear Fuel Complex
NMD	National Missile Defence
NPT	Nonproliferation Treaty
NRI	Non-Resident Indian
NSAB	National Security Advisory Board
NST	Nuclear and Space Talks
OECD	Organization for Economic Cooperation and Development
OOA	Out Of Area (operation)
Ostpolitik	Policy towards the East.
Overkill	Repetitive destruction.
Payload	All devices, including bomb(s), which a missile carries.
PDS	Party of Democratic Socialism
Pearl Harbor	As used here: sneak attack
Pershing	US intermediate-range West Europe-based ballistic missile.
PLA	People's Liberation Army
PNE	Peaceful Nuclear Explosion
PRC	People's Republic of China
Prithvi	Indian ballistic missile.
PSLV	Polar Satellite Launch Vehicle
Pu	Plutonium
PUREX	Plutonium-Uranium Extraction
QDR	Quadrenniel Defense Review
Quantou	PLA's elite 'fist units'.
R&D	Research and Development
RFE	Russian Far East
RMA	Revolution in Military Affairs
"Rogue State"	US term for hostile state.

SALT	Strategic Arms limitation Talks
SDI	Strategic Defense Initiative (Star Wars)
SED	Sozialistische Einheitspartei Deutschlands (former East German communist party)
Shaheen	Pakistani ballistic missile
Silicon Valley	San Francisco Bay Area, hub of IT industry
SIPE	Soldier Integrated Protection Ensemble
SLBM	Submarine-Launched Ballistic Missile
SLCM	Submarine/Sea-Launched Cruise Missile
SLV	Satellite Launch Vehicle
SNDV	Strategic Nuclear Delivery Vehicle
Solvent Extraction	A method of separating plutonium from uranium
SPD	Sozialdemokratische Partei Deutschlands (Social Democratic Party of Germany)
SQ	Significant Quotient
SRINF	Short-Range INF
SS-4, -5	Soviet SRINFs
SS-20	Soviet LRINF
SSTS	Space-based Surveillance and Tracking System
START	Strategic Arms Reduction Talks
Supercompression	A method to produce implosion in a plutonium-based bomb
THAAD	Theater High Altitude Area Defense System
Throw-Weight	Total load capacity of a missile, incl. reentry bodies, warheads and decoys
TMD	Theater Missile Defense
Trust Agency	German agency to reorganize former East Germany's economy
Two-plus-Four Talks	Two-track talks leading to German reunification
U-235	Enrichable Uranium

U-238	Natural Uranium Verification, national technical means of spying by man and machine
Warhead	bomb
WMD	Weapons of Mass Destruction
Zero Option	Reagan's proposal to eliminate all INFs

1

The Cold War

At the end of the Second World War (1939-1945) the character of international politics changed beyond recognition. Great Britain, which used to run a worldwide empire was on the verge of losing substantial chunks of it. Its victory in the war was pyrhic; it was exhausted. So was the Soviet Union. But the iron determination of its dictator Joseph Stalin kept up its massive power, especially military, which built up during its war against the mighty German forces. Traditional power like France and lesser European powers like Belgium , the Netherlands and Italy lay in ruins. The two major challengers to the global Anglo-American colonial and power system, Nazi Germany and Japan,lay deteated. Italy another challenger, had already surrendered to the Westerm Allies in 1943, with Badoglio replacing Mussolini, Only the USA emerged from the world war relatively unscathed, thanks to its geographic remoteness those days from the Old world of the Eurasian landmass.

Soviet military power on the European continent seemed to pose a threat to West Europe. While rolling Hitler's forces back, the Soviets installed communist governments in the East European contries which they liberated. Thus Poland, Rumania, Bulgaria,Hungary and in February 1948, Czechoslovakia, fell into the Soviet sphere of intluence as did the eastern half of Germany. The West became deeply suspicious that if unchecked, Moscow was going to gobble up the rest of Europe. But who could oppose the mighty Red Army? Who had the stamina left to hold up communist revolutionary ideas, backed by power? Only the USA, still fresh, energetic and blessed with abundant resources, seemed able to engage the Soviets. But having finished the war successfully, the USA was initially reverting to its traditional isolationist posture. (`Bring the boys back home') was the mood of the day in America. However, the situation changed. Goaded on by Britain, the US launched its crusade against Moscow and communism worldwide. Thus began the Cold War between the West and the Soviet bloc. This is the immediate background of the Cold War.

The Term Cold War

Suspicion, rivalry, tension and even periodic crises, which looked like a World War III was about to break out, marked the half-century following World War II. Such characteristics were not new in international relations. They had existed in the past with empires rising and vanishing with metronomic regularity. That is what History tells us. What distinguished the post-World War II scenario of rivalry from all past rivalries was the enormity of the danger which it posed to mankind, thanks to the advent of the atom bomb and the super-fast ballistic missile in the last phase of the war. They were continuously developed by the rival sides and promised the instant nirvana of entire nations! Both the USA and the USSR realized that a direct, all-out military confrontation would be suicidal. So the East-West rivalry which spread around the world stopped short of a `hot' war. Hostile postures and threats abounded. But both took great care not to fight each other directly. Hence, the `war' remained `cold'. The Berlin crises of 1948-49, 1958 and 1961, and the Cuban missile crisis of 1962 are among the example of times the examples which the East and the West came dangerously near a war, yet they pulled up from going over the brink. They preferred, however, to fight proxy wars, i.e., taking sides in various regional conflicts.

The Origins of the Cold War

It is hard to determine precisely when the Cold War started. Some scholars trace it back to the Bolshevik revolution of 1917, which spawned the first communist state in the world that firmly believed in the doom of capitalism. Bolshevik Moscow established a precarious peace in the ongoing First World War at Brest-Litovsk (3rd March 1918) with enemy Germany. But soon it turned its energy to bringing capatalism down. The European powers, some of which were capitalist or in any case conservative, and the USA were unhappy at this turn of events in Russia. Even Japan along with several of these powers, sent armed contingents to intervene in the civil war in Russia against the Marxists who were led by Lenin, Trotsky and others. The interventionists failed in their mission. But such intervention by the capatalists and conservatives only reinforced the strongly held Marxist belief that the latter would not tolerate a communist government, that they would do everything possible to root it out. In the view of some scholars, here lay the roots of the Cold War, the ideological antagonism between capitalism and communist.

The more immediate reasons for the Cold War developed during the course of the Second World War itself. Although the German and Japanese challenge gave rise to the Grand Alliance between the Western powers like the UK and the USA on the one hand and the USSR on the other, the underlying mutual suspicion between the two sides never really disppeared. The Grand Alliance was a marriage of convenience, something like the Nazi-Soviet Pact of 1939, which collapsed when Hitler unleashed his massive invasion of the USSR in June 1941, under the code name `Operation Barbarossa'. The overwhelming concern of the Western Allies and the USSR was the defeat of the Axis powers, Germany, Japan, and Italy. Hence, they agreed to bury the hatchet and co-operate. Of course, Japan remained primarily an Anglo-American headache: Stalin did not touch Japan till Hitler was finished. But even as the war progressed there emerged several issues on which the West held views different from Moscow's. These divisive issues contributed to the Cold War too. Let us examine these issues.

We have seen that, as the German forces rolled back from Russia and eastern Europe, the advancing Red Army installed friendly communist governments in the latter region. The future of Poland gradually turned into a bone of contention between the West and Moscow. Two important questions arose. *First,* would Warsaw get a democratic government after the war, or be stuck forever to the emerging Soviet bloc with a communist government? This question cropped up as early as the Tehran Conference of December 1943 among the Grand Alliance partners. And *second,* what would be the future Polish boundary with Germany? The Royalist government of Poland had fled to London. They came to be known as the London Poles and enjoyed British patronage. Moscow, on the other hand, encouraged communist Poles to take charge of the country when it was liberated from the Germans. These Soviet-backed Poles come to be known as the Lublin Poles because they had formed a committee in the city of Lublin. They enjoyed the protection of the Red Army, unlike the London Poles far away across the English Channel. To make matters worse, Nazi Propaganda Minster Joseph Goebbels had announced in 1943 that the Germans had discovered mass graves of some 10,000 Polish Army officers and civilians in the forest of Katyn near Smolensk in Russia; they had apparently been deliberately shot by the Russians. The London Poles demanded an intenational inquiry, which made Stalin furious. So, little love was lost between the London Poles and the Soviets. The later wanted their Lublin Poles to rule Poland in the future. This, of course, did not suit the British and the Americans, but they could do little about the fait accompli that the pro-Soviet Poles had already been ruling over the country since the end phase of the war.

On the second point relating to Poland, Moscow wanted to retain those regions of Poland that it had seized under the secret provisions of the Nazi-Soviet Pact of 1939. It thereby resurrected the old Curzon Line marking the Soviet-Polish border. British Prime Minister Winston Churchill hardly wanted Poland to slip under Soviet control but there was no practical way left to undo this. He was left with little choice but to agree with Stalin that Poland be compensated, at least temporarily, at the cost of Germany. The defeat of the latter was a question of time ever since the Western Allies landed in German-occupied France in June 1944 and started slowly but surely pushing the Germans back from the west. Hence, the new de facto Polish-German boundary was drawn along two rivers, the Oder and the Neisse. The question, therefore, was: would the new Oder-Neisse Line be the de jure, final German-Polish border? The British did not like the idea at all. In fact, Britain has traditionally played the role of a `balancer' in European politics. It never liked the idea of a single nation dominating the European continent. London had gone against Napoleon for this very reason, as it had against Germany in the two World Wars. This time it was Soviet power which seemed to threaten the whole of Europe, much to the distaste of the British Prime Minister. Indeed, when US President Harry S. Truman, who had succeeded Roosevelt following the latter's death in 1945, sent his envoy Harry Hopkins to Moscow in May 1945 to hold frank talks, `Uncle Joe' (Joseph Stalin) aired his suspicion that the British wanted to set up Poland as part of a cordon sanitaire to surround the USSR.

These problems relating to the future of Poland came up again during the Yalta (or Crimea) Conference in the USSR in February 1945. The big three Allied Powers met there. The Soviets were about to transfer the administration of Poland, including the ex-German territories east of the Oder-Neisse Line, to their proteges. Later, at the Potsdam conference during July-August that year, the West finally agreed with the USSR to treat the Oder-Neisse Line as the de facto Polish-German border. Its final legal status would be decided at a future peace treaty with a future German government. In other words, the UK and the USA resigned themselves to the accomplished fact that Oder-Neisse had indeed become the German-Polish border in practice; under the circumstance, the best they could do for Western interests was to keep the question legally open and shelve the issue.

Besides these differences which arose even before the war was over, *Western delay in opening the second front* against Germany made the Russians even more suspicious. The USSR, fighting the mighty German war machine since June 1941, kept on pleading to the West to attack the Germans from the west in occupied France so that pressure on the USSR would lessen. This was the idea of the second front. But Britain and the USA continued to maintain that they were not yet ready to do so. They said they were doing their homework though, i.e. building up sufficient tonnage, including shipping, for a cross-Channel invasion force in south England. Everybody knew that landing in German-occupied Europe would not be a cakewalk, that the Germans would fight back tooth and nail. So it was not before the first week of June 1944 that the Supreme Commander of the West, General Dwight D. Disenhower (later US President), gave the green signal. The cross-Channel invasion in the Normandy coast of occupied France ultimately took place in the face of dogged German military opposition. But Stalin highly resented this delay in opening the second front. In the Soviet view, the West deliberately dragged its feet so that Germany and Russia bled each other and weakened themselves. This would ease Anglo-American domination over a bloodied and weakened Europe Even though the Soviet Union started receiving military aid from the USA under the latter's Lend-Lease Act, it remained convinced of the West's dirty policy of delay in opening the second front.[1]

With these preliminary considerations, let us now continue into the thick of the remarkable history of the Cold War, which shaped all international relations for half-a-century and impacted the lives of countless individuals like you and me worldwide. A good example, from my Calcutta perspective, were the *two* American centers which operated in my native city till the Soviet Union vanished. Even the

Indian capital, New Delhi, had one center; so did Mumbai and Chennai. Why two for Calcutta? Well, the former American director of one them informed me that Calcutta had the largest academic community among all the metros. So the brains of the intelligentsia, and hence their views, had to be influenced to start loving America rather than the USSR, which had its own center of course! Regular seminars and informal meetings with US academics, sometimes with entertainment thrown in, were the regular features of these two centers. With the Cold War over these features have largely disappeared. Today's targets and configuration of the sole center in Calcutta are different. But to get back on track.

Waging The Cold War

The Cold War gathered momentum. Differences widened; suspicions, never totally absent, deepened.

Reparation from a defeated Germany became another bone of contention. At Yalta, Moscow insisted on reparation in kind. There should be bulk withdrawal of German assets. In addition, annual goods deliveries were to be imposed upon the Germans. The Soviets wished $20 billion as compensation, half of which should go to them. Please note that the Russians were not unjustified in demanding such a huge share for themselves. The industrially developed part of the USSR was its European part, and it had been devastated by Hitler's Blitzkrieg or lightning warfare. The USSR suffered the maximum number of casualties among all the nations engaged in the war, with twenty million dead. However, the Western Allies were reluctant to milk Germany dry. They had learnt from a similar situation regarding reparation after the First World War. A broke Germany had to be kept alive by their money! The war-debt question had lingered for long; 'Uncle Sam' had tired of being dubbed 'Uncle Shylock' by the European press. And Germany's over-dependence on the West to borrow of them in order to pay them back in reparation had led to a vicious circle. It proved fatal once the

Wall Street in New York crashed in 1929. That had led to a chain reaction. The economic collapse in the West had directly caused the rise of the Nazi Party in Germany under Hitler, who promised economic recovery to the teeming unemployed of his country. So, disagreement on the reparation issue persisted.

Ultimately, a compromise was reached. It was agreed, in broad terms, that Moscow would receive 15% of "surplus" industries from the western zones of occupation in Germany, in exchange for food and other products from the Soviet zone. Over and above that, 10% of the surplus industry from the western zones were to be shifted to the USSR at no cost to the latter; and Moscow would have 100% control over the industries lying in its own zone. Suffice it to note at this point that a defeated Germany was to be divided into four zones of occupation, as also its capital, Berlin, controlled by the four victorious powers, of which there is more later.

Disagreement also developed on the question of *the future of the East European states*, which came under Soviet domination. The West, especially the USA, insisted on holding 'free and fair' elections in those states to promote the cause of democracy. Moscow also agreed with the need for 'democracy', but its understanding of the word obviously varied from that of the West. The Soviets believed in proletarian dictatorship as a supreme example of true democracy; in their view, the multi-party system of the West and its methods of operation were a sham, just false pretension of the 'bourgeois' government where the capitalists were real wielders of power. While they agreed to hold elections and allow Western observers, the Soviets rejected the US demand that the respective US ambassadors to the East European countries be allowed to supervise the actual process of elections. Let us note here that Moscow's resolve to cling on to its newly created eastern European sphere of influence was fully understandable. Invasions have usually flown on an east-west axis in the continent of Europe. Russia suffered twice at the hands of the Germans in the 20th century, not to speak of Napoleon's invasion of the country earlier. So, Stalin was determined to strengthen and consolidate an East European cordon sanitaire against any future juggernaut from the West. This was the fulcrum of his policy. He ensured that only pro-Soviet communist governments were well entrenched in power in East Europe.[2] The ideological cement would bond best with Moscow's national interest.

Another bone of contention was *the question of membership of the United Nations Organization*, which came into being on 24 October 1945. The US objected to the membership of several East European countries like Finland, Hungary, Rumania and Bulgaria, which had collaborated with Nazi Germany and had been liberated by the Red Army. Even though they now had completely different governments, that did not cut ice with the Americans. The Soviet reply was that if that be so, then Italy, with which the West was hobnobbing after Mussolini's fall in 1943, should also be left out since it had an unbeatable record of fascism and a far closer collaboration with Hitler. Further, at the Dumbarton Oaks Conference of September-October 1944, which laid the groundwork for the UN, the Soviets wanted their 16 republics to become members of the new organization with voting rights for each. The West opposed it. They finally settled for the membership of just two besides the USSR itself, the Ukraine and Byelorussia, at the Yalta Conference of February 1945.

At the Tehran (December 1943) and Yalta Conferences, blood-curdling plans were considered for the dismemberment and permanent weakening of Germany, once the latter was defeated. For example, US plans like the Morgenthau Plan and a military document called JCS 1067, both dreamed up in 1944, and the Yalta Declaration of 12 February 1945, would turn industrialised Germany into a peaceful, sheep-grazing nation, with its famous Ruhr coal mines destroyed and its heavy industry, the backbone of military power, permanently removed. However, at the

Potsdam Conference of July-August 1945, i.e. immediately after the war in Europe had ended, cooler heads prevailed. The victors discarded the idea of dismembering Germany. A major reason was that the German economy was symbiotically linked to those of France, Holland and other countries. An economically weak Germany would impact negatively on the economies of these countries. German coal industry, for example, was essential to run the industries of West Europe.

The Allies agreed to go ahead with the London Protocol of 12 September 1944, and a Supplementary Agreement, which had forwarded the idea of splitting the country into zones of occupation. Each of the Allies would receive a zone. The purpose of creating these zones was not the annexation of German territory but its occupation. The primary aim of occupation was to root out Nazism and 're-educate' the Germans to behave! The British, in a show of solidarity, extended the courtesy to France and gave the latter a piece of the German zone from their own share. Stalin was sarcastic about Paris receiving a zone at all since all it had contributed to the war effort was to surrender to Germany in summer 1940 and, under Marshal Petain, even collaborate with the Third Reich. As a symbol of their decisive victory, each of the four Allies helped itself to a slice of the German Empire's capital, Berlin, which was similarly split into four zones of occupation. The geographical location of Berlin, which was deep within the Soviet zone, subsequently introduced much headache in the West, which had to maintain their three zones in the western part of the city. Their lines of communication ran through the Soviet zone. At Potsdam the four powers decided that, despite the different zones of occupation, Germany would be treated as a single economic unit. This would allow traditional trade, commerce and other exchanges that normally go on within a country, to continue. But this was not to be. Mutual suspicion between the Soviets and the three Western powers soon turned the line along the River Elbe in central Germany, which separated the three Western zones from the Soviet, into a deep political divide. It became, in fact, the most important segment of what Churchill termed as the "iron curtain". The Berlin-based Allied Control Council, which was supposed to jointly administer vanquished Germany, became deadlocked. The abrupt US termination on 12 May 1945 of *the lend-lease supplies* to the USSR added further to Soviet bitterness. Meanwhile, other points of irritation developed with regard to *the Soviet role in Iran, Turkey and Greece*.

In wartime, the British maintained their sphere of influence in the southern half of Iran while the Soviets deployed their troops in the northern part. This arrangement was partly to forestall the German Army Group South, which had entered the Caucasus, from pouring into Iran and then to the Middle East; a grand Cannae or meeting up with Rommel's forces heading across north Africa to the British lifeline of the Suez Canal would be fatal to the West. But after the war was over, the Red Army lingered on in Iran, thereby breaking an agreement on troop withdrawal from that country by both Moscow and London. Stalin's excuse was that he wanted to protect the Baku oilfields by prolonging the deployment of his forces. But things went further than that. Two republics sprang up in northern Iran under the benevolent gaze of the Red Army. They declared themselves independent. These were the Azerbaijani and Kurdish republics, which oriented themselves to Moscow. The latter also demanded of Tehran that joint companies be set up to exploit Iranian oil, with the Soviets holding the majority share. However, pressure by the UK and the USA in March 1946 made Moscow withdraw its troops from Iran. Tehran promptly liquidated the two rebel republics.

Besides Iran, Stalin's gaze also fell upon Turkey. He demanded the return of the districts of Ardahan and Kars, which he said had belonged to Russia between 1878 and the Treaty of Brest-Litovsk of 1918. Not far from Turkey lay Greece, recently liberated from German rule and surrounded by communist states. From 1946 guerrillas began harassing government troops there. They sought and found sanctuaries in neighboring communist Yugoslavia, Albania and Bulgaria. Although Moscow was not directly involved here, and not all who fought the Greek dictatorship were communist, the Cold War mindset of the West saw Soviet hand there, too.

It is against such atmospherics that the speech by Winston Churchill at Fulton, Missouri on 5 March 1946 assumes great importance, even though the arch colonizer had lost Prime Ministership in the previous year. Churchill warned the American audience that the UK could no longer be expected to continue to act as the world's policeman. In the face of the perceived danger posed by an expansionist Soviet policy and the threats posed to West Europe by the Red Army, it was now up to the USA to shoulder the defense of the so-called free world. An "iron curtain" had fallen across Europe, he quipped, thereby making that phrase subsequently famous. Next year, in February, the British government confirmed Churchill's announcement. London informed Washington that it was no longer in a position to continue to help Greece and Turkey against Soviet pressure. President Truman, who was tougher on the Soviets than his late predecessor Franklin D. Roosevelt, responded positively. On 12 March 1947 he promised US help to nations, which were threatened by armed minorities. The immediate context was, of course, trouble with Greece and Turkey, but the 'Truman Doctrine' had implications for US commitments, reaching far beyond those two nations. He did not mention the USSR directly but criticized communism openly. Truman thereby signaled, in effect, that the USA was replacing Britain as the global policeman and would engage Soviet 'aggression' worldwide. In the same year came the economic complement to the Truman Doctrine, i.e., the Marshall Plan or the European Recovery Program. The USA declared that it was willing to provide aid to the European nations to recover from the devastation of the war and rebuild their economy. Moscow shooed away its allies in East

Europe from the great American temptation. Washington must have heaved a sigh of relief that there were no communist takers. So it was the West European nations that fully made use of the plan. Paradoxically, the most successful among them turned out to be West Germany, which created the 'German economic miracle.' While in 1945 the country lay in ruins, by 1955 it was already giving aid to developing countries like India, thanks to the Marshall Plan and characteristic German diligence. The French say that while other nations work in order to live, the Germans live in order to work!

In mid-1947, i.e. a few months after the proclamation of the Truman Doctrine, a US diplomat posted in Moscow published an article entitled "The Sources of Soviet Conduct" in *Foreign Affairs*. It was signed "X" and came to be better known in International Relations parlance as the X-article. The article was an elaboration of the Long Telegram (it was really too long for a telegram!), which he had sent to Washington a year earlier. Its central thesis was that the Marxist ideology fuelled Soviet expansionism, and that the only way to stop Soviet expansion worldwide was to put a ring of "containment" around it. Indefinite frustration at not being able to expand any longer would mellow down the Soviet ideological zeal. This was George F. Kennan's Containment Policy. Along with the Truman Doctrine, it revolutionized US foreign policy. The US abandoned its traditional isolationism and went all out for *peacetime commitments* around the world to stop the spread of communism.[3] One can easily perceive a line leading straight from one commitment to another till the anti-climax of the Vietnam War, which ended in 1973 and forced a rethinking.

The extreme polarization between the East and the West could further be seen in *the Zhdanov thesis*. Andrei Zhdanov was Stalin's ideologue who put forward his two-camp thesis in 1947 at the Cominform Congress. This forum was a resurrected but diluted version of the earlier Communist International (Comintern), the mission of which was to encourage revolutions throughout the world. As Zhdanov saw it, thereby also reflecting Stalin's view, the world had come to be divided into two antagonistic hostile camps, one led by the "peace-loving," socialist USSR, and the other led by the "aggressive," capitalist USA. There was no sitting on the fence. India's nonalignment, for instance, already proclaimed by Jawaharlal Nehru before the country gained independence that year, was therefore highly suspect. Interestingly, a mirror-image situation started dominating the American domestic political scenario. The influential Senator *McCarthy's* Un-American Activities Committee started a witch-hunt in the USA, which gathered momentum in the early 1950s. Anyone not matching his definition of a true American or who had even the slightest socialistic sympathies was automatically suspect. Intellectuals in the USA were harassed as a result, among whom was even the father of the US atom bomb, Robert Oppenheimer!

Meanwhile in the 1940s the three Western zones in Germany gradually merged. Under the US initiative, a new currency was introduced in all three in 1948 called the Deutsche Mark or DM, which replaced the old Reichsmark, which had become highly devalued. The Soviets refused to allow the DM into their zone and responded by a *blockade of West Berlin* (where the three Western zones of the city lay). Thus came the Berlin crisis, which lasted nearly a year (1948-49). Massive airlifts of supplies by the three Western Allies to West Berlin were organized to substitute for the blocked land transport. Even to this day, a visitor to Berlin can see the three-arch memorial to this Herculean effort to feed, clothe and keep warm half a city from the air for almost a year. In the middle of the blockade the West Europeans, who felt threatened by the Soviet action, came together to form the North Atlantic Treaty Organization or NATO in April 1949. The creation of this West European collective security organization under US leadership *added further fuel* to the ongoing Cold War. Moscow saw NATO as a threat to the security of its own bloc. West Germany entered NATO in 1955 to contribute 12 divisions, the organization's largest military contingent. The Soviets immediately responded by creating the Warsaw Pact that very year. The pact then became the Moscow-led East European collective security organization facing NATO across the Elbe River in central Germany.

The Cold War speeded up *the arms race*. In 1949 the USSR broke the US monopoly in atomic bombs by successfully testing its own. In 1952 the US tested the first hydrogen bomb in the Bikini atoll in the Pacific; the Soviets caught up next year, partly at least due to successful espionage. Ever since, both the USA and the USSR continued to build ever more powerful bombs, ballistic missiles, bombers and warships, including missile-carrying submarines, designed to destroy each other's territory. In October 1957 the Soviets launched the first man-made satellite into space, the Sputnik I. This opened up a space race. Most of the initial firsts in space henceforth came, not from the USA, which was desperately trying to catch up, but from the USSR (the first man in space, Yuri Gagarin, 1961, first woman, Valentina Tereshkova soon thereafter, and so on), until America landed the first man on the moon, Neil Armstrong, in 1969.

Meanwhile, a state was founded comprising the three Western zones of occupied Germany, which started functioning from September 1949. It was called the Federal Republic of Germany (FRG). Its 'temporary' capital was located in Bonn on the charming River Rhine. Moscow immediately responded by creating its own German state next month called the German Democratic Republic (GDR). These two German states had limited sovereignty and were allowed to rule at the pleasure of the occupying powers. Berlin already had a special Four-Power status; the control of the two German states over east or west Berlin was severely restricted, even though the GDR declared its capital to be in East Berlin.

Yet another highly significant event took place in October 1949. *China* under Mao Zedong became communist. The ruling Kuomintang government fled the mainland and established itself in the offshore island of Taiwan (formerly known by its Portuguese name of Formosa). The 'loss' of such a huge and important chunk of Asian territory as China to communism, which would only strengthen the Soviet hand and correspondingly weaken that of the West, was particularly shocking to the USA. The latter had long enjoyed business relations with China and carried out extensive missionary activities there; all this would have to wind up now. The communization of China also meant that the Cold War was no longer confined to Europe; it also spread to Asia. This factor, along with the Soviet possession of the atom bomb, gave a new and broader dimension to the Cold War and lent special urgency to the USA's containment policy. Next year, the Korean War (1950-53) led to a dangerous situation where US and communist Chinese troops were killing each other.

The Berlin Crises

We have already seen the blockade of Berlin by the Soviets during 1948-49. Divided Berlin, along with divided Germany, remained one of the most dangerous regions during the entire period of the Cold War because NATO and Warsaw Pact forces directly faced each other there, backed by atomic power on either side. Germany, lying astride the great East-West divide, also became a fertile ground for espionage activities of the two antagonistic blocs, which did little to mitigate mutual suspicion. In November 1958 Soviet communist party chief Nikita S. Khrushchev gave an ultimatum to the West to pull out of West Berlin. The Western presence in the middle of communist GDR territory, and the consequent use of transport and communication lines with the Western zones running through the GDR, were a great source of inconvenience to Moscow and East Berlin. The three Western powers, however, refused to budge, even though Khrushchev had offered to let the UN administer a neutralized West Berlin. The 'ultimatum' created a lot of tension. However, it was allowed to lapse. The Soviets did not take any drastic action. Next year the atmospherics improved visibly. The Soviet leader was invited to visit the USA, which he did. He held talks with then US President Dwight D. Eisenhower, mostly in the relaxed environment of Camp David, the US Presidential retreat. Hollywood also entertained him. A so-called 'Camp David spirit' seemed to have developed between the two rivals. The US tried to impress the Soviet leader with its high standard of living and the magnitude of its production. Khrushchev in turn boasted that the future belonged to socialism and the Soviet Union would overtake the USA before long. However, the Camp David bonhomie did not last long. On 1 May 1960 a high-flying US spy plane, the U-2, was shot down over Soviet territory and its pilot, Francis Gary Powers, captured. The US at first denied espionage but later admitted it. Moscow gleefully gave full publicity to the incident and instituted an international panel of judges to try Powers. Khrushchev also demanded an apology from Eisenhower. The latter refused, stating that the USA had to know what was going on behind the iron curtain so as to be ready for another Pearl Harbor (the sneak Japanese attack in December 1941 on the US naval base in the Pacific island of Oahu in Hawaii). Thereupon the boisterous Soviet leader stomped out of the Paris summit in mid-May and wrecked it.

Yet another Berlin crisis developed in August 1961, when the East Germans erected a wall separating East Berlin from its western part. This measure was felt necessary to stem the tide of refugees fleeing the GDR for the West in search of better living conditions and political freedom. The erection of the wall right under the nose of the three Western powers present in West Berlin was seen as a great provocation effected by the Soviet side. US and Soviet tanks faced each other across streets like the Friedrichstrasse; the slightest provocation from either side might set off a chain reaction leading to a Third World War. Fortunately, both sides kept their cool. Over the following years many East Germans lost their lives at the wall while trying to flee. It was in 1989 that drastically changed circumstances in Europe led to the fall of the notorious Berlin Wall, and that happened literally.

The Korean War

Here are the main facts of the Korean War in a nutshell. After the surrender of Germany on 8 May 1945, Moscow kept its promise to the USA and entered the war against Japan in Asia. In the process of rolling back the Japanese army, the Soviet forces liberated the northern part of the Korean peninsula while the US forces captured the south. An informal line along the 38 degree north latitude divided the two halves. The rest of the story was a repetition of the fate of Germany and Vietnam. North Korea settled for a communist government under Soviet influence, while South Korea obtained a pro-US government. All three countries were divided along ideological lines, which were reinforced by the ongoing Cold War. Needless to say, there was tension and irritation along the 38th parallel. It is not clear who started it first, but in mid-1950 the North Korean forces pushed into the South violating the informal border. The South turned to the USA. Washington mobilized the UN under a General Assembly move called the Uniting for Peace Resolutions. With that approval, the US now led an international UN force to confront the North Koreans. China, only recently turned communist and the immediate northern neighbor of North Korea, sensed danger. It did not want a fellow communist country, and immediate neighbor, to slip under the Western 'imperialists'. So, it sent 'volunteers' —actually regular armed forces — to fight by the side of the North Koreans, just as the US troops were coming to the aid of the relatively weak South Korean forces. This was 'hot' war where capitalist and communist troops were shooting at each other. Despite the USA's nuclear might, the communists put up a good fight for three years. Moscow did not send troops but was quite naturally on the side of the communist powers. Ultimately, the stalemate in the war led to a truce. It basically continues till this day, with mutual suspicion on either side of the border still lingering far above zero. India, incidentally, played a truly nonaligned role in this war by passing on communist China's messages to the USA and sending an ambulance corps to the battle zone.

Berlin and Korea, hence, were among the more significant factors which kept fuelling the Cold War. Following Truman's promise to come to the aid, both economic and military, of legitimate governments threatened by armed minorities (read communists!), and Kennan's Containment Policy, the US started a crusade against communism, which was securely ensconced in the huge landmasses of the USSR and neighboring China and their respective neighbors in East Europe, and in North Vietnam and North Korea. The US gathered a series of bilateral and multilateral security treaties, mostly with nations located along the periphery of the communist states: NATO in April 1949, ANZUS (Australia, New Zealand and US) in September 1951, the Philippine Treaty in August 1951, the South Korean Treaty in October 1953, SEATO (Southeast Asia Treaty Organization) in September 1954, the Formosa Treaty in December 1954, CENTO (Central Treaty Organization) also in the mid-1950's, where the USA, however, took an observer's role, the Japanese Treaty in January 1960, etc. Needless to add, each of these treaties and lesser versions like 'executive agreements', like the USA reached with Pakistan in the 1950's, only reinforced the East-West Cold War mindset.

Before concluding this discussion of the origins and the initial development of the Cold War, let us note that the massive literature on the subject can be divided into two schools of thought, the 'traditionalist' and the 'revisionist'. In the former school belong Elliot Goodman (*The Soviet Design For a World State*), Robert Strausz-Hupe (co-author of *Protracted Conflict*), Bertram Wolfe, (*Communist Totalitarianism*), and many others. They tend to blame the USSR squarely for the Cold War. The revisionists, on the other hand, apportion some blame also to the USA and other factors. Among them are D. F. Fleming (*The Cold War and Its Origins*), Marshall D. Shulman (*Stalin's Foreign Policy Reappraised*), John Lukacs (*New History of the Cold War*), Frederick L. Schuman (*The Cold War*) and Robert G. Kaiser (*Cold Winter, Cold War*). John Spanier's essay, "The Choices We did Not Have" (in Charles Gati ed., *Caging the Bear: Containment and the Cold War*) is a rebuff to the revisionists. Louis J. Halle, however, takes the view that the Cold War simply ran a historic course, which it was kind of predestined to run. So neither side can really be blamed.[3] These theories have been overtaken by dramatic turn of events today. But one thing stands certain. In the immediate post-World War II situation, given that two superpowers emerged, which were radically divided by antagonistic ideologies, the Cold War seemed inevitable.

Readings

1. D. F. Fleming, *The Cold War and Its Origins*, 2 vols., George Allen & Unwin, London, 1961.
2. Walter Lefeber, *America, Russia, and the Cold War*, John Wiley & Sons, New York, 1967.
3. Louis J. Halle, *The Cold War as History*, Chatto & Windus, London, 1967.
4. Adam B. Ulam, *Expansion and Coexistence. The History of Soviet Foreign Policy, 1917-67*, Secker & Warburg, London, 1968.
5. Thomas H. Etzold, John Lewis Gaddis (eds.), *Containment. Documents on American Policy and Strategy. 1945-1950*, Columbia Univ., NewYork, 1978.
6. Philip E. Mosely, *The Kremlin and World Politics*. Studies in Soviet Policy and Action, Vintage, New York, 1960.
7. John Mason, *The Cold War. 1945-1991*, Routledge, Andover, Hants, 1996.

8. Lucius D. Clay, *Decision in Germany*, Doubleday & Co., Garden City, New York, 1950.

9. John Mander, *Berlin. Hostage for the West*, Penguin, Harmondsworth, 1962.

10. Walter R. Sharp, Grayson Kirk, *Contemporary International Politics*, 2 vols., US Armed Forces Institute, Washington, 1944 (provides insights into wartime US world view).

Notes

1. See *The Tehran, Yalta & Potsdam Conferences*, Progress, Moscow, 1969, pp. 7-53. On the Katyn incident, Louis P. Lochner (ed.), *The Goebbels Diaries*, Popular Library, New York, 1948, p. 365.
2. An early compendium of essays on Soviet policy in Philip E. Mosely, *The Kremlin and World Politics*, Vintage, New York, 1960. See Readings for more references.
3. Loius J. Halle, *The Cold War as History*, Chatto and Windus, London, 1967, p. 113.

2

The Cuban Missile Crisis

(October 1962)

Perhaps the biggest confrontation between the two superpowers during the Cold War was the Cuban missile crisis. It was virtually an eyeball-to-eyeball encounter. American authors draw satisfaction from the fact that the Soviets blinked first! But that happened not before the world was brought to the brink of a nuclear holocaust for thirteen days. A diary maintained by the then US Attorney-General Robert Kennedy, President John F. Kennedy's brother, gives fascinating insights into the crisis.[1]

Background

In 1959 Fidel Castro led a successful uprising against the Cuban dictator Batista and ousted him from power. Castro was initially not a communist but surely a nationalist. The change of power in Havana alarmed the USA, which had maintained good relations with the deposed dictator. Washington felt irritated at the revolution and cut off sugar imports from the Caribbean island located just about 90 miles away from the coast of Florida. Now this was a serious blow to the Cuban economy; its cash crop was sugar, the bulk of which it used to sell to its rich, giant neighbor to earn precious foreign exchange. Cuba's plight provided a golden opportunity to Moscow. The USSR began to cultivate Castro and promised various kinds of aid to keep the island republic afloat. The growing Moscow-Havana ties at the turn of the 1960s increased US suspicion that the Soviets were out to fish in the troubled waters right next door. After the brief spell of the 'Camp David spirit', the U-2 incident of 1960 found Superpower relations once again at their 'normal' low. We have already seen that in Chapter One. The Soviets reaped handsome propaganda dividends against Eisenhower and the USA from that incident. Then came elections in the USA. Kennedy replaced Eisenhower in 1961.

As soon as Kennedy started his work as President, the Central Intelligence Agency (CIA) tabled a proposal that it had developed under the previous administration. It related to an invasion of Castro's Cuba by Florida-based anti-Castro Cuban refugees. The US would provide the arms but commit no troops and would pretend to be uninvolved. Kennedy okayed the plan that was not really his. There took place during 17-22 April that year the Bay of Pigs incident. The CIA-trained anti-Castro forces landed in that bay in Cuba. But they were promptly defeated and rounded up by Castro's forces. Though US forces were invisible, even a child could guess who was behind the attempted coup and where these men had come from. A failure so early into his office put Kennedy to shame. The victory of Castro, by now a Soviet friend, was perceived as an indirect victory for the USSR. Moscow issued warnings that it stood firmly by Havana. In June Kennedy and Khrushchev met in Vienna. The latter revived the Soviet differences with the West over Berlin and other issues. It was far from being a pleasant summit. Moscow also stepped up supplying what it termed as 'defensive weapons' to Havana. Young Kennedy probably itched to get even with Khrushchev. His 'chance' came soon enough, in October 1962.

Soviet Missiles in Cuba

French intelligence tipped off CIA Director John McCone that the Soviets might be secretly deploying strategic missiles in Cuba. The CIA watched carefully the large volume of Soviet shipments to the island republic. The suspicion was not confined to the CIA headquarters in Langley alone. Speculation over the nature and meaning of Soviet shipments generated a "heated domestic debate"[2] in the USA in 1962. On 4 and 13 September Kennedy announced, in response to the debate, that there was no evidence of the presence of offensive Soviet missiles in Cuba. Were such missiles to be discovered, however, he warned, "the gravest" consequences would follow. [3] The Soviet government also responded by denying the supply of strategic offensive missiles to Cuba, for instance, on 11 September. On 26 September the US Congress resolved to prevent Cuba from "endangering" US security. On October 13 the Soviet Ambassador in Washington, Dobrynin, again assured the US that there was no question of Soviet strategic missiles in Cuba. The very next day a high-flying US reconnaissance U-2 aircraft photographed installations in Cuba in the course of a routine overflight. Upon later analysis these turned out to be Soviet-built strategic missile bases, very typically trapezoid in structure. On the morning of 16 October Kennedy came to know. He then called his advisors together and asked what options he had to respond to this perceived Soviet challenge. The options ranged from "do nothing" to "surgical air strike" to destroy the missile bases. On 20 October, a Saturday, after careful deliberation Kennedy settled for a middle path, a naval blockade of Cuba. He announced the latter move to the world two days later and insisted that the missiles already in Cuba must be promptly removed. To avoid problems under International Law the blockade was euphemistically termed "quarantine".

Eyewitness: This author had the opportunity to board the Forrestal-class aircraft carrier called *USS Independence* (CV-62), which had *led the blockade,* in San Francisco Bay in summer 1989. Though old now, it is incidentally still active in the Pacific region as part of the US Seventh Fleet.

Although there are more modern carriers now in service with the US Navy like the *Nimitz*-class, the following data on the *Independence* will give you an idea of the awesome power of a carrier. There are 5,000 crew aboard the 78,000-ton (fully-loaded displacement) ship. There are many departments like air units, deck crew, maintenance, etc. Even a chapel and a post office operate aboard! It is impossible for any one crew member to know the rest of the 4,999 people well. So each unit wears color-coded uniforms for easy recognition. Among the aircraft it how operates are Phantoms, Corsair, Intruder, E2-C Hawkeye AWACS (for early warning and electronic warfare) with their huge radome or dish on top, helicopters, etc. The single building, called the island, is on the starboard (right) side. The 'air boss' controls all flight operations from there. The rest of the huge deck, the size of several football fields, serves as flight deck for aircraft. The carrier's electricity consumption could easily meet the consumption of a small town in the USA!

There followed six days of intense international crisis when World War III seemed almost imminent. On 23 October Khrushchev condemned the US blockade as sheer piracy. The crisis gathered momentum when it was reported that Soviet merchant ships and six submarines were heading for the US navy-patrolled quarantine line. US anti-submarine warfare (ASW) units made the Soviet submarines surface even as Washington and Moscow were talking to each other through official and private channels to defuse the high tension. Khrushchev wrote a relatively soft and highly emotional letter to Kennedy on 26 October, which promised that he would withdraw the missiles if the US gave an assurance not to invade Cuba. But his letter next day, again addressed to Kennedy, had a tougher tone and added that the 15 US Jupiter missiles in Turkey must also be removed in exchange![4] The US side selectively listened to Moscow's counter-demands, extended a secret pledge not to invade the island but chose to ignore the October 27 letter (the Soviet demand on the Jupiters). However, the US secretly assured the Soviets that it would remove its Jupiters after the Soviets had removed their missiles from Cuba. Meanwhile Washington went ahead with the mobilization of air, sea and land forces in Florida to signal Moscow that an invasion of Cuba would be imminent if the Soviets failed to agree on withdrawal by the deadline of 28 October. On that day, much to the relief of the world, Khrushchev finally agreed to withdraw the offensive missiles from Cuba. These are the bare facts of the crisis in a nutshell. A number of puzzles related to the episode were highlighted in Graham T. Allison's excellent study of the crisis.[5]

Reasons for the Crisis

Why did the Soviets place the missiles in Cuba, right next door to the USA? The immediate reason is known now. During a visit to Bulgaria, then Soviet Defense Minister Malinovsky pointed out to Khrushchev that, across the Black Sea in Turkey, there were US missiles pointed at the USSR. Khrushchev then wondered aloud to his companion why could not Moscow do the same to the US, i.e. deploy missiles near it? It was then that Cuba came up as a good site. The Soviets overcame Castro's initial hesitation. The missiles would serve as a *defense of Cuba* but there must have been *other reasons* behind the secret Soviet move. These, however, mostly lie in the realm of informed speculation.

First, the Soviets probably wanted to create a strong bargaining chip regarding Berlin. They could ask the West to agree to their proposals on Germany—e.g., pull out of West Berlin and recognize the GDR—by using their missiles as a bargaining counter. *Second*, they would want the US missiles to be removed from Turkey; this they achieved. *Third*, strategic missiles in Cuba would test US nerves. If the US attacked Cuba to remove the latter, it would create an uproar all over Latin America and contribute to the unpopularity of the USA. US domestic opinion could also turn against the government. Moscow could then take advantage of a politically divided US and make bold moves in Berlin. *Fourth*, future Bay of Pigs would not happen; the US would have to consider Cuban-Soviet strategic retaliation. *Fifth*, the US-Soviet strategic balance would be tipped in Moscow's favor once the US accepted the deployment of the missiles as an accomplished fact. Indeed, missile early warning time would be cut down to a matter of minutes for the USA, given the proximity of Cuba. The US-Canadian radar network for half-an-hour of early warning of a Soviet missile attack was based on the assumption that hostile missiles would come hurtling over the North Pole. The US was little prepared for a ballistic missile attack from the southeast instead! *Sixth*, it would be more efficient, and cheaper, for Moscow to rely on the medium-range and intermediate-range ballistic missiles (MRBMs and IRBMs) in Cuba than on their cumbersome intercontinental ballistic missiles (ICBMs) based in the USSR. The latter were not accurate and took a long time to be liquid-fuelled and readied. *Finally*, Moscow also probably relied on the perceived 'missile gap', which was the US anxiety of the late 1950s that the USSR was far stronger in ballistic missiles.

The Conseqences Of The Crisis

An offshoot of the crisis was that *'crisis management'* became a popular term. Kennedy projected himself to the outside world as a cool-headed crisis manager who steadily and surely reached his goal in a highly uncertain, even dangerous, environment. Actually, his brother confesses that the President was shaking in his boots! More important consequences were as follows. *The fall of Khrushchev* in 1964 was at least partly due to his retreat over Cuba. The Soviet withdrawal of their missiles widened *the Sino-Soviet conflict*, which was beginning to show from the 1960s. Beijing thought that Moscow's act was most cowardly; it was not becoming of the leader of the socialist bloc to retreat in the face of American threat. Next, the US by uncompromisingly demanding Soviet missile pullout reiterated the *Monroe Doctrine* of the 19th century. The doctrine had been developed to discourage European powers from meddling in the American continents and establishing spheres of influence there.

Of great importance was the lesson that both the Superpowers learned about the role of conventional weapons. The valuable lesson that the crisis taught, was that *conventional weapons still had their use* in the nuclear age. The first US move was to surround Cuba with its conventional navy. If, on the other hand, a country were to get rid of its conventional forces and rely only on nuclear force, then a confrontational move would have to begin by exploding, or threatening to explode, an atom bomb. That would mean suicide for both the antagonists. In the Cuban case, the Soviets, in 1962, had no ocean-going navy to match the huge US navy. Their missiles were neutralized by the threat of US missiles and long-range bombers. Soviet conventional forces could not prevent a US invasion of Cuba. Both geography and long-range overseas force-projection capability were against them. So Moscow had little option but to back down. The USSR subsequently built up a huge ocean-going navy under Admiral Sergei Gorshkov. By the 1970s and later, their navy became a formidable force, despite certain geographical handicaps that separate the various Soviet fleets widely from each other. A most important reason for this *Soviet naval buildup* was certainly the lessons learnt in Cuba.

The Cuban missile crisis made the Soviets in subsequent years soft-pedal *the Berlin question*. No more Berlin crisis took place, as mentioned earlier. Both Washington and Moscow realized how close they had come to the brink of disaster. So they got together in 1963 and established *the hotline*, a direct connection of communication between the two capitals. This would enable the top leaders to talk to each other directly in a crisis. In the missile age time is at a premium because once launched, the missiles of the two Superpowers would just take thirty minutes to destroy each other's territory, as already noted. Once the worst was over in 1962, the era of *détente*, or relaxation of tension, seemed to begin next year. Besides the hotline, the US and the USSR reached a *grain deal*, under which American grain would be supplied to the Soviet Union. The two sides, along with Britain, also signed *the partial nuclear test-ban treaty*. Thereby they agreed to refrain in future from testing nuclear bombs in the earth's atmosphere.

But Kennedy was assassinated in late 1963. Khrushchev fell from power next year. The two Superpowers, with different leaderships in each, soon continued to develop friction over issues like Vietnam, the Middle East, and the strategic arms race. Détente in the immediate post-Cuban years turned out to be short-lived indeed. Before winding up, we should note that the literature on the Cuban missile crisis hardly mentions the Cuban role in it! In the big game of the Superpowers little Cuba had virtually no role to play except playing host to the elusive missiles. Havana had no control over them. Castro in fact was very annoyed with Moscow since the latter had agreed to pull out the missiles without even bothering to consult Havana beforehand. [6]

READINGS

1. Graham T. Allison, *Essence of Decision: Explaining the Cuban Missile Crisis*, Little, Brown & Co., Boston, 1971.
2 McGeorge Bundy, *Danger and Survival*, Affiliated East-West Press, Indian edition, New Delhi, 1989.
3. Roger Hilsman, *To Move a Nation. The Politics of Foreign Policy in the Administration of John F. Kennedy*, Doubleday, Garden City, New York, 1967.
4. Henry M. Pachter, *Collision Course. The Cuban Missile Crisis and Coexistence*, Praeger, New York, 1963.
5. Robert Kennedy, *Thirteen Days. A Memoir of the Cuban Missile Crisis*, New York, 1969.

6. *Problems of Communism*, Special Ed., Washington DC, Spring 1992 (contains several articles and 25 letters between Kennedy and Khrushchev, released only in 1992).

NOTES

1. Robert F. Kennedy, *Thirteen Days: A Memoir of the Cuban Missile Crisis,* New York, 1969.
2. McGeorge Bundy, *Danger and Survival*, Affiliated East-West Press, Ind. ed., New Delhi, 1989.
3. Kennedy's statement of 4 Sept. 1962. Readers interested in hi-tech espionage should read about the US U-2 program in "The Oxcart Story," *Studies in Intelligence*, Vol. 26, No. 2, Summer 1982, pp. 1-22, www. foia.ucia.gov.
4. The aging Jupiter missiles were slated to be removed in any case.
5. Graham T. Allison, *Essence of Decision. Explaining the Cuban Missile Crisis*, Little Brown and Co., Boston, 1971, pp. 102-113. Allison cites several puzzles relating to the Soviet missile adventure in Cuba.
6. On this and related issues, which came to light only after the Soviet collapse, see *Problems of Communism,* Washington, Special Edition, Spring 1992, Vol. XLI. Henceforth *POC*. This issue of the POC is entirely devoted to the Cuban missile crisis and contains the Kennedy-Khrushchev correspondence.

3

The US-Soviet Détente

Early Attempts at Détente

Stalin died in March 1953; the post-Stalin era ensued. On 8 August Soviet leader Malenkov announced that war was no longer inevitable in the nuclear age; the inevitability of a war between capitalist and socialist blocs had hitherto been a cherished ideological dogma of the Stalinist era. The Malenkov speech showed a certain softening of posture in the Kremlin. But questions pertaining to Germany, Indochina, Korea and other issues continued to divide Moscow from the West. In 1954 the Berlin conference of the four big powers failed to agree on Germany. In July next year they again conferred in Geneva. Moscow wanted to disband both NATO and the Warsaw Pact. It also wished that all foreign troops be withdrawn from the European countries. But the latter provision meant that, while the US would have to go home, the Red Army would still remain within striking distance of West Europe. Differences also cropped up in the arms control issue, over questions of inspection and controls. The US favored the latter measures but the USSR was more concerned about its sovereignty being thereby compromised. The participants could only agree on a truce in Indochina. The French defeat by the communist North Vietnamese in 1954 at Dien Bien Phu, and the emergence of two mutually antagonistic states on either side of the 17th parallel in Vietnam, were the outstanding problems there. In the Western view, it not only meant the end of French influence in the Indochina peninsula but also the rise of communism there, which would only widen Moscow's sphere of influence. The US dissociated itself from the Geneva arrangements because it feared that the communists would use them as a wedge to infiltrate Southeast Asia.

Turning to Europe, Moscow was keen that West Germany not join the US-led NATO. The Soviets held talks with the West German leader Konrad Adenauer in Moscow in 1955. The latter, incidentally, used his special train to confer confidentially with his aides because the Germans feared that the official Soviet guesthouses were full of 'bugs' (eavesdropping microphones)! The Soviets agreed with the Western powers to restore Austria's sovereignty and remove all troops, along with other occupation troops, from that country in exchange for its neutrality. This was achieved under the Peace Treaty of 15 May, a rare occasion when the Red Army moved out of a country into which it had entered. One reason for this liberal Soviet gesture could have been to impress upon West Germany that German reunification would also be possible and the Soviet troops could also pull out of German soil, if Bonn kept out of the US-led NATO. However, the West German leaders under the conservative Christian Democratic Party thought otherwise. Adenauer wanted to secure West Germany first with US help, even if that meant perpetuation of the division of his country for an indefinite future. In his view, a neutralized Germany, which was left without US/Western protection and existed in the proximity of the Soviet-led socialist bloc would invite disaster for its newly established democracy and freedom. So, these Soviet attempts soon after Stalin's demise at reaching some kind of an understanding with the West fizzled out.

In early 1956 Nikita S. Khrushchev, who had meanwhile emerged as the Soviet leader, criticized Stalin for his policies in a secret speech at the 20th Congress of the Communist Party of the Soviet Union (CPSU). He went even so far as to banish the dead demigod's body from the prestigious mausoleum, where only the topmost leaders rest into eternity. The congress became subsequently known for its *'destalinization'* and *'revisionism'*. Khrushchev was supposed to have turned Lenin and Stalin upside down. For Khrushchev, like Malenkov before him, war was no longer inevitable between the capitalist and socialist blocs. So, peaceful coexistence was possible. Further, the parliamentary road to socialism was also possible. This meant that the communists the world over could, and should, fight elections to get to power; it was no longer necessary to seize power from the capitalists violently, which had been the hitherto held belief. The results of this changed attitude were reflected in the behavior of the various communist parties. The Communist Party of India (CPI), which had been very militant and had led uprisings in Kakdwip and Telengana, turned docile. That in turn disenchanted the more militant elements, who would soon look up to a dissenting China and break away to form the CPI (Marxist) party in the 1960s. Khrushchev's 'revisionism' gradually led to a worldwide split of the hitherto monolithic communist movement centred in Moscow. It was the latter's differences with communist China, and not those earlier (since 1948) with Marshal Tito's Yugoslavia, which eroded Moscow's monopoly hold over world communism. But that is another story (more details in Chapter Four). Here we note the relative softening of the post-Stalin Soviet stance although the fundamental rivalry with the capitalist system was never given up.

The next, and more successful, appearance of detente was in 1963, following the Cuban missile crisis, as already seen. The hotline connecting the Superpowers was established, a grain deal signed between them as also the partial nuclear test ban treaty along with the UK. But this détente also petered out due to the Western and Soviet side-taking on a plethora of issues worldwide, notably the Arab-Israeli conflict in the Middle East and Indochina. A more spectacular phase of US-Soviet détente came in 1969, with the Republican President Richard M. Nixon taking office. Nixon had lost to Kennedy in the race for President. Now, having realized his ambition, he was determined to make a mark on contemporary events. He embarked upon what he termed as "an era of negotiations". Nixon chose as his National Security Adviser the Harvard Professor of German Jewish descent, Henry A. Kissinger. Together, they made up an interesting team, as reflected in their respective memoirs[1], and added a fascinating chapter in US relations with Moscow and Beijing.

Before proceeding further, let us take a brief but close look at the French word *détente*. The *Concise Oxford Dictionary of Current English* defines it as "easing of strained relations esp. between States". The word came in vogue to describe US-Soviet relations following the Cuban missile crisis. The English-speaking world, however, mistook it as something like *entente* or friendly relations. Whatever the dictionary meaning, détente in practice turned out to be an odd mixture of cooperation and confrontation, especially in the Nixon era. Détente did not mean that the problems dividing the two nations had vanished. It was more accurate to say that détente was a starting point for conciliation and accommodation, not the end product but the process. The misunderstanding of the word, and its somewhat simplistic and facile interpretation, especially played up by the Western media, contributed not least to a great deal of disillusionment later.

The Reasons for Détente at the Turn of the 1970s

The Vietnam War was the most important factor for the USA to negotiate a détente policy by the time Nixon came to power in 1969. The background to the increasing US involvement in the remote Southeast Asian country was as follows. After the Second World War the French, who had colonized Indochina consisting of Vietnam, Laos and Cambodia, but had themselves been lying prostrate under Nazi jackboots since summer 1940, returned to the peninsula. But the Viet Minh, under Ho Chi Minh's leadership, challenged the past colonial masters. At the Battle of Dien Bien Phu in 1954 they decisively defeated the French. With the French pulling out, the US stepped in to fill the vacuum. The Americans feared the spread of communism in Indochina and the rest of Southeast Asia, the 'domino theory', given Ho's Moscow-affiliations and the proximity of communist China to Vietnam. We have already noted that the latter, like Germany and Korea, had come to be de facto divided. Ideological and power struggle of the Cold War created and consolidated that division. The northern half of the country governed by Hanoi was socialist, the south administered from Saigon was anti-communist and pro-West, whether it was Emperor Bao Dai or his series of short-term successors; the latter came in and out of power usually via violent coups. In fact, though the US was supposedly backing Saigon after the French said "au revoir", it really could not be sure just whom it was backing. The Saigon governments, including that of Ngo Dinh Diem, never lasted long enough to provide the stability to meet the challenges from the north as well as from within the south. The better organized and spirited North Vietnamese armed forces posed a serious challenge across the 17th parallel to Saigon. There were Viet Cong guerrillas in the south itself, especially in the Mekong delta region, who also proved to be formidable foes to both the South Vietnamese forces as well as their US friends. Eisenhower bequeathed to Kennedy the policy of supporting Diem to counter Ho Chi Minh, who wanted to unite the country and establish socialism. That was also the aim of the Viet Cong's political arm, the National Liberation Front (NLF), which was founded in December 1960. Although the Southeast Asia Treaty Organization (SEATO) was supposed to protect South Vietnam, it was in reality ineffective, barring its US forces. So, the fears of Eike (Eisenhower's nickname) and State Secretary John Foster Dulles of falling dominoes if communism could not be halted at the 17th parallel also permeated the subsequent US administrations. As Kissinger was to testify later, Hanoi wanted not only the unification of Vietnam but also to dominate Laos and Cambodia, i.e., the whole of Indochina. [2] In neighboring Laos the Eisenhower-backed government stood little chance against the better organized Pathet Lao guerrillas; a 1961 Geneva agreement to neutralize Laos did not work. As the war in Vietnam progressed, North Vietnamese supplies kept pouring into the south meant for the Viet Cong. These came through the Ho Chi Minh Trail, which ran through Laotian jungles. Despite heavy US bombing of the trail, the supplies could not be stopped; the Vietnamese carried them on their bicycles or even on their backs while sidetracking the bomb craters![3] It was a picture of the poor but defiant holding his own against the hi-tech of the rich.

The US started getting militarily more involved under Kennedy. During 1961, the latter's first year in office, the number of US military advisers in South Vietnam shot up from 4,000 to 10,000.[4] In 1964 there allegedly took place attacks on two US destroyers by North Vietnamese torpedo boats[5] in the Gulf of Tonkin. Kennedy's successor, the big Texan Lyndon B. Johnson, then got the US Congress to make a declaration in August, which was branded the Gulf of Tonkin resolution. It warned that the US was prepared to commit its armed forces to defend its Southeast Asian allies. On 7 February next year came a Viet Cong attack on Pleiku in the central highlands. Johnson immediately escalated. He ordered bombing communist targets. He also threw off all pretense regarding military advisers and started sending regular US forces to Vietnam. Soon the US role in the North-South conflict in Vietnam widened. From 23,000 troops deployed in 1964 the number jumped to 200,000 in 1966 and peaked over 500,000 in 1967.[6] The US armed forces became heavily engaged in combat against the communists. The US bombing tonnage during 1965-71 over Indochina amounted to 6.3 million tons. That was equal to three times all the bombs dropped by the US Air force in Europe, Asia and Africa during World War II![7] US military expenditure shot up to well over $150 billion during 1965-70, largely due to the war.[8] But this was partly guerrilla warfare, and guerrillas cannot be recognized! It was also a civil war, with political issues involved. And political issues cannot be solved by purely military means. The US mania for quantification, with which Social Scientists are familiar, led to futile 'body counts' of the dead enemy! What such cold statistics miss, however, is that for every enemy dead, there will be several others like his relatives and friends who will take up arms! The end was nowhere in sight. The inefficiency and corruption of the South Vietnamese forces also contributed to America's dilemma, not to speak of continued instability in Saigon itself. The net result was that as the 1960s wore on, the US got increasingly involved in the war under Johnson, invested heavily in men and materiel but without a light at the end of the tunnel. The morale of the North and the Viet Cong remained superbly high. No amount of bombing and use of other hi-tech gadgets by the leading world power against them could break them. The number of body bags with dead soldiers arriving in the US from Vietnam increased. The US suffered a total of 200,000 casualties, including 30,000 dead,[9] in that war. The communist Tet offensive of early 1968 shook the Americans. US public opinion was outraged. Many Americans had only the vaguest notion about Vietnam and cared even less whether that country turned communist. US youths, including the student community, who were required to go to fight in the tropical jungles 10,000 miles away and against an often invisible enemy, soon let loose campus riots and dodged military draft. Anti-war protest movements, defiance of authority, 'flower children', LSD drugs and the beatnik and hippie cults mixed strangely with ideas of Mao and Marcuse. This phenomenon spread worldwide. Also thanks to the media, especially TV, which brought live footage of the war right into US bedrooms, a significant part of the US public opinion sharply turned in favor of getting 'the boys back home'. Any US government, which could not get the country out of the Vietnamese quagmire would be committing political harakiri. Johnson escaped by foregoing a second term of Presidency. Hanoi doomed his chances for a re-run for Presidency. It was now up to Nixon and his Kautilya, Dr. Kissinger, to devise a way out for the USA but without losing face. One of the first significant moves by Nixon relating to the ongoing Vietnam war was to declare, on 25 July 1969 in the Pacific island of Guam, that henceforth Asians would have to fight their own wars; the US would not like any more Vietnams. This came to be dubbed as *the Nixon Doctrine* or the *Guam Doctrine*. It signaled clearly that the US was fed up with the war and that it wanted to go home from Vietnam.

Hanoi was fully aware of the US dilemma and was in no mood to give Washington an exit permit easily, least of all on the latter's terms. This had already been found out when US representatives opened talks with those of Hanoi in May 1968 in Paris. Both sides remained adamant, and Saigon was especially opposed to the NLF's participation in any talks.[10] So Nixon and Kissinger thought up the idea to talk directly to the two main sponsors of Hanoi, the communist big brothers of the USSR and also China. *Hence came détente.*

The strategic arms race was another important factor, which gave momentum to détente between the USA and the USSR. Each side relied for deterrence on a mix of three types of offensive arms called the triad. The mix varied with each Superpower. The triad consisted of land-based ICBMs, sea-based SLBM-submarines, and long-range bombers. (ICBM and SLBM stand for intercontinental ballistic missile and submarine-launched ballistic missile, respectively). The Soviets relied more on their ICBMs than bombers, while the latter remained a US favorite despite their relative vulnerability and slowness compared to ballistic missiles. Both sides went on stockpiling and ever improving these weapons to the point of 'overkill'. Also in the 1960s the development of the anti-ballistic missile (ABM) by both sides gathered momentum. These were supposed to shoot down incoming hostile missiles but their reliability remained dubious. Both Washington and Moscow felt the need to slow down the arms race; a lot of money was going down the drain without assuring either side commensurately greater security. In fact, Johnson had initiated, way back in 1967, arrangements for strategic arms negotiations. But the talks, scheduled for 1968, were postponed due to a spurt in East-West tension over the Soviet military intervention in Czechoslovakia that year. The liberal experiments under Alexander Dubcek appeared to endanger the communist dictatorships in East Europe. Hence came the intervention. The Strategic Arms Limitation Talks (SALT), however, began in late 1969 in Helsinki and culminated in the US-Soviet SALT I Treaty, which included the agreement to limit ABM defense of both sides. Nixon and Brezhnev signed the treaty in Moscow on 26 May 1972. Under SALT I the US agreed to put a ceiling to its ICBMs and SLBMs at the combined number of 1,710. The Soviets were permitted 2,350. Their rate of building SLBM-submarines had been a source of particular worry for the USA.[11] The discrepancy between the two sets of figures was the result of various complicated calculations, including the fact that the US led in MIRV technology. These were multiple independently-targetable re-entry vehicles, which meant that each MIRVed missile could lob several bombs, each heading for a different target. MIRV thus had a multiplier effect. Bombers were not in the picture but the juvenile ABM was. Each side was permitted to protect two sites with ABMs. Subsequently this was brought down to one site for each by mutual agreement. This meant that each agreed to remain open to attack by the other. Hence, the nuclear threats would cancel each other out and neither would dare to initiate a suicidal attack. This was the 'mutual assured destruction' or MAD doctrine, also known variously as 'balance of terror', the 'nuclear balance', etc. SALT signaled that the US was now ready to accept strategic parity with Moscow.

A third major reason for détente was *trade*. Although Western commercial firms loathed the communist system where they would go out of business, they were more than interested in investing in the enormous Soviet bloc. The

USSR and its East European allies, after all, promised a huge market. Some of America's West European allies were already into trade with the USSR. So why should US companies and banks lag behind? Nixon's slogan of 'an era of negotiations' encouraged the idea that the Cold War need not be a total road block. There were ways to bypass it and establish cooperative linkages. Indeed, there was even encouragement from Moscow itself. At the 24th CPSU Congress in early 1971 Leonid Brezhnev launched his "peace offensive". He positively encouraged the West, including the US, to invest in a variety of projects in the USSR and also to introduce technological know-how. We shall come across some of these projects when we discuss the consequences of détente.

Political factors played no less a role in spawning détente. On 2 and 15 March 1969 armed clashes took place between the Soviet and Chinese border guards along the Far Eastern River Ussuri on the island of Damansky (Zhen Bao for the Chinese). This was a startling occasion when communist 'brothers' were not merely exchanging hot words but live bullets and killing each other for the first time. In all, there would be over 400 skirmishes along the Sino-Soviet border in 1969. The Ussuri River clashes marked a high and dangerous point in the Sino-Soviet conflict. But the twin incidents of March were a godsend for Nixon who had taken office barely two months earlier. His adviser, Kissinger, who was a devotee of Prince Metternich and had a penchant for the classic European-style politicking, was no less thrilled. This was a great opportunity to exploit the Sino-Soviet conflict and maneuver carefully to reach US foreign policy goals like exerting pressure on Hanoi. So, Kissinger set up and started using his 'backchannel' quite frequently, i.e., negotiating confidentially with Soviet Ambassador Anatoly Dobrynin. The State Department, which was officially in charge of US foreign policy, was often left in the dark. Nixon for his part visited Rumania later in 1969 to set up a channel of communication with Beijing. It was well known that only

Bucharest among the Warsaw Pact countries maintained good relations with Beijing and even enjoyed a limited degree of independence of Moscow. But the Soviet secret service, the KGB, was very active in East Europe, including Rumania. So, the US looked around for, and found, a channel better than the leaky one in Bucharest. It was Islamabad.

The US continued to send various signals to communist China at the turn of the 1970s to indicate that it was interested in talks with the latter. Hence, between 1969 and 1972 Nixon was simultaneously talking with both the communist adversaries, Moscow and Beijing, who were at loggerheads with each other. It became a classic case of a big power triangle. Nixon's chief and immediate concern, as noted, was Vietnam. Nixon and Kissinger aimed to use the influence of Moscow and Beijing with Hanoi to soften it up so that the US could get out without irreparable damage to its prestige. Also, Germany's new Social Democratic government under Willy Brandt and his adviser, Egon Bahr, was rushing headlong into its own détente with Moscow. Bonn's rapid move with its Ostpolitik (policy towards East Europe), which received encouragement from Moscow, raised eyebrows in Washington. But if the Germans were going ahead with détente, why should the Americans lag behind, even though the Cold War was on? Just as US attempts to open up China made the Soviets anxious, so did the Soviets smile at West Germany, a close ally, cause concern to the USA.

However, Moscow was equally keen on détente with the USA. About a month after Nixon's historic visit to China in February 1972, North Vietnamese forces launched an offensive against the south across the demilitarized zone (DMZ), which ran along the 17th latitude, and from Laos and Cambodia. Hanoi was clearly getting edgy in view of Nixon's rapidly developing links with Moscow and Beijing. The offensive made Nixon face a dilemma. If he did not hit back, the US would appear in a bad light, especially to its allies. If on the other hand he did retaliate, the Soviets might cancel the upcoming summit in Moscow. But Nixon went ahead and gambled. He ordered the bombing of communist targets, including Hanoi and the Haiphong harbor. But Moscow did not cancel the upcoming détente summit with him in May.[12] There was far too much at stake for Moscow to cancel or postpone it. The Soviet leaders made the right noises against the US action but kept the summit on top of their agenda. There were indications that Kissinger's policy of isolating Hanoi by driving a wedge between it and its two communist sponsors was having an effect. Kissinger reports that disagreements had arisen especially between Hanoi and Beijing.[13] Peace at last came to Vietnam, after protracted negotiations, with the signing of an accord in Paris on 23 January 1973. Kissinger even got the Nobel Peace Prize for his role in the peace effort.

Another political reason for détente was the US acceptance of the socialist bloc as an accomplished fact. At this time, détente marked a clean break with the past US tradition of taking Soviet and Chinese aggressiveness for granted. From Truman to Johnson that assumption had remained largely accepted, reinforced by Cold Warriors like Dean Acheson and John Foster Dulles, not to speak of the somewhat neurotic Senator McCarthy. But the Nixon Administration acknowledged that communism was here to stay. So it was better for Washington to hammer out an arrangement with it, to accommodate it, rather than continue to pretend that it would not last or that life could go on without it. The US had to reshape and adjust its foreign policy taking the reality of the Soviet bloc into account. Nixon and Kissinger opted for a carrot-and-stick approach; cooperation with Moscow, and opening up China, as far as possible; opposing the USSR and denying it rewards when the latter did not listen.

Hence, developing understandings with Moscow and Beijing, and accepting their respective status while at the same time using the animosity between them, became the dominant characteristics of US détente policy. These strong, sometimes even contradictory, connotations widely varied from the simplistic dictionary meaning of the word détente, i.e. the relaxation of tension. There were both relaxation and additional causes to be tense, a mix found in the Nixon-Kissinger policy.

The Results of Détente

In the first half of the 1970's the US-Soviet détente bore fruit. It progressed on a number of fronts. At times it mitigated the Cold War, e.g., the holding of talks itself was an achievement. At other times détente ran parallel to the Cold War, e.g., during the Yom Kippur War, named after a Jewish holiday, when the Arabs attacked Israel in 1973. The two superpowers again took sides, the US backing Tel Aviv, the Soviets Cairo. As we noted earlier, Nixon's Moscow-visit and the SALT I agreement of May 1972 were two initial landmarks of détente. A number of other bilateral cooperation agreements on environmental protection, medicine, space, science and technology, incidents at sea and commercial relations accompanied SALT I. [14] The two sides agreed to set up a joint commercial commission to reach the goals of mutual grant of the most-favored-nation (MFN) status in trade, to make available government credits and find other ways of promoting business. A nearly $1 billion-grain deal was signed under which the US was to supply massive amount of grain, mostly fodder, to its foe.

In April 1973 came a Soviet agreement with the giant firm called US Occidental Petroleum Co. on long-term deliveries, on credit, of plant and technology for producing high quality fertilizers in the USSR. Already 13 large US firms and banks were operating in Moscow that year. A Soviet trade mission was opened in Washington. The Soviets welcomed US participation in the Kama Auto Works; 80 contracts were signed with 67 US firms on that project. In June Brezhnev paid a visit to the USA. Although he was supposed to represent the poor proletariat worldwide, he had a weakness for Western technical products like fast cars![15] So the US side presented him with a Cadillac, which was the epitome of US capitalism! Among others, a joint trade and economic council was envisaged during the visit and set up the following year. Among its functions would be the promotion of links between the scientific and technical organs of the two countries. In June 1974 Nixon paid a second visit to the USSR. Energy research, housing construction and the development of an artificial heart were among the items on which the two sides agreed to cooperate. They further agreed to *ban all underground nuclear tests above 150 kilotons* from 31 March 1976. This was an improvement upon the Partial Test Ban Treaty of 1963, mentioned earlier, which had only banned atmospheric tests but permitted unrestricted underground tests. There was also a startling agreement, as early as that year, on banning 'weather warfare'. It revealed that science had advanced so far that manipulating weather as a weapon had become thinkable! Besides, there seemed to be good prospects of tapping the huge natural gas deposits of Tyumen in western Siberia and the Yakut region. It seemed entirely possible that in future Californians in the west coast of the USA would be cooking with Siberian gas. Further, in 1975 the US spacecraft Apollo and its Soviet counterpart Soyuz docked together in space, apparently taking détente to new heights. But that was not to be.

The Decline of Détente

In August 1974 President Nixon was forced to resign over the Watergate scandal.[16] With him went the chief architect of détente. There was no dearth of critics of Nixon's détente policy. Some of them were influential senators like Jackson from the state of Washington. The critics leveled their guns at the détente policy of Nixon and Kissinger on the following grounds.

First, the critics did not like less number of strategic weapons for the USA than those permitted to Moscow under

SALT I. That the US was ahead in MIRV technology, which, among other factors, made up for the shortfall, did not cut ice with them. On paper, inferior numbers *looked* inferior. Hence, Jackson and others demanded absolute parity in the number of missiles. They made Nixon's successor Gerald Ford rush to Vladivostok in late 1974 and persuade Brezhnev to agree to new figures for their respective missiles. The result was the Vladivostok Accords, which set an absolute parity and took the ceiling higher to 2,400 missiles for each, with a subceiling of 1,320 MIRVs. This was a strange kind of strategic arms *limitation* where the ceiling on arms was revised upwards!

Second, the grain deal, the largest in recorded history, pushed up bread prices in the USA since much grain was going out to the USSR. This was what critics said. They also felt that the price charged for the grain was less than the market price. This meant that the US taxpayer was subsidizing grain for the USA's enemy number one!

Third, there came the Jackson-Vanik Amendment to the Trade Act, which barred the US Administration from granting MFN status to the USSR so long as the latter did not maintain a rate of voluntary Jewish emigration that would be considered satisfactory by Washington. Moscow was offended. This was interference in Soviet domestic affairs. Soviet Jews, like good Jews everywhere, wanted to migrate to Israel, the post-war Jewish homeland, but Moscow rarely permitted emigration of its citizens; there also might have been a built-in historical prejudice against the Jews at work behind the restrictions on Jewish migration, a prejudice which had long been part of European history. Also, Moscow's Arab friends would thoroughly detest an increase of Jewish population in the territory to which they laid claim. Moscow agreed to permit 35,000 Jews to migrate annually. Jackson demanded 100,000.[17] Senator Jackson also co-authored another amendment that put a ceiling of $300 million on all loans offered to Moscow. The carrot side of the US détente policy, hence, was becoming too short. The stick side also suffered because post-Vietnam USA was in a great mood for slashing military budgets, even though the Soviets were reportedly increasing theirs.[18] And the Congress was gleefully busy devising various kinds of curbs on Presidential powers because Nixon had ordered unauthorized bombings in Indochina and had overreached in Watergate. Thus the executive branch was weakened, which in turn might have served as a disincentive for détente to Moscow. In the US view, the USSR became very bold in the second half of the 1970s, in terms of expanding both its military spending as well as spheres of influence in Third World regions like Africa.

Fourth, critics identified détente with Kissinger's 'backchannel' diplomacy, i.e. secret talks with the Soviets. Sometimes even the US Embassy in Moscow was left unaware of the mysterious Dr. Kissinger's arrival and talks with the Kremlin leaders. The regular US bureaucracy of the State Department, the Foreign Service people, for example, resented this. They were being left out of important action. Although Bill Rogers was supposed to be in charge of US foreign policy as the Secretary of State, it was actually Nixon's National Security Adviser who was running the show. Besides this natural bureaucratic resentment, *the US ethos* has a distaste for intrigues and realpolitik or power politics. Traditional European politics is seen by US public opinion as distasteful and unbecoming of America's ideal of openness. Among the idealistic President Wilson's 14 Points was one which demanded 'open covenants openly arrived at.' That way, Wilson had championed glasnost (transparency in governmental dealings), preceding Gorbachev in this by seven decades, although their contexts were different. But what did this German Jewish immigrant, an admirer of Metternich, do? In the land of openness Kissinger introduced old-fashioned secret, even conspiratorial, diplomacy. The very term 'backchannel' suggets this. Nixon backed him up. So, despite the enormous influence that Kissinger came to wield in the US government, resentment at his unconventional diplomatic maneuverings piled up. Détente became associated with his style of functioning (which often left his colleagues in the dark!) and that of Nixon, who suffered disgrace over his habit of secret eavesdropping in Watergate. No wonder that Ford, at one point, said he was throwing the very word détente out of his vocabulary, so unpopular had the word become by the mid-1970s. Hardliners cried out that it was a sellout to *the mischievous USSR*, that the latter had no intention of playing fair, that it was cheating the USA, lulling it into a false sense of peace, and was bent as ever on spreading communism. The CIA then made itself very visible. It made an upward revision of Soviet military expenditure in 1977, which alarmed the USA. A related concern was *Moscow's active involvement*, politically, economically and militarily, in several conflicts in Africa (as in the case of Somalia versus Ethiopia in the strategic African Horn; in Yemen, various leftist national liberation movements like the MPLA engaged in a civil war against UNITA in Angola, where, incidentally, Cuban forces joined up with the MPLA, etc.). The US saw these as further signs that Moscow was not interested in détente but was using it as a cover to hide its aggressiveness.

The appearance of *a new generation of heavy ICBMs* seemed like the Soviets were preparing for a winnable nuclear war by sharpening their first strike and counterforce capability.[19] Even though President Jimmy Carter signed the SALT II Treaty with Moscow, this move towards détente was overtaken by *Moscow's support* for the Vietnamese-backed installation of the Heng Samrin government in *Phnom Penh* in early 1979, followed in December that year by direct Soviet military intervention in *Afghanistan*. America's close ally, *Shah Reza Pahlavi* had been ousted earlier in 1979. Washington now faced an enormously hostile Persian Gulf state under Ayatollah Khomeini instead. *The USA's 'twin pillar' policy* in the Gulf, that of cultivating the two oil-rich states of Saudi Arabia and Iran, thus crumbled. On top of this disaster another unsavory possibility now stared

Washington in the face. The Soviet Air Force was now deployed in Afghanistan within striking range of *the West's jugular vein*, the oil-rich Persian Gulf. Militarily, this meant that Moscow could cut off oil supplies to the West and Japan; many West European states and Japan in particular were significantly dependent on the Gulf oil for their economic activity and high standards of living. *All these factors piled up against any more détente*. Even Jimmy Carter, who seemed to be relatively soft on Moscow, proclaimed, in January 1980, a doctrine which came to be tagged to his name. Against the background of a newly hostile Iran and the Soviet military presence in neighboring Afghanistan, *the Carter Doctrine* declared the Persian Gulf to be lying within the USA's 'vital sphere of interest.' He warned that the USA would use *all means* at its disposal to remove any threat to the region. Since he did not use any disclaimer and a resort to nuclear weapons could not be ruled out. Carter also quickly made up most of the remaining differences with China in a hurry. His National Security Adviser, Columbia University Professor, Polish-born Zbigniew Brzezinski, acted energetically to move closer to China as a warning signal to Moscow. The built-in historic Polish dislike of the Russians informed Brzezinski's activities as Carter's adviser (it is said that the Poles do not know what to fear more, German invasion or Russian liberation!). But Carter was perceived to be weak. The failed military attempt to rescue American Embassy hostages in revolutionary Iran only smeared his image further. Ronald Reagan, a B-grade Hollywood actor, burst into the US Presidency in 1981 by blasting the Soviet Union and promising that the US would again flex its muscles. His Hollywoodish showmanship seemed to have impressed the American public. It was instrumental in jumpstarting another round of super Cold War from the early 1980s.

Readings

1. Richard Nixon, *RN Memoirs*, Grosset & Dunlap, New York, 1978.

2 Henry Kissinger, *White House Years*, Little, Brown & Co., Boston, 1979, and *Years of Upheaval*, Little, Brown & Co., Boston, 1982.

3. Raymond Garthoff, *Détente and Confrontation: American-Soviet Relations from Nixon to Reagan*, Brookings, Washington, 1985.

4. Harry Gelman, *The Brezhnev Politburo and the Decline of Détente*, Cornell Univ. Press, Ithaca, 1984.

5. Coral Bell, *The Diplomacy of Détente: The Kissinger Era*, St. Martin's Press, New York, 1977.

6. Alvin Z. Rubinstein, *Soviet Foreign Policy since World War II: Imperial and Global*, Little, Brown and Co., Boston, 1985 (2nd ed.).

7. Norman A. Graebner, *America as a World Power*, op. cit.

Notes

1. Richard Nixon, *RN Memoirs*, Grosset & Dunlap, New York, 1978; Henry Kissinger, *White House Years*, Little Brown & Co., Boston, 1979.

2. Kissinger, *ibid.*, p. 433.

3. Discovery TV, 10 Feb. 2001, 9. 30 pm. Indian Standard Time (IST). All times henceforth are quoted in IST except specified otherwise.

4. Norman A. Graebner, *America as a World Power. A Realist Appraisal from Wilson to Reagan*, Universal Book Stall, New Delhi, 1984, p. 230.

5. Ibid., calls the alleged attacks "doubtful," pp. 235-6.

6. Ibid., pp. 236-7.

7. Raphael Littauer, Norman Uphoff (eds.), *The Air War in Indochina*, Beacon Press, Boston, 1972, pp. v-vi.

8. Bruce Russett, Harvey Starr, *World Politics. The Menu for Choice,* Vakils, Feffer & Simons, Bombay, 1986 (2nd. ed.), fig. 13. 1, p. 334.

9. The fancy hi-tech devices used in the Vietnam war have been described by Uphoff and Littauer, op. cit., and General William C. Westmoreland (who led the US forces in Vietnam), in *A Soldier Reports*, Doubleday, Garden City, N. Y., 1976, pp. 281-283. Also Graebner, op. cit., p. 237.

10. These initial talks bogged down to discussing seating arrangements, and how to avoid even symbols of a four-sided (as Hanoi wanted) versus two-sided (as US and Saigon preferred) meeting, the shape of the negotiation table, etc.! Ibid., p. 247.

11. Kissinger, op. cit., pp. 196-8. SLBMs continued to be a major issue after SALT I. See Strobe Talbott, *Endgame: The Inside Story of SALT II*, Kalyani Publishers, Ludhiana, pp. 161-3.

12. Kissinger, op. cit., pp. 1097-1123.

13. Ibid., p. 1113.

14. Texts in US Information Service, *President Nixon in Moscow. A Summary of Major Statements and Agreements During President Richard Nixon's Visit to the Soviet Union, May 22-30, 1972*, pp. 4-10 (no place and date of publication).

15. Nixon gave Brezhnev a Cadillac "for his auto collection," and received a hydrofoil in exchange. Kissinger, *op. cit*., p. 1224.

16. The hotel Watergate in Washington housed the Democratic Party headquarters. Nixon, the Republican President, had allowed it to be 'bugged' so that eavesdropping on confidential talks within the

Democratic Party became possible. Two *Washington Post* newsmen leaked the Presidential indiscretion. The following scandal spread like wildfire and led to Nixon's resignation as President.

17. Kissinger, *Years of Upheaval*, Little, Brown & Co., Boston, 1982, Ch. XII.

18. Ibid.

19. Kissinger, writing in the 1970s, mentions the 'heavy' Soviet SS-9 and SS-18

    ICBMs, for which the US had no equivalent. *White House Years*, op. cit.,

    pp. 812, 1218.

4

Confrontation and Reconciliation: China's Relations with the USSR and Russia

Historical Background

Batu Khan's Mongol armies overran Kievian Russia during 1237-40 and ruled the region for 200 years. It is said that the later Soviet control over Outer Mongolia was in revenge. In 1689 Russian Tsar Peter the Great signed the Treaty of Nerchinsk with the Chinese Emperor. The treaty halted Russia's imperial expansion in the Amur Valley and the Siberian maritime areas, regions in the Far East where the interests of the two giant neighbors confronted each other. Nerchinsk marked a diplomatic victory for China. However, the situation changed subsequently.

Since 1854, Russian diplomat Muraviev was busy settling all border questions in the east. In the Crimean War (1853-56) England and France attacked Russia's Pacific Fleet base at Petropavlovsk. This brought the Russians down the River Amur as a vital artery for supplies to the defense of the fleet as well as the Kamchatka Peninsula in April 1854. The Manchu frontier forces did not stop the Russians. Amur's left bank was vital to Russia and hence occupied. On 28 May 1858 Muraviev forced China to sign the Treaty of Aigun, which sealed Russia's claim to all territories left and north of the Amur. Russia wished the river to be the border separating Siberia from Manchuria. China was unhappy with the loss of the Ussuri country. Two weeks later, in June, Russia's diplomat Putiatin and three Western powers signed four commercial treaties at Tientsin with China.

On 14 November 1860 a tottering Chinese regime, under the Treaty of Peking, gave away to Russia territory east of the Rivers Ussuri-Amur, while finding it difficult to bring under control the Taiping rebels in the central coast. Taking advantage of China's weakness, England and France occupied Peking. The shrewd Russian diplomat Ignatiev promised China that he would intervene with the Western duo to prevent further destruction like the looting and burning of China's summer capital. He charged a price, however, for his 'services', viz., Russian possession of the Manchurian coastline.[1] The 19th century is replete with instances of the increasing foreign stranglehold over China. Russia was a cheerful signatory to China's 'unequal treaties'. In fact, Wang Tao, a journalist with a checkered and somewhat quixotic career, had already advocated, in 1879, the setting up of a kind of 'containment' of Russia's hunger for expansion in Asia in alliance with Japan, Annam, Siam, the latter two being today's Vietnam and Thailand, respectively and Burma.[2] But after China's disastrous defeat by Japan during the 1894-5 war, China and Russia signed a secret 15-year treaty, on 22 May 1896, of mutual military aid with specific reference to future Japanese threat. Of special worry to the Russians was the Trans-Siberian Railway, which they had began constructing in 1891. Russian troops participated in the suppression of the Boxer rebellion against the docile Manchu regime four years later. Russia, however, showed no less greed than its other ten co-signatories to exploit a weak China, when on 7 September 1901 it signed a Protocol designed to milk that country dry.[3] Three years later, the Russo-Japanese war broke out over rivalry to control northeast China, in which both Russia and the USA were also interested. The war was fought on Chinese soil. Chinese hopes to develop a modern navy with Russian help were shattered, however, with the latter's defeat, including naval disasters, at Japanese hands. This brief look at the past Sino-Russian relations enables us to understand the bitterness on China's side when in March 1969 armed clashes broke out between the two communist neighbors, which went beyond the exchange of polemics to the exchange of live ammunition, which we have seen in Chapter Three.

The Marxists came to power in 1917 in Russia, and in 1949 in China. There followed a decade of Sino-Soviet friendship, sealed by the Friendship Treaty of 1950. But this association was a troubled one, for a variety of reasons, among which *Chinese resentment* of Russia's relatively benevolent ties (including arms supply) with the rival Kuomintang forces (to fight the Japanese) was one; another was Khrushchev's ideological 'revisionism' of 1956, in addition to the incompatible personalities of Khrushchev and Mao. There followed three decades of Sino-Soviet rivalry, which, with the USA, as an active third player, forged a unique big-power triangle that strongly influenced international relations. The Soviet military intervention in Afghanistan in December 1979, just a year after the beginning of the Soviet-backed Vietnamese military intervention in Kampuchea, made Sino-Soviet relations, which were already suboptimal, take a nose dive. It is noteworthy that post-Mao China gradually stressed less on ideological issues in its dispute with Moscow. The outstanding issues for Beijing in the 1980s became the questions of Soviet troop withdrawal from Afghanistan and Outer Mongolia, Vietnamese military pullout of Kampuchea, and Soviet military build-down along the 4,500-mile Sino-Soviet border, especially in its eastern sector. The fiery debates on who was the 'real' communist of the earlier decades faded out. This post-Mao scenario was prevalent when the radical Soviet reformer Mikhail Gorbachev came to power in 1985. Gorbachev's advent and the subsequent collapse of the USSR in 1991 gave Sino-Soviet/Russian relations a startlingly new dimension.

Gorbachev and China

Zhou Enlai and Mao died in 1976, the former on 8 January and the great chairman on 9 September respectively. Both veterans were 82. The revolutionary Maoist era in the People's Republic of China came to an end. Moscow hoped for improvement in relations, halted its anti-Chinese polemics and waited. But to its disappointment there was no abatement in open anti-Soviet pronouncements from Beijing. The post-Mao leaders like Hua Guofeng and others poured cold water over Soviet hopes of better ties by, inter alia, publishing Mao's hitherto secret derogatory comments on the Soviets from earlier times.

Relations seemed to marginally improve with a Sino-Soviet trade agreement signed annually under Deng Xiaoping in post-Mao China, even though Deng showed little inclination to cultivate Moscow. The Soviets were allowed to lay wreaths to the memorial to Soviet soldiers who had fallen in 1945 in Manchuria, while Moscow permitted Chinese boats carrying vegetables and coal to sail past strategic Khabarovsk, a route which had been forbidden since the late 1960s.[4] But following the Kampuchean and Afghan crises, China allowed the 30-year Friendship Treaty with Moscow to lapse in 1980. It also dropped border talks with the latter to register its strong protest over the Soviet military presence in Afghanistan. The following two years saw several Soviet attempts during Brezhnev's last days to normalize relations.[5] Beijing cautiously responded to some of these overtures, partly propelled by irritation over the Reagan Administration's pro-Taiwan policy. The uneasy relationship continued but the controversy over Afghanistan, Kampuchea and the border remained unsolved. Meanwhile, China's domestic power structure was changing after Mao. In less than a month following his death, the ultra-left 'gang of four', including his widow Jiang Qing and their other sympathizers, were rounded up with the help of Mao's bodyguard unit under Wang Dongxing. The new leadership led by Hua, which took power in October 1976, opened up the country for modernization under Deng's guidance in 1978.

Things started looking up with the advent of Gorbachev. On the eve of his assuming office of the General-Secretary of the CPSU (12 March 1985) Gorbachev categorically stated at an important party meet that "we would like to see a considerable improvement of relations with the People's Republic of China and believe that, given reciprocity, much improvement is quite possible".[6] That he meant business was evident three months later when, in a speech honoring his Vietnamese counterpart Le Duan, he declared that normalization of relations between Moscow and Hanoi on the one hand and Beijing on the other was worth striving for and that the Soviets and the Vietnamese had made "constructive proposals" in this regard. When in October a message arrived from Deng Xiaoping, via Rumanian leader Nicolai Ceausescu, that Vietnamese pullout from Kampuchea would pave the way for a Sino-Soviet summit, the Soviets put pressure on Hanoi to comply with Beijing's wishes. This Soviet arm-twisting of its ally for China's sake became evident when, in April 1989, Hanoi declared it was ready to withdraw its troops, thus smoothening the way for the sixth Sino-Soviet summit the following month.

Meanwhile, Gorbachev's report to the 27th CPSU Congress in early 1986 and his Vladivostok speech of 28 July that year had echoed once again his "new political thinking" about international relations in general and about China in particular. Gorbachev indicated that his country was now turning towards the Pacific. In July 1987 Moscow adopted a long-term economic development plan for the Soviet Far East, Buryatia and Chita. Gorbachev was keen to integrate these regions with the bouncing economies of the Asia-Pacific Region (APR), including China, which were becoming a major center of world economy (some of these Asian 'tigers', of course, underwent a serious economic crisis subsequently in 1998). The latter's operation of 'special economic zones', tailored to boost exports and thereby earn hard currency, was of special interest.[7] Trade with APR amounted to only 8% of total Soviet trade in 1986, whereas US trade with the region was over 30% of the US total, exceeding the latter's trade volume with even Europe. A Sino-Soviet agreement was reached on processing Soviet Far Eastern raw materials in joint ventures based in China for export to the markets in Japan and Southeast Asia. Moscow also promised to freeze its intermediate-range nuclear force (INF) level in Asia and cut naval exercises in the Pacific, which were two other sources of anxiety for China. Gorbachev even toyed with the idea of an Asia-Pacific security and cooperation conference modeled on the European conference in Helsinki. He pushed through the acceptance of the Thalweg principle regarding the disputed River Amur, where the Chinese were long asking for the main navigation channel as the border. The Soviet military had been resisting it so far, for fear of putting Khabarovsk, a major military base, in jeopardy.

The US-Soviet INF Treaty of December 1987 (we shall see its details in Chapter Six) took into consideration the anxiety of China and Japan regarding the USSR's Asian INFs. Then came *the Sino-Soviet summit* of 15-18 May 1989, which marked a turning point in bilateral relations. This was a summit between the two giant communist neighbors after a lapse of three decades. It was noteworthy that the Chinese did not harp too much on preconditions. After all, in April 1988, the Soviets had agreed in Geneva on total military pullout of Afghanistan by February 1989 and, as we have already seen, Hanoi removed the Kampuchean obstacle two months later. In December 1988 Gorbachev had announced at the UN that three-quarters of the Soviet troops based in Mongolia would withdraw within two years as part of overall Soviet military draw-down. He announced a 500,000 troop cut in the Soviet armed forces, 40% of this in the Soviet Far East. The pullout of Mongolia began the day Gorbachev began his Beijing summit.[8] So, the Chinese had ample reason to be satisfied with Gorbachev's forthcoming attitude, his 'new political thinking' and advocacy of 'reasonable defense sufficiency' even though his Beijing-visit triggered a massive pro-democracy movement in China and the resultant Tien An Mien square massacre.[9] Lingering differences over the composition of a future government in Phnom Penh, a future mechanism for regular military consultations, and Gorbachev's pet theme of an Asia-Pacific security and cooperation conference did not prevent a wider agreement to improve trade, not only bilaterally but in an all-Asia context, and also in overall relations. A political angle to improving bilateral relations was the apparent resurrection of US-Soviet détente (the INF Treaty and other agreements like those over Germany and Europe). Beijing certainly would not have liked Moscow to lean too much towards Washington. Also, lower Sino-Soviet tension and a peaceful border would enable China to divert resources from defense spending to economic development. Further, if US support for Taiwan weakened, Taipei might turn to Moscow. This had to be forestalled by improving relations with the latter.

Sino-Russian Relations in the 1990s

Following the Soviet collapse in 1991, China's relations with Russia, the leading post-Soviet state in the Commonwealth of Independent States (CIS), were configured in ways radically different from the past. The new configuration was, of course, also influenced by other events in Europe like the reunification of Germany a year earlier and the rapid collapse of Marxism in East Europe. The bilateral relations over the past decade can be analyzed under three headings: trade and economics, defense and politics.

Trade and Economic Relations

Gorbachev's visit to Beijing in May 1989 was returned by the then Chinese Premier Li Peng the following April. The summit in Moscow spawned a long-term agreement on boosting trade, economic and scientific cooperation till 2000

A. D.[10] The Chinese also extended a credit worth 250 million rubles to Moscow to buy consumer goods from their country. In turn the Soviets agreed to float a loan to help build two 1-million megawatt nuclear power stations in China, followed in 1992 by an agreement on nuclear fusion research[11], and signed a protocol on future Foreign Minister-level talks. Bilateral trade stood at $3. 7 billion in 1990, not counting the unmeasurable border trade, thus registering an eight-fold increase since 1978. However, reports soon circulated that the Chinese consumer goods flowing to the Russian market, e.g., shoes, padded jackets, meat and other food products, were often of poor quality.

Border Trade

Trade on the border plays a significant role in bilateral relations, especially between the Russian Far East (RFE) and the adjoining areas of China (Manchuria). Under Gorbachev Moscow opened the border to China in 1988, with the result that Chinese workers started migrating to RFE in search of work. The presence of a large military force hitherto had led to RFE's relative economic prosperity. Chita, Khabarovsk and Vladivostok were big centers of the Soviet military, equipped as they were, inter alia, with surface-to-surface strategic missiles (SS-12, 800 km range, SS-4, 1,600 km range) and 43 divisions of the army based in Central Asia, Transbaikal, Siberia and the Far East military regions. Besides, the army's tank divisions, motorized infantry, two parachute divisions (near Khabarovsk), and air force units were based in the region, including Mig-25 Foxbat squadrons, all facing China. So did the 60 combat ships and 100 submarines of the Soviet Pacific Fleet, mainly based in Vladivostok. A second railway line, the Baikal-Amur Mainline (BAM), was under construction further north of the old Trans-Siberian Railway to ensure logistic movement for these half-a-million people from west to east across the vast Russian territory.[12]

However, with the Gorbachev-initiated Soviet military draw-down in Europe and Asia and the subsequent Soviet collapse, RFE's economy suffered. Exodus of Russian workers began in the 1990s. Hence, RFE had to depend on migrant labor from abroad, e.g., North Korea, Vietnam and China. These workers, mostly cheap contract laborers, were given '3-D' jobs (dirty, dangerous, difficult) shunned by the Russians.[13] As many as 30,000 Chinese workers were legally employed in RFE, while only a few hundred Russians worked in China. About one million Chinese live along the border and in Siberian cities, and over 200,000 in RFE. The close economic and other ties of RFE with the Soviet Central Asian states weakened following the Soviet split in 1991. Consequently, economic ties with neighboring China dramatically increased. While RFE's trade with China was only 1% of the total Russian trade in 1985, it shot up to almost 34% in 1992. This is also due to strong complementarity between RFE and northeast China. However, RFE's growing dependence on trade with China and the need for migrant labor from China worried its local governments. The governor of the Khabarovsk Krai (district) Viktor Ishaev, for example, was vociferously anti-Chinese. These local leaders feared that, given RFE's decreasing population and the growing economic and demographic influence of the Chinese there, China may ultimately develop a stranglehold on the region. This fear also had historical roots. RFE was traditionally underdeveloped and under-populated and surrounded by more powerful neighbors. The local governors, in fact, resented Moscow-Beijing ties and agreements affecting RFE, and on occasion had even defied their central government. They were lukewarm towards the Tumenjiang Delta project, which would involve the cooperation of Russia with North Korea and China. Nevertheless, Moscow's interest in trade with the Asia-Pacific region (APR) was seen in the fact that about a third of its trade was conducted with that region. Moscow also hoped to enter the Asia-Pacific Economic Council (APEC) with China's help.[14]

Overall Trade

Russo-Chinese trade increased to $7. 7 billion in 1993, i.e., by 31% over the preceding year. However, Russian trade accounted for only 4% of total Chinese trade. Despite 'vigorous' border trade, especially with the northeast Chinese provinces of Heilongjiang and Jilin, the barter trade system remained a major obstacle. The quality of goods from both sides was usually shoddy, and Russia continued to have difficulty in paying in hard currency. Indeed, China's military trade with Russia not only served its national security interest but also helped Moscow cope with its financial difficulties.[15] Russia's stagnating economy provided a sharp contrast with that of China's largely successful experiment with 'socialist market economy'. The latter's GNP grew at a whopping 19. 5% annually during 1990-95, and continued at an average of 9% till 2000. Way back in 1979 China created Special Economic Zones (SEZ) with low taxes and cheap land and labor to lure foreign investment. By 1989 nearly 22,000 joint ventures operated there.[16] During the first half of 2000 its exports and imports reached record levels, with an increase in foreign exchange reserves by nearly $4 billion, all of which totaled $50 billion.[17] In contrast, Russia's inflation rate was rising by 30% every year. With 7 out of 10 companies evading taxes, tax arrears amounted to $200 billion annually.[18] Even Germany, Russia's biggest trade partner and creditor, poured cold water on Moscow's expressed hope that its $42 billion debt, much of it inherited from the Soviet era, would be written off during the G-8 summit in Okinawa in July 2000.

It was the stated objective of both Moscow and Beijing to create a market economy and achieve integration into the world economic system. They recognized that they should take advantage of their "unique geographical proximity and economic complementarity" to promote bilateral trade and technical cooperation while substituting "cash transactions" (read hard currency payments) for barter.[19] It was publicly acknowledged that improvement was needed in "means of payments". Indeed, China had agreed to delay repayment of loans incurred by the USSR in 1990 and 1991 and to work out a solution to other loans payable by post-Soviet Russia. Ever since former Premier Li Peng's visit to Moscow in April 1990, mentioned earlier, many high-level visits took place between Russia and China. They spawned a large number of economic, technical and military cooperation agreements. As noted, a significant dimension of Russia's very willing arms sales to China (and to other nations like Iran and India) was to ease its financial difficulties. Moscow's worldwide arms sales totaling $6. 4 billion, though trailing behind the USA's $21. 3 billion, was ahead of several other European arms peddlers like Germany ($2. 7 billion).[20] The Chinese market, along with the Indian, figured prominently in the Russian sales figures, even though China was downsizing and streamlining its large armed forces. Supply of nuclear fuel to China constituted another segment of Russia's bilateral trade with the latter country.[21] Moscow would also like to build a pipeline to sell China natural gas from its huge west Siberian natural gas deposits.

It is interesting to note official Chinese commentary while reporting on the G-8 nations. The commentaries invariably mention, separately, the "leading industrial nations", i.e., the rich seven, "and Russia", the only poor in G-8. It reflects contempt, as famously depicted by Klaus Mehnert in *Moscow-Peking*, mixed perhaps with pity, a deep-running historic-cultural superiority complex of the Middle Kingdom towards its northern neighbor, whose total foreign debt burden amounted to $120 billion.[22] In mid-July 2000 Russian President Vladimir Putin signed yet another set of trade agreements while visiting Beijing.

However, China's Russia-trade lagged far behind its trade with the West. Its US trade alone was ten times its trade with Russia. A major reason for this was that both these countries generally looked up to the West for hi-tech products rather than to each other. In addition, Western products made under license in China found convenient export outlets in flourishing Western and other markets. Nevertheless, China ranked as Russia's second largest trade partner after Germany.

Defense Relations

The Soviet military draw-down along its border provided China with relief in the north. It now had a freer hand in the east, i.e., Taiwan and the Paracels and Spratlys, and in the south, the Bay of Bengal and the Indian Ocean. China was also quick to take advantage of the post-Soviet chaos in Russia. To be sure, Beijing had bought Soviet arms worth $130 million during 1982-86, despite cool relations with Moscow. During Li's Moscow-visit in April 1990, both sides agreed to develop "military-economic relations", an oft-repeated phrase in subsequent summits. Other high-level visits, including those affecting defense ties, followed. Several defense cooperation agreements came in November 1993 and December 1995.[23] While Soviet-successor Russia remained in a poor state of political and economic organization, China set up recruiting offices there to procure arms. Hi-tech Russian arms were meant to help modernize China's armed forces, the People's Liberation Army (PLA), and not least its elite 'fist units' called quantou. This was in keeping with shifts in China's military doctrine from the Maoist 'people's war' to 'people's war under modern conditions' to 'limited war under hi-tech conditions.'[24] The Chinese sometimes even bypassed Moscow's central authority and struck direct deals with Russia's individual arms factories. Russian arms hitherto supplied had included MI-17 helicopters, SU-27 air superiority fighter jets (involving $1. 7 billion in 1992-96), $2 billion SU-30 multirole fighters (so far received only by India), Il-76 transport aircraft, Mig-29s and probably also advanced Mig-31s. Moscow had granted licenses to manufacture some of these in China. In mid-1992 the two neighbors agreed to cooperate on nuclear fusion research, as has already been seen. Other Russian arms supplied included tanks, submarines (including Kilos), SA-10 and SA-300 surface-to-air missiles, Moskit missiles for Sovremenny-class destroyers, AA-10 air-to-air missiles, and probably anti-satellite satellites.[25] Russia would also supply AL-31 FN turbofan engines for China's fourth-generation F-10 fighters to boost their range. The arms trade turnover reached $2 billion in 1994, the year when both sides agreed to retarget their missiles away from each other. A US State Department estimate for 1998 pegs the value of Russia's arms supply to China to $2.5 billion.[26]

Reports suggested that both Beijing and Moscow were developing new-generation ballistic missiles. The Russian Topol-M (NATO code-named SS-27) is a case in point. The 1990s saw a remarkable proliferation of military cooperation agreements, including one at the time of former Russian leader Boris Yeltsin's sixth summit in 1999 and the present leader Vladimir Putin's in July 2000. At the latter summit, the phrase "strategic partnership" was ritually repeated, and talks were partly devoted to national security cooperation.[27] Russia became China's largest arms supplier. A major motive for Russia was, of course, to earn hard currency and dispense with barter, which brought in poor quality Chinese goods, as we have seen already. Another was to ease relations with a difficult neighbor. Supply of military hardware and technology was a also a means to pay back debts as well as have China's support on a number of issues in the post-Cold War world dominated by the USA.

The Chinese navy was partly equipped with Russian destroyers and submarines, as noted. Further, it had plans to build two 48,000-ton Kiev-class short-take-off-and-landing (STOL) aircraft carriers by 2005, each equipped with 28 aircraft.[28] China was boosting its anti-ship C-802 missile's range. Beijing began its blue-water navy exercises way back in 1986 with its North Sea Fleet in northeastern Pacific. Next year came another exercise in the western Pacific. Beijing also set up an Ocean Observation Station on the Yongshu Reef in South China Sea to protect the Nansha Islands. In response, Vietnam, Malaysia and the Philippines began occupying several islands. China, meanwhile, continued to shift from the Maoist strategy of coastal defense to offshore operations, thanks to its military cooperation with Moscow. It focused on the development of amphibious capability for its navy. Given China's dispute with Southeast Asian states over the Spratly and Paracel islands, it is little wonder that the Foreign Ministers of the Association of Southeast Asian Nations (ASEAN) hastened to sign the Manila Declaration on an international code of conduct in the South China Sea. While Hanoi was an enthusiastic signatory, Beijing withheld its endorsement and submitted its own draft on the conduct to ASEAN in October 1999.

Beyond this, *India* also had reasons to be wary of China's increasing naval power. The Chinese had set up a naval base in the Coco Island courtesy Myanmar, from which Beijing could, inter alia, monitor India's missile tests in the Bay of Bengal. The Chinese navy was openly displaying its ambition to develop into a long-range blue-water force. In late July 2000 a guided-missile destroyer and a supply ship from the South China Sea Fleet steamed to Tanzania. Their crew played football with the hosts! This was the first time that Chinese ships visited the African continent in half-a-century.[29] Coming to think of it, you do not need warships to play football, so the mission of the visit certainly went beyond a friendly match or two! In early August 2000 the Chinese navy carried out an exercise to test the wartime readiness of civilian ships. Beijing's active military cooperation with the Burmese military regime was also a source of worry for India, since its turbulent northeast was next door to Myanmar. Of equal concern was the spurt in Chinese naval activities, particularly in the Bay of Bengal, and the show of flag in the Indian Ocean. Meanwhile, three months after Kozyrev's visit, reports emerged that Russian defense experts were to train the Chinese armed forces in the use of Russian arms and that Chinese personnel would attend Russian military schools.

In July 1994 a further agreement came on avoiding accidental military confrontation. In September Jiang Zemin was the first Chinese President to visit Russia in 37 years. The ensuing Joint Statement of 3 September reiterated that of 18 December 1992, on no-first-use and no targeting of nuclear weapons against each other.[31] In April 1997 the two sides, along with Kazakhstan, Kyrgyzstan and Tajikistan signed two agreements on confidence-building measures (CBM) along their borders and on mutual troop cuts. These were hailed as being of "great significance" and as representing a new model for regional peace. The "strategic partnership" clause was ritualistically inserted in the Sino-Russian Statement on International Issues.[32] Along with the drastic Soviet troop cuts, the then Russian Foreign Minister Andrei Kozyrev's reiterated in January 1994 no-first-use of nuclear weapons against China (which was reciprocated). Russia's continued weapons sales and high-level mutual visits, and defense ties between Moscow and Beijing further cemented bilateral relations. These were further strengthened when the Defense Ministers of both sides, along with those from the Central Asian states like Kazakhstan and Turkmenistan, met in early August 2000.[30] It is to be noted that, like India, China was not satisfied buying off-the-shelf arms but wanted large-scale military technology transfer from Russia.

Political Relations

The past half-a-century had been eventful in Sino-Soviet/Russian relations. While in 1949, when mainland China turned communist, the development brought cheers, bilateral relations had already started to move downhill by 1959, when Khrushchev paid a visit to Mao. In March 1969 the two neighbors were firing at each other on the Ussuri. The death of Zhou and Mao in 1976 brought no significant change in bilateral relations, even though the Soviets seemed to have hoped for it. Post-Mao China remained hostile towards Moscow's "hegemonism". In 1979 the Kampuchean and Afghan crises took Sino-Soviet relations on a further nosedive. Things, however, started looking up with the appearance of Gorbachev in the Kremlin in 1985, as has been noted earlier in this account. The 1989 summit was an indicator of an upturn in future relations. It was also announced that year that ninety percent of the festering border dispute had been resolved.

At the turn of the new millennium the two permanent members of the UN Security Council share much in common in their global view. Their political differences, which were enormous in the past and fuelled the big-power triangle along with the US, are hardly visible today. Yeltsin's visit to Beijing in December 1992 set the tone for bilateral relations, which urged each side to respect the other's right to pursue its domestic policy as it saw fit.

There are many similarities between Russia and China in terms of the problems they face. Both are large, multinational states. With the end of the Cold War, Gorbachev's preaching of glasnost and perestroika, and the spread of democratic fervor worldwide, each of them faces the dilemma of striking the right balance between granting liberty to its citizens and at the same time maintaining effective control over fissiparous forces. In facing this challenge, Russia before Putin was hobbling but China managed to maintain a better balance, which worked, even though at times it trampled over human rights, notably the Tien An Mien Square massacre in 1989.

Both sides understand how difficult it is to keep the centrifugal forces in a multiethnic society in check, once even partial freedom is granted. The rapid balkanization of Yugoslavia, Czechoslovakia and the mighty USSR itself, as well as the disappearance of communism as a force to reckon with from the entire region of East Europe, are a reminder of that harsh reality. So, it is small wonder that Beijing, unlike the West, officially supports Russia's military campaigns against the Chechen rebels. Moscow in turn keeps reiterating its full support for Beijing against the show of independence of "breakaway" Taiwan and the independence movement for Tibet.[33]

In the economic sphere, both Russia and China are trying to cope with the novel experiment of converting their command economy into a market economy. They have discarded their past ideology in doing so. Despite the inevitable socio-economic dislocations that they face, China's performance is by far superior. Moscow, indeed, can learn from Beijing how to minimize chaos and transit to market economy[34] or, as the Chinese prefer to call it, "socialist market economy". Russia can also count on China's support for its goal of joining APEC. In the defense sphere, as we have already seen, close cooperation with China provides Russia with income, as well as a source of outlet for its abundant weapons.

Besides economic and defense ties, it is resentment against the West, especially the USA, which brings Moscow and Beijing together politically. China resents the US-led NATO bombing of its embassy in Belgrade, the Western/US criticism of the human rights situation in the country, the US backing of Taiwan, and the talk in Washington of creating the National Missile and Theatre Missiles Defenses (NMD/TMD). We shall read about these ballistic missile defense plans in Chapter Six. The question of extending TMD to Taiwan irks Beijing tremendously. At this writing in March 2001, new irritations have developed. The Bush administration is irked over the Chinese arrest of US scholars. In early April 2001 a snooping US spy plane collided midair with a Chinese F-8 jet fighter, caused the death of its pilot; and the US plane itself force-landed on China's Hainan island in a crippled condition. The Chinese detained the 24-member crew of the EP-3A Aries II for several days and surely examined the aircraft's hi-tech spying gadgets. The incident increased the level of Sino-US irritations all the more since Beijing kept demanding an apology from the US, but Bush was not willing to go that far. Beijing in turn felt irritated at the defection of an army officer and Bush's plans to sell arms like sophisticated AEGIS-class destroyers and anti-missile radars to Taiwan. These types of friction have continued through mid-2001 although the Chinese Vice-Premier visited Washington in February and Bush was invited to China in fall.[36]

Moscow shares many of these and other resentments against the USA, related to the NMD/TMD issue, for US criticism of its military action against breakaway Chechnya, for the US-led bombing of Russia's Yugoslav 'brothers' during March-June 1999, and for allegedly taking advantage of its post-Cold War role as the sole superpower. For Moscow, Western/US criticism of Russia over Chechnya is seen as undue interference in its domestic affairs. The US plan for NMD is taken to be a violation of the 1972 ABM Treaty, which was a major pillar of US-Soviet cooperative relations. The bombing of Milosevic's Yugoslavia and other forms of US involvement in global issues are perceived as an exercise in hegemonism. So, Moscow has been vociferous in recent years about the need to move away from a 'unipolar', US-dominated world and to create a 'multipolar' one, in which China and India should play an important role. Indeed, the Russians have even talked about a Moscow-Beijing-New Delhi triangle. But this idea has not met with overt enthusiasm in the other two capitals. Moscow also resents NATO's eastward expansion. It suspects that this is a design to control East Europe, Transcaucasia, and Central Asia, regions still considered to be of considerable importance to Russia, given their mutual historical, economic and other ties.[35] So, Moscow and Beijing share a number of common perceptions of the structure of present world politics, of which anti-US sentiment forms a significant part; this, of course, notwithstanding their otherwise close ties with Washington, hence forming a far milder version of the big-power triangle of the 1970s and 1980s.

To sum up, Sino-Russian relations at the turn of the new millennium register far better and business-like relations[37] than those in the past. Barring the vagaries of international politics, they seem to promise a largely cooperative future.

Readings

1. Paul H. Clyde, Burton F. Beers, *The Far East*; 6th ed., Prentice Hall of India, New Delhi, 1981.

2. *An Outline History of China*, Foreign Languages Press, Peking, 1958.

3. Yu Teng and John K. Fairbank, *China's Response to the West: A Documentary Survey 1839-1923*, Atheneum, New York, 1970.

4. Harold C. Hinton, *Peking-Washington: Chinese Foreign Policy and the United States*, SAGE, Washington, 1976; "The United States and the Sino-Soviet Confrontation," *Orbis*, Vol. XIX, No. 1,Spring 1975.

5. Herbert J. Ellison, "Changing Sino-Soviet Relations" *Problems of Communism* (*POC*), Washington, May-June 1987,Vol. XXXVI, No. 3, pp. 17-29.

6. Mikhail S. Gorbachev, *A Time for Peace*, Richardson & Steirman, New York, 1985.

7. Steven M. Goldstein, "Diplomacy amid Protest: The Sino-Soviet Summit," *POC*, Sept-Oct 1989, Vol. XXXVIII, No. 5, pp. 49-71.

8. Won Bae Kim, "Sino-Russian Relations and Chinese workers in the Russian Far East," *Asian Survey*, Vol. XXXIV, No. 12, Dec. 1994, pp. 1065-6.

9. Clay Moltz, "Regional Tension in the Russo-Chinese Rapprochement," *Asian Survey*, Vol. XXXV, No. 1, 1995, pp. 512-520.

10. Li Peng's speech at the 21st Century Forum in Beijing, Sept. 1996, reprinted in *China Report*, Delhi, Vol. 33, No. 1, Jan-Mar 1997, p. 119.

11. Nimmi Kurian, "Defense modernization in China," *International Studies*, New Delhi, Vol. 37, No. 3, July-Sept. 2000.
12. US Dept. of State, *World Military Expenditures and Arms Transfers 1998*, Washington, Table III, p. 168.
13. John W. Garner, "The Chinese Communist Party and the Collapse of Soviet Communism," *China Quarterly*, London, no. 133, Mar 1993, pp. 25-26.
14. Felix N. Yurlov, "Problems of Security in the Post-Cold War World", *World Affairs*, New Delhi, Vol. 4, No. 2, April-June 2000, pp. 42-56.

Notes

1. For a brief history of Sino-Russian relations, see Paul H. Clyde, Burton F. Beers, *The Far East*, 6th ed., Prentice Hall of India, New Delhi, 1981, pp. 104-5.
2. Ssu-Yu Teng, John K. Fairbank, *China's Response to the West: A Documentary Survey 1839-1923*, Atheneum, New York, 1970, p. 136.
3. *An Outline History of China*, Foreign Languages Press, Peking, 1958, pp.270-3; *Konferenzen und Vertraege*, Part II, Vol. 3, 1492-1914, 2nd. ed., A. G. Ploetz Verlag, Wuerzburg, 1958, p. 384.
4. "China wieder vernuenftig," *Der Spiegel*, Hamburg, Vol. 33, No. 11, 12 Mar. 1979, p. 146.
5. See Herbert J. Ellison, "Changing Sino-Soviet Relations," *POC*, Vol. XXXVI, No. 3, May-June 1987, pp. 17-29.
6. Mikhail S. Gorbachev, *A Time for Peace*, Richardson & Steirman, New York, 1985, p. 18.
7. Ellison, op. cit. Mikhail G. Nossov, "The USSR and the Security of the Asia-Pacific Region. From Vladivostok to Krasnoyarsk," *Asian Survey*,

University of California, Vol. XXIX, No. 3, March 1989, pp. 252-267.

8. John W. Garver, "The "New Type" of Sino-Soviet Relations," *Asian Survey*, Vol. XXIX, No. 12, Dec. 1989, p. 1138; Indian Express, 29 Sept. 1990.

9. See Steven M. Goldstein, "Diplomacy Amid Protest: The Sino-Soviet Summit," *POC*, Sept. -Oct. 1989, No. 5, Vol. XXXVIII, pp. 49-71; Garver, op. cit., pp. 1136-52. Hardliners within the Chinese government like Li Peng ordered the military to crackdown on the large gathering of protesters, mostly young people. Tanks were fielded to bulldoze over them.

10. *The Indian Express*, 29 Sept. 1990.

11. *Times of India*, 23 June 1992.

12. Drew Middleton, "Geheimnis, eingehuellt in ein Raetsel," *Der Spiegel*, vol. 33, No. 11, 12 Mar. 1979, pp. 156-166.

13. Won Bae Kim, "Sino-Russian Relations and Chinese Workers in the Russian Far East," *Asian Survey*, Vol. XXXIV, No. 12, Dec. 1994, pp. 1065-6.

14. Truneo Akata, Russia in Asia in 1994. An Emerging East Asian Path," *Asian Survey*, Vol. XXXV, No. 1, Jan. 1995, p. 100.

15. *Strategic Digest*, New Delhi, Vol. XXX, No. 5 May 2000, p. 573. PRC's 800 million dollars deals with Moscow on supply of four Sovremenny-class destroyers first signed in 1996, which started arriving in Feb. 2000.

16. The SEZs include Hainan island, the Zhu Jiang Delta, nearby Shenzhen, South Fujian Triangle with Xiamen, the Minnan Delta, the Chang Jiang Delta with Shanghai, the Shandong Peninsula and the Liaodong Peninsula, all located in the South and east of coastal China. *National Geographic* map on China, July 1991, Vol. 180, No. 1, p. 110A; David Backman,

"China in 1994, Marking Time, Making Money," *Asian Survey*, Vol. XXXV, No. 1, Jan. 1995, p. 40; Chinese Central TV (CCTV), 31 July 2000, 11 p. m.; Li Peng at the 21st Century Forum, 4-6 Sept. 1996, *China Report*, Delhi, Vol. 33, No. 1, Jan. -Mar. 1997, p. 119. According to CCTV, with steel, oil and other industries showing profits, growth in 2000 is expected to be around 7.5%. 22 July 2000, 9. 15 p. m. However, China's economic reforms are also creating dislocation like unemployment. The official figure is 12 million, as of Feb. 2000, CCTV, 29 Feb. 2000, 9. 45 p. m.

17. CCTV, 31 July 2000, 10. 30 p. m.

18. Deutsche Welle TV (DWTV), 21 July, 5. 50 p. m., 26 Aug. 2000, 11. 30 p.m.. Putin told Russian Duma, on 8 July 2000, that the country's weak economy and declining population were among the biggest problems that needed a strong central government. DWTV, 8 July 9. 30 p. m.; BBC TV, 10 July 2000, 9.50 p. m. Russia is even considering receiving nuclear waste from abroad to earn 5-6 billion dollars. The Russian nuclear fuel reprocessing cost is $300/kg., compared to $1,000/kg. in the West. Strategic Digest, Vol. XXIX, No. 7, July 1999, p. 1126. According to a CIA report, the 1998 Asian financial crisis hit Russia hard. Its oil export sharply declined and an exodus of foreign investors took place. Production dropped by 4. 6%. In 1999, however, the country's output increased for the second time only since 1991, by an official 3. 2%. www.foia.ucia.gov.

19. Boris Yeltsin-Jiang Zemin's joint statement following the Joint Statements of 18 Dec. 1992 and 3 Sept. 1994, *China Report*, Vol. 34, No. 2, April-June 1998, p. 240.

20. DWTV, 21 July 2000, 5.50 p. m.

21. CCTV, 3 Mar. 2000, 10.45 pm.

22. DWTV, 22 July 2000, 9.50 a. m. The G-8 summit in Okinawa in July 2000 decided to make Russia a full member. DWTV, 26 July 2000, 10.15 p. m.

23. 1,000 Russian scientists were reportedly working in China in the 1990's. Strategic Digest, Vol. XXX, No. 9, Sept. 2000, p. 1266. Nimmi Kurian, "Defense Modernisation in China," *International Studies*, New Delhi, Vol. 37 No. 3, July-Sept. 2000, p. 250.

24. Ibid., p. 245. While the People's Liberation Army cut its manpower in the 1980's and 1990's from 4.2 million to 2.5 million men, paramilitary and reserve forces (latter 1.2 million) would still bring the total to 4.6 million men. Ibid., p. 246.

25. *Strategic Digest*, IDSA, New Delhi, Vol. XXIX, No. 2, Feb. 1999, pp. 258-9. In Jan. 2000, Russo-Chinese talks were held on a joint missile defense system and Chinese use of a Russian military space-based system. *Strategic Digest*, Vol. XXX, No. 5, May 2000, p. 632. But there is resistance within the Russian military in supplying the technology for the new SU prototype multi-role fighter Project 1-42. *Strategic Digest*, Vol. XXIX, No. 4, April 1999, p. 591.

26. US Dept. of State, *World Military Expenditures and Arms Transfers 1998* (*WMEAT*), Washington, Table III, p. 168.

27. CCTV, 3 Mar. 2000, 10.45 p. m. on Russian Deputy Premier Kievanov's meeting with Chinese President Zemin, when they reiterated their "strategic partnership"; 22 July 2000, 9.15 p. m., on Putin's visit.

28. The present author is grateful to the University of Hawaii's *SUPAR* (Soviet Union in the Pacific-Asia Region) program for its bulletins containing information on the early 1990s. See also Sheldon W.

Simon, "East Asian Security: The Playing Field Has Changed," *Asian Survey*, Vol. XXXIV, No. 12, Dec. 1994, pp. 1047-63.

29. CCTV, 28 July 2000, 10.30 p. m. On India's reaction, Ashok Kapur, "China and Proliferation: Implications for India," *China Report*, Vol. 34, Nos. 3-4, July-Dec. 1998, p. 406.

30. CCTV, 1 Aug. 2000, 8.30 p. m.

31. Akata, op. cit., p. 102; Zemin-Yeltsin Joint Statement, *China Report*, Vol. 34, No. 2, April- June 1998, pp. 240-1

32. *Xinhua* text, 23 April 1997, reproduced in *China Report*, ibid., pp. 249-250.

33. Among a host of joint statements emanating over the past decade, see, for example, the one signed by Presidents Boris Yeltsin and Jiang Zemin. *China Report*, Vol. 34, No. 2, April-June 1998, p. 240.

34. China under Deng Xiaoping opened up its economy from 1978 but resistance from hardline conservatives like Deng Liquin was overcome finally in 1992, at the 14th party congress. John W. Garner, "The Chinese Communist Party and the Collapse of Soviet Communism," *China Quarterly*, London, No. 133, Mar. 1993, pp. 25-26.

35. Felix N. Yurlov, "Problems of Security in the Post-Cold War World," *World Affairs*, New Delhi, Vol. 4, No. 2, April -June 2000, pp. 42-56.

36. *CNN.com* and *ABCNews.com*, 3 April 2001.

37. Beijing considers Putin, the ex-KGB operative and judo black belt, a practical man with whom one can do business. In China, the coastal elite are becoming increasingly prominent on the political scene, thanks to the country's economic development along the coast. Premier Zhu Rongji is an economic expert, while President Zemin is partly trained in Russia and

speaks Russian. Hans-Georg Wieck, " Jiang Zemin tritt nicht aus dem Schatten von Deng Xiaoping," *IndoAsia*, Sachsenheim, Vol. 39, No. 4, 1997, pp. 4-5.

5

The Sino-US Rapprochement

In the 19th century the Chinese and Americans interacted with each other more closely than would appear to the uninitiated. There were Chinese settlers in Pacific-facing California who mostly found odd jobs as working hands. Their traditional pigtails were a butt of ridicule in the USA, as vividly portrayed in such novels as *The Sand Pebbles*. The word 'shanghai', in fact, entered American vocabulary but as a verb and in the negative sense of kidnapping or inducing someone to do something by underhand methods. The Americans also went to China, chiefly as missionaries and to do business. In fact, in 1899 the US Secretary of State John Hay sent an 'Open Door letter to the then major powers like the UK, France, Italy, Germany and up-and-coming Japan. It declared that all nations must have equal opportunity to trade with China. The US, yet to 'arrive' as a big power, was clearly in a mood to expand its business horizons while steering clear of the Old World, i.e., European, politics and intrigues. Missionary and trade ties with China grew.

With the birth of the communist party in the 1920s, and its subsequent growth, civil war marked much of the decades in the 20th century in China till 1949, when the latter turned communist. The ruling Kuomintang (KMT) and the communists had frequent violent encounters, even as Japan entered the scene with its puppet Manchukuo government, which it set up in Manchuria during 1931-32. In the course of World War II the US provided material help to China to fight the Japanese. Dumdum airport at Calcutta, incidentally, played an important role in enabling materiel to fly over the

Himalayan 'hump' in India's northeast, where bad weather often made these supply missions hazardous.[1] Though the US military aid went to the KMT, that did not prevent communist leader Mao Zedong from praising the Allied role in the war in April 1945 since the latter, particularly the US, fought against China's enemy, Japan.[2] At the end of the war, however, the KMT preempted the communists by occupying several regions evacuated by the Japanese like the lower Yangtze valley, Manchuria etc., and with US help. This embittered the Chinese communists vis-à-vis Washington. One reason why the Maoist communists supported Stalin in his conflict from 1948 with a defiant Tito, the Yugoslav guerrilla fighter and leader of the country after the war, was to strengthen Moscow's stand against the USA.

When the communists captured power in China in October 1949 and ousted the US-backed KMT from the mainland, the Americans were upset. Their long missionary and trade ties with the country would now have to be severed. China, for them, was 'lost'. As already noted, the Korean War broke out in mid-1950. The USA and communist China found themselves pitted against each other in the war. For three long years, casualties on both sides increased mutual bitterness. On 27 June the US extended its protection to Taiwan, the offshore island where the KMT now ruled and claimed to represent the whole of China. In 1954, during the Battle of Dien Bien Phu, in which the communist Viet Minh forces defeated the French colonialist troops, Beijing helped Ho Chi Minh with material support. This in turn only confirmed the then prevalent US fear that the communists were all set to take over the globe. State Secretary John Foster Dulles played up the alleged Chinese threat to create the SEATO as a collective security body for the defense of Southeast Asia. From the mid-1950s the US Seventh Fleet stationed in the Pacific began patrolling the Taiwan Straits. This enraged Beijing, since it considered Taiwan as an integral part of China, the KMT illegal, and the US protection of Taiwan and the naval patrolling as gross interference in China's domestic affairs. Periodic Chinese bombardment of other offshore islands like Quemoy and Matsu, to defy the US and the KMT, precipitated crises in the mid-1950s and in 1958. Not only did the US and China maintain no embassies in each other's capitals, the permanent seat in the Security Council reserved for China was given to Taipei, not Beijing. The US and its Western friends were enormously influential in the immediate postwar years and decades; they took every precaution to keep the People's Republic of China isolated.

Opening to China

Despite all the bad blood between Washington and Beijing, however, their representatives opened secret talks in Warsaw in September 1958. These talks lasted off and on through the next decade. The result was zero. Each side stuck to its own formal official position. This is well portrayed in the memoirs of the then US Ambassador in Warsaw, Jacob Beam, in his book *Multiple Exposure*. Negotiations cannot succeed if there is no give and take. Also, the Soviets were probably kept well informed about the talks by the Poles, who where Moscow's allies. By the mid-1960s the US got increasingly involved in the Vietnam war, as we have seen. The Sino-Soviet conflict was also out in the open. In mid-March 1966 a tacit understanding developed between China and the USA, that as long as the latter refrained from carrying out raids on Chinese territory, Beijing would not directly intervene in the Vietnam war (unlike in the case of the Korean war). During 1966-68 the Chinese got busy with their Great Proletarian Cultural Revolution (GPCR). It was anything but cultural in the classic sense of the word. Mao let loose bands of young hooligans who turned the country, including the bureaucracy, upside down. Xenophobia gripped the country and ambassadors were withdrawn. China became inward-looking. Relations soured with many countries, including the USA. Things looked up somewhat when the peak of the GPCR passed.

Then came the Ussuri River clashes of March 1969, between the Chinese and Soviet border guards. We noted that. We also noted that the Nixon Administration, freshly installed in power, sought to use the Sino-Soviet conflict, which had now turned physical, to serve several Realpolitik purposes, the foremost of which was a decent exit from the Vietnam imbroglio. As also noted, the US set up several channels of communication with Beijing, including Bucharest and the more successful one of Islamabad. Various signals, by gestures and messages, were sent to Beijing between 1969 and 1971, to indicate US interest in talks with the latter. In fact, in 1967 Nixon, then a presidential aspirant, had already written in the prestigious US journal *Foreign Affairs* that, in future, the US should reorient its China policy and bring the latter country out of 'its angry isolation.' The Chinese started responding cautiously. In the October 1970 celebrations of the founding of the People's Republic, US journalist and author Edgar Snow, who was sympathetic to the communists of China, was given a prestigious seat next to China's great helmsman Mao. That was the Chinese way of saying that Beijing was quite willing to open talks and relations with Americans who treated it more gently than hitherto. Another Chinese signal came in April 1971. A mediocre US table-tennis team playing in Japan suddenly received an invitation from China to come and play there! The US government gave clearance, the US team then went visiting the communist rival, and lo and behold, they were received by no less a person than Prime Minister Zhou Enlai himself! The incident was promptly branded as *'ping-pong' diplomacy* by the international media. *Time* magazine called it "the ping heard round the world". Nixon responded with glee. On 14 April the US announced that it was lifting the 21-year embargo on trade with China and other restrictions on visa and currency relating to visit there.

The US perseverance had paid off. Agha Hilaly, the Pakistani Ambassador in Washington, passed on to Kissinger a written message from Beijing. It was a strange sheet of paper; it had nothing in print, like a letterhead, and was entirely handwritten. There was no logo, no bureaucratic seal, or anything else to show it came from a government. And, on top of all this, it was unsigned too! So, it could hardly be construed as an official letter. Nevertheless, it said in effect that China was willing to accept the US offer of sending an envoy to Beijing to open talks. The non-official nature of the document showed that those Chinese leaders who favored a new beginning of relations with the USA did not want to reveal themselves on paper lest there be a premature leak. In retrospect, it seems certain that the highest Chinese leaders were divided on whether to improve relations with the USA or with the USSR. In fact, the coup attempt by Marshal Lin Biao, the chief of the People's Liberation Army (PLA) and successor-designate to Chairman Mao, a few months after Kissinger's secret visit to Beijing in July 1971, clearly revealed the split. Lin Biao tried to fly away to the USSR when the coup failed but was reportedly shot down over Mongolia.

Polo I

In any case, the question now was: who was going to be that historic envoy to communist China? Whoever was chosen would immediately come to world limelight, write his memoirs and laugh all the way to the bank! After keeping his Secretary of State Bill Rogers and National Security Adviser Kissinger in suspense for a while, Nixon finally chose the latter to make the historic dash to Beijing. Codenamed *Polo I*, it was kept a super secret, barring a few privileged like General Yahya Khan, the Pakistani military dictator, and a few of his closest associates. Since Kissinger was much in the news those days, the snooping newsmen had to be shaken off. So Kissinger ostensibly embarked upon an Asia tour, was scheduled to visit New Delhi and then Islamabad. The plan was that he would feign stomach trouble in the Pakistani capital and pretend to take a few days off his busy schedule. But he actually developed one in Delhi though he kept up a bold face and did the circuits dutifully. Then in Islamabad he complained openly of his ailment, Yahya picked up the cue and offered him a Presidential retreat for rest. All this play-acting was meant for the benefit of newsmen who were always 'all ears'. In the dark of the night, old Henry dashed off by car to the military section of the Islamabad airport. He boarded a Pakistani aircraft where, to the shock of the accompanying US Secret Service men, his bodyguards, *Chinese* military officers received him![3]

Kissinger's main mission was to prepare an even greater event that would send shock waves round the world. This was Nixon's forthcoming visit to Beijing in February 1972. It would be the first time that a US President, and a dyed-in-the-wool anti-communist Republican one at that, would go to communist China. The implications for both US allies and the USSR would be enormous. On July 15, 1971, Nixon appeared on prime time TV to tell the world that right at that moment his envoy, Dr. Kissinger, was visiting Beijing. Polo I spawned another momentous event. In October, thanks to US string-pulling, communist China replaced the USA's faithful ally Taiwan in the UN Security Council's permanent seat. It was about this time that the abortive coup by China's top military leader took place. Kissinger's opening of China also caused some hard calculations in *New Delhi* under Indira Gandhi. Trouble with Pakistan over the newly declared Bangladesh in East Pakistan was brewing. Millions of Bengali refugees were pouring into neighboring India to escape Islamabad's military repression. The South Asian subcontinent was clearly headed for a drastic solution of the problem as 1971 wore on. War between India and Pakistan seemed inevitable as long as Islamabad did not mend its ways and concede to Bengali nationalism. But New Delhi was worried about the growing Washington-Islamabad-Beijing axis. China and America could create considerable trouble for India in its military confrontation with Pakistan. China had already developed specially close relations with the latter ever since its 1962 border war with India; both Beijing and Islamabad had a border problem with India and quite naturally rallied together. And the US was grateful to Yahya

Khan for the services rendered to open up China. Hence, to counter that axis, India turned to Moscow. The latter in turn had its own border and ideological problems with China and thoroughly disliked Islamabad's close security cooperation with the USA. Hence, it did not take long for the USSR to sign a Friendship Treaty with New Delhi in August 1971. The key clause, of mutual assistance if either side faced a threat, provided the Indian Prime Minister Mrs. Indira Gandhi the required insurance cover she needed against any possible third party intervention. The Indo-Soviet treaty, hence, was the direct result of the US-Chinese connection and Pakistan's linkage with it.

The Nixon Visit

But to revert to Sino-US relations: during 21-28 February 1972 President Nixon visited the People's Republic of China. The visit sent, as mentioned, shock waves throughout the world. Nations had to recalculate their relations with the two states involved and adjust their foreign policies accordingly. While his team of foreign policy experts met separately with their Chinese counterparts, Nixon naturally was doing the top circuits among the Chinese hierarchy. He was especially keen to meet Chairman Mao, who had already become a legend worldwide. Mao had become the symbol of protest, primarily against the US war in Vietnam. From Tokyo to Calcutta, from Berkeley to Jadavpur, from Sorbonne to other universities, students went on a rampage on campus. This was the era of 'flower children', beatnik culture, hippies and LSD. Pop songs preached peace and love, not war. And a major symbol of this esoteric mixture of subcultures and war protestors was Mao. Strangely enough, Mao had never stepped outside his country, barring a stray visit to the USSR. Nixon had even learnt by heart a few of Mao's poems during the long hours of his flight. While he was keen to meet the Chairman, he also could not afford to forget that he was the most powerful executive in the world, representing a superpower. At one point upon his arrival in Beijing he was shaving. "Henry" (Kissinger) burst in and urged him to rush to the Chairman who had granted him an audience. But Nixon, the US President, had to show that he did not come to kowtow. He says in his memoirs that he took his time shaving, and unhurriedly boarded the car waiting to take him to Mao!

The encounter with the latter in his simple abode has been vividly described in the memoirs. Mao's niece, who had studied in the USA, acted as interpreter. Nixon recited a few lines from one of Mao's poems to please the latter. Mao was duly pleased and said he liked rightists like Nixon but had problems with pseudo-socialists, meaning the Soviets. It was a strange meeting. A rightwing Republican leader striking bonhomie with an ultra-leftist whose slogans were that political power grew out of the barrel of a gun and that the US with all its atom bombs was a 'paper tiger'!

Meanwhile Kissinger and Premier Zhou Enlai, along with their advisers, thrashed out a number of issues. The result of their toil was *the Shanghai Communique*. It stated the US and Chinese positions on a variety of issues.[4] *First*, the two sides agreed to disagree on Vietnam. And, what was unusual for a communique, their respective views were incorporated; usually a joint communique includes propositions agreed upon by the signatories. *Second*, the US agreed to decrease its military presence in Taiwan, as tension in the area diminished. This was a compromise between Beijing's stand that it had the right to liberate Taiwan and the US commitment to defend the latter. *Third*, both sides agreed to respect the territorial integrity and sovereignty of other states. *Fourth*, neither state was to dominate the Asia-Pacific region and were agreed to oppose any third power trying to do so (read Moscow!). *Fifth*, a disclaimer was added, viz., Sino-US relations were not directed against any other state. Such disclaimers are actually intended to have the effect of anything but soothing the nerves! They have the nuisance value of increasing worry, in this case, that of the Kremlin. Kissinger must have delighted in the inclusion of this clause.

Sixth, and most important for Beijing, the US recognized that China was one and that Taiwan was part of China. This last clause sounded great but was actually hollow. No one disputed that China was one country, least of all Beijing or Taipei. Taiwan, as an island and therefore as a geographical entity, most certainly belonged to the larger geographical entity of China. Nobody doubted that. The key question, however, was political. *Who* represented that one China (including the island of Taiwan)? Was it the People's Republic of China (Beijing) or the Republic of China (Taipei)? The Shanghai Communique simply skirted that key question and left a void. The US had too many significant business, security and other ties with Taiwan to renounce them all at one stroke. The Taiwanese also had powerful friends in the US Senate, who would oppose too drastic a move against Taipei. The US must have successfully urged upon Beijing these limits on its maneuverability. So Beijing was satisfied, for the time being, with the US declaration that it would not play a two-China game. The Chinese have one of the oldest histories in the world. And they have learnt the value of patience. They surely were confident that ultimately, at some point of time in future, the Americans would have to veer around to their point of view and grant what they wanted regarding the Taiwan question. After all, it was the Americans who came running to them. And Beijing had already replaced Taipei in the UN Security Council, and this with American connivance, something which was unthinkable even a few years ago.

Various ties rapidly built up between the USA and communist China as *the result of the Nixon visit* in 1972.[5] RCA Global Communications set up that year two permanent ground stations for satellite communication in China. Following up its easing of trade with China the previous year, on 22 November the US lifted ban on its ships and aircraft from visiting the People's Republic. In January 1973 came the Paris Peace Agreement ending the war in Vietnam and paving the way for US troop pullout. Next month Kissinger again visited Beijing. While in March Sino-

Soviet talks on navigation in the border rivers met with a deadlock, the Chinese released the last three US prisoners. On 1 May the US and China opened liaison offices on each other's territory; they would act as substitutes for embassies and facilitate communications. On the US Independence Day, 4 July, Chase Manhattan Bank announced that it was establishing ties with the Bank of China. Four days later, parcel delivery service began between the two countries. In November Kissinger was again in China, but this time as the Secretary of State, a position he held since August.

Relations Level Off

But relations leveled off, and were even sometimes jolted, in the subsequent years. Nixon was out over the Watergate scandal. In April 1975 the State Department cancelled a Chinese troupe's scheduled visit to America since its program contained a song on the liberation of Taiwan. In January 1976 Zhou died of cancer. Mao died in September. A new post-Mao era was beginning in China. Meanwhile the Chinese were irritated with President Ford. They deliberately ignored him and sent an aircraft to pick up Nixon to come and visit their country, even though the latter was out of power. Jimmy Carter succeeded Ford in the November 1976 elections. Though Ford had, on Kissinger's advice, approved the sale of two Cyber 172 computers to China, Carter allowed the sale to lapse. The computer question arose because the US did not want to help proliferate nuclear weapons nor their refinement by nuclear-aspirants like China. The latter, in turn, was disappointed that Washington was apparently doing precious little in the face of growing Soviet political and military involvement in troubled regions of Africa, including the strategic Horn of Africa in the 1970s. In May 1977 the US and China opened talks on another major issue besides Taiwan, that of unsettled mutual financial claims. Three months later Carter's State Secretary, Cyrus Vance, went to Beijing for talks but these were largely sterile.

Next year relations looked up somewhat. In April the US announced sale of wheat to China; the first time had been in 1974. In May Carter's National Security Adviser Brzezinski, whom we have already met, paid a visit to China and, among other things, inspected the long Sino-Soviet border. At one point he pretended to see the (Russian) bear on the other side! With his anti-Russian hawkishness, the Columbia Professor hit it off with the Beijing leaders. He also roped in the Japanese and got the Sino-Japanese Friendship Treaty to be signed on 12 August. There was nothing wrong with a friendship pact except that in international relations they often mean ganging up on a third party! This was no exception. The Chinese had long insisted on retaining an 'anti-hegemony' clause in it, the reason for Japanese procrastination so far. The word 'hegemony', everyone knew, was the Chinese code for the USSR. Japan, to be sure, had its own frustrations with Moscow over the Kurile islands in the north, which the Soviets had captured at the end of World War II. At the same time, they did not want to be seen to be joining China in its anti-Soviet campaign. However, Brzezinski managed to overcome Japanese hesitations and the clause was retained. The signing of the treaty received a great deal of media exposure. Brezhnev and his Foreign Minister Gromyko were hardly in a celebrating mood that night!

The Indochina Crisis

The situation in Southeast Asia worsened over the Indochina crisis that was meanwhile brewing.[6] It affected China too and got enmeshed in the US-USSR-China triangular politics. What happened was this. In 1975 the North Vietnamese and the south-based Viet Cong launched an offensive and united the country under communist rule. Hanoi became the capital of united Vietnam, now renamed the Socialist Republic of Vietnam. Saigon was rechristened Ho Chi Minh City. Simultaneously, the communist Pathet Lao in neighboring Laos and the Khmer Rouge in Cambodia captured power. So the whole of Indochina turned Red! So far this was fine. But what turned out to be not so fine was Hanoi's 'socialist reconstruction'. It hit the ethnic Chinese Hwa community in the south, who were mostly businessmen. Since free enterprise was taboo under socialism, this community was adversely affected. These Chinese, as well as Beijing, suspected anti-Chinese motives behind Hanoi's ideological pretensions. After all, China and Vietnam had a long history of mutual bad blood. The Chinese had tried to subjugate Vietnam time and again but the latter had thrown off Beijing's yoke at the slightest opportunity. So the Chinese suspicion was well founded. The Hwa started fleeing the country, which raised eyebrows in Beijing.

Another source of conflict developed within Indochina. With the successive foreign interventions having ended with the US pullout, old historical quarrels came back. Laos had no problem kowtowing to the Vietnamese who were the most powerful country in Indochina. But Cambodia's historic suspicion of Vietnamese attempts at domination increased. Pol Pot, the communist leader in Phnom Penh, oriented his country and ideology to Beijing. The latter was pleased. But Pol Pot's Khmer Rouge government earned notoriety by introducing drastic measures to reorganize society along strict ideological lines. Urbanites were forced to move en masse to the countryside to serve the rural economy there. Any dissent was removed by breaking, literally, the skull of the dissenter. Indeed, mass graves with thousands of broken skulls became the hallmark of the Pol Pot regime. The film *Killing Fields* depicted the plight of the Cambodians well. Tension, buried so long as foreign intervention was going on in the peninsula, revived between Hanoi and Phnom Penh, even though both confessed to Karl Marx and Lenin. So, as the second half of the 1970s wore on, Hanoi faced increasing tension with Beijing as well as its protégé, Phnom Penh. Like the situation in South Asia in 1971, when everyone could sense another round of war between India and Pakistan, war seemed imminent in Indochina seven years later. And just as New Delhi had taken out an insurance policy with Moscow prior to the war, so did Hanoi. On 3 November 1978 Hanoi signed a Friendship Treaty with the USSR. This was a sensation since Hanoi had kept clear of signing such treaties either with Moscow or with Beijing during the peak period of US intervention and bombing. What was the need for such a treaty now? The answer was absolutely clear. This was Hanoi's insurance policy taken out in case China intervened when Hanoi got busy in Cambodia. Moscow had no hesitations in 1971. It also had none this time. After all, these Friendship Treaties were a nice way to consolidate and even widen its own spheres of influence and a smart move against the emerging Sino-US axis. The Vietnamese action came next month. Cambodian military commander Heng Samrin revolted against Pol Pot, with full Vietnamese support. Phnom Penh fell to Samrin's forces early next year; the Khmer Rouge fled to the mountains and jungles of neighboring Thailand. The domination of Hanoi over the entire Indochina peninsula was now complete by early 1979.

Beijing was outraged. Not only did the Vietnamese oust its protégé, Moscow had played a highly incendiary role by giving the go-ahead signal. Hence, the Cambodian episode was an indirect Soviet victory as well. China's post-Mao strongman Deng Xiaoping rushed to the USA in February 1979 and used US platforms to issue public warnings that Vietnam must be 'taught a lesson'. This was somewhat to the embarrassment of the Carter Administration since Deng made it seem like China and the USA were ganging up on Hanoi. Even if that were actually the case, Washington was not crazy about showing it. Indeed, Chinese troops crossed the border into north Vietnam and fought a limited, indecisive border war but were smart enough to turn back after a short spell of battles. After all, everyone knew how doggedly the Vietnamese could fight, be it against the French or the Americans.

Impact on Sino-US Relations

It was the Soviet-Vietnamese political move in late 1978 and the impending turmoil in Cambodia that accelerated Sino-US relations. In late 1978, against the background of the growing Indochina crisis, Brzezinski negotiated with the Chinese Liaison Officer in Washington, Chai Zemin, and reached certain momentous agreements in December.[7] *The joint communique* dated 15 December dropped the controversy over the US right to sell weapons to Taiwan— hitherto a sore point for Beijing. Most importantly, the Carter Administration filled the gap left open by Nixon's Shanghai Communique, viz., *the question of who represented the whole of China*. The US now hurried to agree, with the rapidly mounting crisis in Indochina and the Soviet Friendship Treaty with Hanoi in the background, that there was one China and that *China was represented solely by the People's Republic, not Taipei*. The Carter Administration further agreed to pull out its troops from Taiwan and sever all government-level relations with Taipei within four months of the establishment of full diplomatic relations with Beijing! These relations were scheduled for 1 January 1979. The US also agreed to terminate its Mutual Defense Treaty with Taiwan. However, America would continue to maintain non-governmental relations with the island republic; after all, US trade with the small island nation amounted to $11 billion. The US got precious little from China in exchange for all these concessions. It did not manage to extract a pledge that China was not going to liberate Taiwan by force, a long-standing sore point in US relations with Beijing. The latter had continued to insist on its right to do so.

The main reason for the rapidity with which these concessions were granted to China was, of course, to signal Moscow and Hanoi that they would have to face the combined countervailing power of the USA and China. There was bad news all over for the USA and partly also for China in 1979. The fall of the Shah in Iran, a US ally, the

Vietnamese triumph in Cambodia with Soviet backing, and the Soviet military intervention in Afghanistan along with the suspected massive rearmament of the USSR worried both Washington and Beijing. Soviet power seemed on the rise, and the two felt that this had to be stopped. Also, the US Congress did not like Carter granting so many concessions to communist China at Taiwan's cost. So it rushed to pass the Taiwan Relations Act in March 1979 to shorten its leash on the Administration. The Act provided that the US would continue to maintain cultural, commercial and other ties with Taipei, provide defensive weapons, maintain force to prevent a violent takeover of the country, and that stability and security in the area was in US national interest. [8] But Beijing's chief goal in its relations with the USA was achieved. It had already obtained the permanent Security Council seat in the UN, then extracted from Nixon the pledge to a one-China policy, and now managed to remove the haze on who was the real China. In other words, the US went out of its way to accommodate it in the mainstream of world community. Moscow, unwittingly, played an important role in bringing the two together.

A postscript is in order here. The old controversy over whether the People's Republic of China has the right to 'liberate' Taiwan, by force, if necessary, continues. As Chinese Premier Zhu Rongji explained to a press conference in mid-March 2000, if the question of Taiwan's reunification with mainland China continued to drag out, "how can we not use force?"[9] In July Chinese President Zemin told former US Defense Secretary William Cohen visiting Beijing that Taiwan remained a most important issue. Cohen assured him that Washington supported the 'one-China principle'.[10] Though business and communication ties had improved between China and Taiwan with the former trying to actively promote cross-straits relations, the question of Taiwan's 'liberation' remained a sore point between the two and between Washington and Beijing. Let us note here that we have already seen some more recent data (as of March

2001) on Sino-US relations at the end of the previous chapter.

Readings

1. Harold C. Hinton, "The United States and the Sino-Soviet Confrontation," *Orbis*, Vol. XIX, No. 1, Spring 1975.
2. Richard Nixon, *RN Memoirs*, op. cit.
3. Henry Kissinger, *White House Years*, op. cit.
4. Congressional Quarterly, *China. US Policy since 1945*, Washington, 1980.
5. Jyotirmoy Banerjee, "Moscow and the China Card," *IDSA Journal*, New Delhi, Vol. 12, No. 1, July-Sept. 1979, pp. 1-42.
6. Zbigniew Brzezinski, *Power and Principle: Memoirs of the National Security Adviser 1977-1981*, Farrar, Straus, Giroux, New York, 1983.

Notes

1. In my campus of Jadavpur University in south Calcutta, there are still a few armored personnel carriers lying around, partly overgrown by grass, from those days. Many areas of south Calcutta, including its famous 'lake' region, as well as Dumdum airport area were filled with US military installations and camps during the war.
2. Mao Zedong, "On Coalition Government," (April 1945), in Mao Tse-tung, *Selected Writings*, National Book Agency, Calcutta, 1967, pp. 243,285-6.
3. Kissinger, *White House Years*, op. cit., Ch. XIX, pp. 733-787.
4. Ibid., Ch. XXIV, pp. 1074-96.
5. For highlights of Sino-US relations till 1980, see Congressional Research Service, *China: U.S. Policy*

since 1945, Washington, 1980, "Chronology," pp. 75-264.

6. Jyotirmoy Banerjee, "Moscow and the China Card," *IDSA Journal*, Vol. XII, No. 1, July-Sept. 1979, pp. 1-42; and "Indonesia, Malaysia and the Indochina Crisis: Between Scylla and Charybdis," *China Report*, Vol. XVII, No. 1, Jan. -Feb. 1981, pp. 41-73.

7. Details in Zbigniew Brzezinski, *Power and Principle. Memoirs of the National Security Adviser. 1977-1981*. Farrar, Straus, Giroux, New York, 1983, pp. 191-233.

8. Text of the Act in Congressional Research Service, op. cit., pp. 41-43.

9. CCTV, 15 Mar. 2000, 9.15 p. m.

10. CCTV, 14 July 2000, 10.30 p. m.

6

The INF Treaty: Salt, Start, Star Wars and NMD/TMD

THE INF TREATY

Among the various US-Soviet agreements on limiting strategic weapons, the Intermediate-range Nuclear Force Treaty stands out as the first and only one, which wiped out an entire class of ballistic missiles. So let us turn our attention to it first.

About early 1977 the Soviets started deploying a new type of intermediate-range missiles in Europe called the SS-20. It was a modern, solid-fuel, mobile ballistic missile equipped with three MIRVs. Its range covered all of Western Europe, even from bases located inside the USSR. The SS-20 caused immediate concern in West Europe. This was because the US no longer enjoyed strategic superiority over the USSR. So, were the Soviets to fire their INFs at West European targets, would the US (dare to) retaliate? Would the latter risk New York and Washington for an attack on Paris and London? The West Europeans felt acutely the need for an upgraded INF based on their territory; the old US Pershing I missile lagged behind the SS-20 in striking power, accuracy, mobility and by other criteria. Hence, they perceived that the new Soviet missile was upsetting the balance of strategic power. On 12 December 1979, after much consultation, NATO decided on a *'dual track'* strategy to counter the SS-20 threat. One track would be holding talks with Moscow on correcting the INF imbalance. Should the first track fail to achieve results, the second track would be activated, i.e., West Europe would receive 464 ground-launched cruise missiles (GLCMs) and 108 Pershing II missiles from the USA to match the SS-20s.

Then began a series of diplomatic maneuverings by the USA and the USSR. On 18 November 1981, Ronald Reagan, who had meanwhile assumed Presidency, proposed the '*zero option*'. This meant that the US would cancel INF deployment in West Europe if Moscow agreed to eliminate all its SS-20s as well as its lesser-range SS-4s and SS-5s. At the ensuing talks in Geneva that opened on 30 November, the US thus sought global elimination of the INFs on both sides. But Moscow wanted to retain some and suggested 300 missiles for each side. It also wanted to count the French and British nuclear forces within the US total! It was just a mutual hoodwinking game. The US was giving away nothing but wanted the Soviets to remove theirs already in place. So the Soviets wanted to retain at least 300 missiles and to add up all Western INFs under the 300 ceiling. This they did in the full knowledge that Paris, which jealously guarded its independence and its force de frappe or strike power, would absolutely turn the proposal down. The US also wanted that Moscow refrain from shifting the INFs to Asia; this was partly because China and Japan became worried that an agreement on Europe might entail such shift. That would mean Soviet INFs at *their* doorstep! Finally, Washington was firm on detailed verification procedures.

Track one failed. So, from November 1983 the new INFs started arriving in West Europe from the USA. The Soviets, in protest, walked out of the INF talks. The deadlock lasted till January 1985. However, the superpowers entered a new series of talks from March 1985 called the Nuclear and Space Talks (NST), which included the INF issue. The Soviets maintained their 1983 position till the advent of Gorbachev in mid-1985 following Soviet leader Chernenko's death. In October the new Soviet Communist Party chief called for a freeze in the INF deployments of both sides while visiting Paris, followed by the 'deepest possible' cuts. He further announced that Moscow was phasing out the SS-4s and removing some SS-20s from combat status. The next month, Gorbachev and Reagan met in *Geneva* and agreed to *an interim agreement* while the US maintained its goal as being the total elimination of the INFs. In October 1986 they met again, this time in *Reykjavik*, Iceland, and agreed to cut down long-range INFs (LRINFs) to 100 warheads for each side but with none in Europe. But there were some disagreements over short-range INFs (SRINFs). The Soviets also agreed to some key verification elements. But then they went ahead and linked progress on the INF agreement to US restraining its ambitious program of Strategic Defense Initiative (SDI or 'Star Wars'). In June next year the US proposed total elimination of short-range INFs. On 23 July came a major breakthrough. Gorbachev suggested *'double global zero'*, i.e., for both sides to totally destroy their INFs. He agreed to the elimination of the 100 LRINFs hitherto permitted, and all the SRINFs, provided the US did the same. The Soviets also dropped the link with British and French INFs and SDI! One wonders how Gorbachev managed to convince the Soviet military leaders to accept such a drastically reduced position vis-à-vis their chief rival. Bonn also hastened to clear the last obstacle in the path of an agreement. Chancellor Helmut Kohl signaled his readiness to dismantle the 72 Pershing I-A missiles deployed on West German soil. The path now led straight to the INF Treaty, signed by the US and Soviet leaders on 8 December 1987 in Washington. Next year, on 27 May, the US Senate gave its consent to the ratification of the treaty. It came into force on 1 June.

The INF Treaty consists of a preamble and 17 articles. Three other documents signed at the same time are also considered to be part of the treaty, e.g., the Memorandum of Understanding on the Setting of Initial Data, which contains information exchanged between the two signatories on their respective INF assets. The treaty affected not only the Superpowers but also their allies. This was because the missiles were based in the UK, West Germany, Belgium, Holland and Italy on the Western side, and in East Germany and Czechoslovakia on the Soviet side. A total of 20 missile facilities in these states became subject to inspection.

Achievements

The INF Treaty eliminated an entire class of missiles, not all of which were obsolete. All missiles with the range of 500-5,500 kms. were scheduled to be eliminated. This schedule was subsequently carried out. In fact, under Gorbachev's 'new political thinking' Moscow started withdrawing its missiles from East Germany and Czechoslovakia from February-March 1988 even before the treaty came into force— a goodwill gesture. The Soviets were required to eliminate a total of 1,766 missiles, including 809 LRINFs; the US figures were 846 and 677, respectively. A novelty lay in *verification.* It was unprecedented in depth and scope. Most of the procedures for verification set a unique record in international relations and was to continue for thirteen years. Moscow got the right to carry out 240 inspections in the USA and West Europe; the quota for Washington was fixed at some 400 inspections in the USSR, East Germany and Czechoslovakia. The US quota was more because the USSR had to eliminate a greater number of INFs. Similarly, the Soviets were permitted to inspect 32 facilities in the USA. The latter could carry out verification in 117 facilities in the USSR. A Special Verification Commission was set up to deal with questions of compliance with the treaty provisions. The inspectors on both sides were given all the rights to monitor the observance of the treaty. On 2 July 1988, the US began continuous monitoring at the Soviet Votkinsk Machine Building Plant. The Soviets began theirs at the USA's Hercules Plant Number 1 in Magna, Utah.

It should be noted that even before the treaty was signed in December 1987, the two sides had set up Nuclear Risk Reduction Centers, on 15 September that year. These centers also served the needs of the INF Treaty when it was signed. Among the functions of the center was the issuing of notifications of any forthcoming missile launches. This also helped enhance confidence-building measures or CBMs between the two hitherto arch rivals. The strict and detailed verification procedures of the treaty were unthinkable in pre-Gorbachev Soviet Union, where super-secrecy, particularly in defense matters, had long been a matter of routine. The fact that Moscow under Gorbachev agreed to the drastic verification regime revealed the scope and depth of the Soviet leader's propagation of glasnost (transparency or openness) and perestroika (reconstruction).

The INF Treaty, by eliminating a whole class of missiles, stimulated interest in reaching agreements in other areas of arms control, e.g., the Strategic Arms Reduction Talks or START, which dealt with longer range missiles like ICBMs. In fact, while the Soviet and US leaders met in Washington to sign the INF Treaty, they also agreed to rev up and complete the START talks as early as possible. The treaty became a symbol of the end of the four decades long Cold War. In addition, it helped reveal serious Soviet economic weakness, as borne out by other events and ultimately leading to the collapse of the superpower. The irreparable economic ailment must have been the major driving force behind Gorbachev's highly unconventional liberalism.

Readings

1. *The First Anniversary of the INF Treaty,* (no author), Novosti, Moscow, 1989.
2. US Information Agency, *A Chronology of United States Arms Control and Security Initiatives: 1946-1990,* Washington DC, May 1990 (henceforth *Chronology-I*).
3. Lynn E. Davis, "Lessons of the INF Treaty," *Foreign Affairs,* New York, Vol. 66, No. 4, Spring 1988, pp. 720-734.
4. US Arms Control & Disarmament Agency, "The INF Treaty: What's In It?" *Arms Control Update,* Washington

DC, January 1988, No. 3.

5. US Dept. of State, Bureau of Public Affairs, Secretary Shultz, *The INF Treaty: Strengthening US Security*, Washington DC, Current Policy Series 1038.

SALT II

We have already seen SALT I and the 1974 Vladivostok Accords, which set up a framework for the next SALT round, i.e., SALT II, discussed in Chapter Three. We have also noted that instead of limiting the ceiling of strategic weapons, SALT I raised them at Vladivostok. In that Soviet Far Eastern port city, the two superpowers agreed that the 2,400 strategic launchers permissible for each side would also include heavy bombers, which had been excluded from the 1972 SALT I. The US B-52 and the Soviet Bison, Bear and the new Tu-26 Backfire constituted the heavies. Moscow dropped its insistence on including the US Forward Based Systems, meaning bombers based in West Europe, in the US total. In January 1976, the US agreed to count bombers carrying air-launched cruise missiles[1] or ALCMs against the MIRV subceiling of 1,320 permitted in Vladivostok, if Moscow counted its Backfire bombers against the same. But in the latter's view, Backfires were purely tactical weapons; the US opposed that definition by insisting that they could be refueled in mid-air to increase their range (to reach the US mainland) or land in Cuba, Moscow's friend. On 16 June, Soviet leader Brezhnev offered a statement to President Carter, which in US view became part of the SALT II agreement. He promised that Moscow would neither increase the Backfire's range nor its production rate of 30 bombers per year. The US took the statement as a binding commitment. With the 'cruise versus Backfire' controversy thus out of the way, there came the SALT II Treaty on 28 June 1979. It was signed in Vienna. The treaty counted missile-carrying bombers within the MIRV subceiling.[2]

SALT II was a larger and more complex document than SALT I. It consisted of the treaty proper, a Protocol, 'Agreed Statements and Common Understandings' on the treaty, a Memorandum on the data base, and a Joint Statement on SALT III (which never came). The treaty proper, along with the Agreed Statements, lay down detailed limits on items like missile silo dimensions, MIRVs, missile telemetry encryption,[3] and so on. Remarkably, Moscow finally agreed to a database, based on which subsequent talks were expected to be held. The treaty banned both flight-testing and deployment of mobile ICBMs and air-to-surface ballistic missiles (ASBMs). It also prohibited certain types of MIRVed cruise missiles, e.g., sea-launched and ground-launched cruise missiles (SLCMs and GLCMs). It stipulated that any new MIRVed ICBMs could have a maximum of 10 and SLBMs 14 warheads each. The grand total of strategic launchers permitted to each side decreased to 2,250 from the Vladivostok ceiling of 2,400. The MIRV subceiling remained pegged at 1,320 but counted the long-range and heavy B-52 bombers carrying cruise missiles with a range exceeding 600 km. The Soviet Backfire bomber was not included in the treaty but in a statement only, as mentioned earlier.

The two sides agreed to use their 'national technical means' (read espionage, whether by humans or machines like spy satellites) to monitor each other's compliance with the treaty. They also agreed to set up a Joint Consultative Commission to handle any complains by either side.

Critics, however, pointed out that SALT II could not achieve substantial cuts in the main armaments programs of the two superpowers. They also pointed out that while the treaty cut the number of delivery vehicles from 2,400 to 2,250, the number of warheads and throw-weight levels (the total payload capacity of a ballistic missile, including re-entry bodies, warheads and decoys) were allowed to rise. Finally, critics alleged that the treaty was not adequately verifiable.

Readings

1. Henry Kissinger, *White House Years*, op. cit.
2. Richard Nixon, *RN Memoirs*, op. cit.
3. Strobe Talbott, *Endgame: The Inside Story of SALT II*, Kalyani Publishers, Ludhiana,1979.
4. *Chronology-I*, op. cit.

START I

With Ronald Reagan coming to power in 1981, SALT came under fire. Reagan, largely to prove he was smarter than his predecessor and would make the Soviets dance to his tune, announced that he wanted *reductions*, not merely limitations, of strategic weapons. Undoubtedly he thereby hoped to gain political mileage, within his country as well as in the wide world. A significant portion of world public opinion, even in countries allied to the US, had been crying hoarse against the over-armament of the two superpowers. Protest movements were common worldwide. On 29 June 1982, a new round of talks began between the Soviets and the new US government. The latter even changed the nomenclature of the talks from SALT to START with apparent emphasis on reduction. Strategic Arms Limitation Talks gave way to Strategic Arms Reduction Talks. Reagan's premise was that the existing Soviet advantage in land-based ICBMs was 'unfair', since these were more accurate and combat-ready than SLBMs or bombers. Reagan wanted a one-third cut of warheads for both sides, thereby bringing down their number to 5,000 for each. ICBMs could have a maximum of 2,500 warheads. He proposed a limit of 850 deployed ballistic missiles and equivalent bomber levels, including the Soviet Backfire. On 8 December 1983, however, the Soviets walked out of the START talks in Geneva to protest against the US deployment of the INFs in West Europe. Next month the Reagan Administration complained of Soviet violation of the SALT agreements, e.g., in missile telemetry encryption and in the deployment of a large phased-array radar in Krasnoyarsk in central Siberia.[4] It also alleged that the Soviets were going ahead with massive rearmament, partly in violation of SALT.

***Eyewitness*:** Talking about ballistic missiles, you can see the granddaddy of all ballistic missiles, the V-2, still standing tall in the Deutsches Museum in Munich or the Smithsonian Aerospace Museum in Washington DC. I visited an even more interesting yet less known site. This was the German wartime underground V-2 assembly plant, dug deep inside the Harz Mountain in central Germany at Nordhausen. Codenamed Dora, it was a concentration camp using slave labour to work inside the kilometers-long factory. You can see real V-2 parts and related machinery, videos about life in the camp, torture chambers, crematoria, etc. The whole 'museum' looked very much like such scenes from Hollywood!

START again came up during US-Soviet Nuclear and Space Talks (NST) in March 1985. The US remained focused on deep cuts of strategic missiles. Reagan had reiterated as much during his second inaugural speech as President two months earlier. In September that year, Moscow tabled its own START proposal. It contained elements which it called 'strategic' but the US disputed its view. On 1 November came another US proposal. It focused, among other issues, on reducing the throw-weight of missiles, re-entry vehicles, and mobile ICBMs (since the latter were difficult to verify). On 21 November, Reagan and Gorbachev, meeting in Geneva, agreed to the principle of 50% cuts in the nuclear arms of both sides. But in May, Reagan again complained of Soviet violations of SALT, announcing that the US force structure would be geared to actual Soviet buildup. In June, the Soviets proposed an 'interim' agreement on cuts that would fall short of the goal of 50%. In fall that year, the US responded positively to this, though it reiterated the ultimate goal of 50% reduction. During 11-12 October, the two leaders met again, this time in Reykjavik in Iceland. The Soviets found Reagan's Strategic Defense Initiative (SDI or Star Wars program) an impediment. However, they agreed to limit the strategic nuclear delivery vehicles (SNDVs, i.e., missiles and bombers) to 1,600 and the nuclear warheads for them to 6,000 for each side. Later that month the US put forward a proposal incorporating the areas agreed at Reykjavik. Moscow replied with its own proposal next month that wanted to limit SDI. In May and July 1987, further drafts were submitted by the US and the USSR separately. Following many more proposals and counter-proposals, US State Secretary Shultz and Soviet Foreign Minister Zhevardnadse reviewed the drafting of the START Treaty text in Moscow. Remaining differences revolved around verification, counting of nuclear-armed, long-range ALCMs, limitation and verification of SLCMs (submarine-launched cruise missile) and mobile ICBMs.

Finally START I was born. The signatories were the USA and the Soviet-successor states of Russia, Ukraine, Kazakhstan and Belarus. The last three were admitted into the treaty under the Lisbon Protocol of 23 May 1992, since they played host to nuclear missiles in the former USSR. The treaty was signed by Presidents Bush and Gorbachev on 31 July 1991 and entered into force on 5 December 1994 following ratification. The demise of the USSR caused much of the delay. The treaty permitted a maximum of 1,600 SNDVs each for the US and Russia, and 6,000 'accountable' warheads each. Russia was required to limit the number of its heavy ICBMs in fixed silos to half the number possessed by the former USSR. Following the stipulations of the treaty, Kazakhstan in 1995 and Ukraine and Belarus got rid of their nuclear weapons the next year. Their weapons were sent to Russia for destruction.[5] START I required that all the stipulated reductions be completed within seven years after the treaty entered into force, that is, in December 2001. When completed, the treaty will have achieved 30-40 percent cuts in the strategic arsenals deployed at the time the treaty was signed.

START II AND III

START II and III were conceived in continuation of the START I Treaty and involved the USA and Russia only. START II was signed on 3 January 1993. But, by its own provisions, Start II could be implemented only after Start I came into force. Start II provided for a ban on all land-based, MIRVed ballistic missiles by 1 January 2003. According to the treaty, the overall ceiling on deployed strategic warheads is supposed to come down to 3,000-3,500 by 2003, with a cap of 1,750 for SLBMs. But more than numerical cuts, its qualitative provisions are significant. These ban heavy ICBMs and MIRVs, thereby substantially reducing first-strike capability.[6] They are expected to reduce the deployed strategic offensive arsenals of the US and Russia by around two-thirds of their 1990 levels. The two START treaties are to run simultaneously.

However, START II ran into ratification problems. The US Senate took its time, then ratified it in January 1996. But the Russian parliament, the Duma, held it up as of 1998. The Duma was reluctant because its provisions would leave Russia with about 1,000 warheads less than the permissible limit. By certain calculations, the US could reload its missiles and bombers to produce a force far more powerful than Russia's. Further, NATO's eastward expansion, ratified in spring 1998, provoked a segment of the Duma to deny ratification. However, on 14 April 2000, Sahara TV reported that the lower house of the Russian parliament had approved START II. On 4 May, Putin got it ratified. But Russia has complained, in February 2001, that the US has not signed protocols relating to a number of agreements on cutting the number of offensive strategic weapons.

Meanwhile, August 1999 marked the beginnings of START III, which basically would involve more cuts. In fact, Russia proposed the figure of 1,500 missiles for each side as against the 2,000 to 2,500 figure envisaged under START III. The new US President George Bush, who took office in January 2001, has also offered deeper cuts than those envisaged for START III but under his plan for a National Missile Defense or NMD. During the second half of 2000, the Russians repeated several times that they wanted to get on with START III. But they were evidently frustrated, since the US procrastinated even though Moscow had cleared the START II Treaty. In fact, from late 1998, Russia started deploying a new long-range, lightweight, mobile ballistic missile, which carries a single warhead. It is called Topol-M. NATO has codenamed it SS-27.

President Vladimir Putin, the former KGB operative in East Germany who speaks fluent German, later head of the Russian secret service, the FSB, and a karate black-belt, wants to make START III "simple". Instead of a separate and new treaty, he proposes to amend the other two STARTs. Both approaches have been debated in Russia since 1997 but currently the amendment version prevails. For Putin, cuts in strategic weapons would depend upon continued observance of the ABM Treaty, which was part of SALT I. This means capping the US proposed NMD/TMD (Theater Missile Defence). Senior Russian officials have also maintained that Moscow's START III proposal would include US non-strategic nuclear weapons based in Europe. Either they are to be withdrawn to US territory, or should count against the Russian-proposed 1,500 ceiling. Colonel-General Vladimir Yakovlev, commander of Russia's Strategic Missile Force (SMF), gave an interesting twist to Moscow's thinking on START III in November 2000. He put forward the idea of a single limit on offensive and defensive weapons. This would mean an inverse relationship between the two— the more you have of the one, the less you are allowed of the other. The more robust the defense system, the fewer the offensive weapons. This would indirectly limit the size of the US NMD.

There are various speculations and conjectures going on over START III in both the USA and Russia. The latter, for example, seems to want both mobile ICBMs and SLBMs as highly survivable second strike weapons. It would also like to put MIRVs on the mobile ICBMs, which START II has banned, allowing only SLBMs to be MIRVed.

However, we should note here that it is one thing to sign on the dotted line, but quite another thing to implement the massive and complicated work of eliminating nuclear weapons. Russia lacks the funds, facilities and sometimes the technology for the denuclearization programs it has undertaken to carry out. America's Nunn-Lugar program for Cooperative Threat Reduction (CRT) has been providing funds and technology to Russia to accomplish some of the START goals of elimination. During the first half of the 1990s, the US provided $400 million annually to Moscow for the purpose, totaling $1. 6 billion till 1995.[7]

READINGS

1. USIA, *Strategic Arms Reduction Talks. Chronology 1881-1988*, May 1988 (henceforth *Chronology-II*).
2. *Chronology-I*, op. cit.
3. *Strategic Digest*, New Delhi, Vol. XXXI, No. 2, Feb. 2001, pp. 187-9.
4. Jyotsna Bakshi, "Russia's National Security Concepts and Military Doctrines: Continuity and Change," *Strategic Analysis*, New Delhi, Vol. XXIV, No. 7, pp. 1266-84.5.
5. US Department of State, Bureau of Public Affairs, *Security and Arms Control: The Search for a More Stable Peace,*

June 1983, Sept. 1983; *A Short Guide to U. S. Arms Control Policy*, Oct. 1984.

STRATEGIC DEFENCE INITIATIVE (SDI) or STAR WARS; NMD/TMD

The Need for a Shield

As we have already seen, Reagan was bent upon promoting his pet thesis that the Soviets were going ahead with developing more powerful and more accurate ballistic missiles like the monstrous SS-18 and the SS-19 and bombers like the Blackjack. But it is the missiles that worried him most. A single SS-18 could carry 30 nuclear warheads. They would amount to an enormous megatonnage of explosive power. Together, only these two types of missiles in the Soviet arsenal were stated to be capable of far exceeding the power of the entire US missile and bomber forces combined![5] Their warheads totaled over 5,000, not counting those on other types of missiles and bombers. Some of the even more advanced, fifth generation Soviet missiles were mobile, making them hard to detect. Besides, as we have seen in the context of the Krasnoyarsk radar, the CIA raised the panic level a few notches higher by announcing that the Soviets were building a network of nine new large phased-array radars, including the one at Krasnoyarsk, to enhance their ballistic missile defense. This perceived increase in Soviet offensive and defensive capability, in Reagan's view, clearly indicated that Moscow was preparing for a first strike capability against the USA. Indeed, the Soviets had never officially adhered to the MAD doctrine, though in actual practice US-Soviet strategic relations came to be based on mutual deterrence. In any case, the US was concerned that the heavy Soviet missiles were capable of destroying America's second strike or power of retaliation, even those US Minuteman missiles which nested in super-concrete underground silos ('hardened' silos). The US alleged that the growing Soviet ballistic missile defense system made it increasingly difficult for the US to attack the Soviets' hardened missile sites. Moscow, on the other hand, was constantly improving, and adding to, its offensive missile power. The aging B-52 bombers, or the more modern stealth B-1s, to be sure, could launch low-flying cruise missiles at Soviet targets from a safe distance. But the Soviet SA-10 surface-to-air missiles (SAMs) and Foxhound fighter jets, which had a look-down, shoot-down capability, could defeat any cruise penetration of Soviet air space. So, in Reagan's view, Moscow was enjoying an unfair advantage in both offense and defense. This was intolerable.

The following story fits into the present context. Once Reagan visited the North American Aerospace Defense Command (NORAD) headquarters in Cheyenne Mountains, Colorado. During his conversation with the officers there, he asked what they could do with all their elaborate tracking systems and missiles and bombers at their command, if a single Soviet missile was found to be heading towards the USA. Could they stop it? The answer was purely negative. Reagan took his cue from there. The USA, a superpower, lay open, quite voluntarily, to a Soviet attack. The only means of defense was not physical defense, for this was ruled out by MAD, but deterring the enemy from attacking in the first place. If the enemy, however, was not deterred and launched its missiles, then the US would remain as helpless and vulnerable as an overturned cockroach! So, on 23 March 1983, Reagan announced his multi-billion dollar Strategic Defense Initiative or Star Wars program. He wanted to build an elaborate protective shield for the US mainland to physically guard against a missile attack. It would be a layered ballistic missile defense and involve satellites and an assortment of other weapons based in space as well as ABMs based on the ground.

SDI Architecture

To make the maze of SDI simple, let us note that a *ballistic missile's flight* has broadly four phases. These are, first, *the boost phase*, when the missile lifts off amidst much fire and smoke. This is its 'signature' and is the easiest time to detect it by heat-sensitive infra-red sensors aboard satellites hovering overhead in space. The second phase is called *the post-boost phase*, in which the booster rockets release the 'buses' containing MIRVs, i.e., several warheads. The boosters fall away, having burnt themselves out. The buses then speed through space and start releasing their deadly passengers, i.e., the bombs or warheads (MIRVs), each heading for an independent target on the ground, thousands of miles away. Next is the continuation of the second phase, and is called *mid-course*. The warheads, which have emerged from the buses, are now flying through space. This phase lasts the longest of all the phases, clocking a total of just about 30 minutes! The fourth and last phase is *the terminal phase*. Here, the warheads re-enter the earth's atmosphere and home in on their assigned targets. SDI, therefore, was conceived as a multi-layered defense system.

Each phase of the hostile missile must have a particular defense configuration against it. Ideally, an offensive missile should be destroyed in its first, or boost, phase. This is because, as already seen, it leaves a huge 'signature' and is therefore easy to target. Its destruction in this phase would also mean the destruction of the warheads it is carrying, all in one shot. Once the 'bus' releases the warheads in space, the problem becomes more complicated. The SDI defense weapons in space would now have to detect and track, or 'acquire', individual warheads, and then destroy them. Most SDI weapons in the first three phases of the hostile missile's path will be space-based systems, like satellites. In the fourth and last phase, those warheads that have so far managed to hoodwink the defenses would have to encounter ground-based anti-ballistic missiles, possibly in combination with space-based systems. SDI proponents like Jastrow assert that killing the incoming warhead about 100,000 feet above US soil in this last or terminal phase would still be safe for the Americans below.

As of 1987, experts considered, among others, the following research programs for Phase I of SDI: the ground-based surveillance and tracking system (GSTS), the boost surveillance and tracking system (BSTS), the space-based surveillance and tracking system (SSTS), battle management/ command and control, and communications (BM/C^3), the space-based interceptor (SBI), and the exo-atmospheric reentry vehicle interceptor subsystem (ERIS).[8] The R&D on SDI would be a multi-national one, pulling in the best technologies available, whether in the USA or among its allies in West Europe and Japan. Simultaneously, the US START talks strategy was geared to make the Soviets reduce their heavy missile force. With SDI, Reagan was throwing away the long stabilized MAD doctrine. The Soviets were upset over SDI; in their view, that program would give the US an unfair advantage in the balance of nuclear power. Moscow, to keep up with the Joneses, nay, to survive at all, would have to build its own missile defense shield (which the US alleged it was already building!). After all, if one side has only a sword while the other has both a sword and a shield, then the latter has a distinct edge. Reagan was keen to build a shield and also blunt the Soviet sword by means of SDI and START respectively.

The SDI program during 1983-88 cost in the neighborhood of $11 billion. A presidential study, one of three, called the Defense Technology Study, pegged the cost of funding the program's feasibility, from October 1983 over the next five years, at $26 billion. As a White House release in January 1985 entitled "The President's Strategic Defense Initiative" put it, the SDI was a program of intensive research into advanced defensive technologies, with the aim of eliminating the ballistic missile threat. [9] The State Department elaborated, in June, that the program aimed at a *defense-*

reliant nuclear balance. The Department, reflecting Reagan's policy, was in an expansive mood. It announced that SDI was meant not only to enhance US security but also that of its allies. Even the Soviets were welcome to join and share it![7] In November, the US tabled a proposal to the Soviets to join in an 'open laboratories' program. The program would pave the way for exchange of scientific information and visits to each other's research institutions and labs. Earlier, in March, the US had invited a total of 18 allies to pull in their talent and resources into SDI research. The British were the first to accept the US offer to join SDI research in December 1985, followed next year by West Germany, Israel and Italy, and by Japan in July 1987.

A variety of experiments with emerging and futuristic technologies were carried out. An excellent read on these technologies, written in easy language, is Jastrow's book, which you can find in the Readings list. In December 1985, the Eastport Study Group reported to the SDI Office that it was entirely possible to develop computer battle management hardware and software. The technologies tested involved a variety of lasers, particle beam, electromagnetic railguns, many other 'smart' weapons (e.g., 'smart pebbles', or small bullets or shells, which can home in on an incoming target by means of sensors) and, of course, supercomputers, which would see the larger picture of battle in space and manage the defense effort. There were to be weapons satellites, i.e., soldiers, doing actual battle. Behind them, deep in space, would hover battle-management satellites, i.e., the Generals, coordinating their activities. As Jastrow explained:

> *Reacting quickly to the attack, tracking the Soviet missiles and warheads, aiming our guns, keeping the master file on thousands of warheads and decoys, shifting our forces from one region to another with the vicissitudes of battle— all these*

tasks carried out simultaneously will require several billion operations, or basic units of arithmetic and thought, per second. The newest computers are already close to this capability and computing speed is not expected to be a major problem for our defense. [10]

Critique of SDI

Skeptics, however, had their doubts. They included eminent scientists like Carl Sagan. They doubted whether the system could be much more than 50% foolproof. Even if one assumed its 90% effectiveness, 10% of the then existing 10,000 Soviet nuclear warheads was 1,000. The latter number were enough to destroy the US. Further, the SDI 'shield' would simply tempt the adversary, the USSR, to concentrate more on the quality and numbers of their offensive missiles to saturate and overwhelm defense. They could also deploy space mines to destroy a large number of US defense satellites carrying sensors, weapons and other objects. Again, SDI was a shield against high ballistic trajectories. But the US would still remain vulnerable to nuclear weapons delivered by bombers, ground-hugging cruise missiles, and even motor boats or private aircraft! Critics pointed out that a small nation or a terrorist group would be more likely to deliver bombs by suitcase rather than by ICBMs! As Sagan observed sarcastically, "The Soviets, with many firsts in space technology, are unlikely to sit on their hands while the U.S. spends decades developing SD!".[11] It is not difficult to imagine that in a threat scenario they could put thousands of decoys along with their 10,000 real warheads to confuse US battle management satellites. The decoys would form part of 'penetration aids'. Sagan, incidentally, observed that the terminology of the nuclear arms race, including other phrases like 'release simulation' (a 'bus' releasing MIRVs), was increasingly taking on "phallic imagery," which suggested a psychosexual element on both sides![12]

Regarding decoy warheads, however, Jastrow maintained a different view. In his opinion there were technologies available to distinguish between the real thing from the false one. The differences would lie in their heat difference, speed and other variables. But, then, the Soviets could make the dummy warheads appear real. That way, the argument for and against could go on forever. Another line of criticism against SDI is that the computer programs for battle management would be so complex that humans would not be able to write them. They must be written by other computers. But going by track record of errors in civilian space programs, would such a super-complex system managed by machines run faultlessly? This question verges on theology, something like: is there a God? The answer to our question seems increasingly to depend on how much faith one has in error-free technology. Skeptics were more inclined to follow Murphy's law: if anything can go wrong, it probably will. Moreover, by some estimates, the cost of SDI, if it is in place, would climb to a trillion dollars. That was a lot of money for a dubious system, argued the critics. Again, if satellites were based increasingly deeper into space to make them difficult to reach, these 'dark' satellites might eventually lead to the militarization of the solar system and make the Outer Space Treaty of 1967 redundant. In the view of the skeptics, SDI could not protect the US. It could be "overwhelmed, underflown, outfoxed," would flagrantly violate arms control treaties signed by the US, was "ruinously expensive," jeopardized space exploration and increased the chances of nuclear war". Other than that, it's a great idea," observed Sagan.[13]

NMD/TMD: THE LATEST SOURCE OF CONFLICT

With the gradual reconciliation between the superpowers on a number of issues, especially after the advent of Gorbachev in 1985, the end of the Reagan era, and the Soviet collapse in December 1991, Star Wars faded. Research on ballistic missile defense, however, did not totally stop. The US concern over what it calls 'rogue' states (Iraq, Iran, North Korea and others) and their missile programs kept a diluted version of the program going. Former President George Bush, father of the junior Bush now sitting in the White House, had a ballistic missile defense (BMD) program in place called Global Protection Against Limited Strikes (GPALS). But the massive Reagan-era budget for SDI-type research was drastically slashed. However, even during Clinton's Presidency the question of installing a National Missile Defense (NMD) for the USA proper and a Theatre Missile Defense (TMD) for its allies came up. The US kept up a limited research program. In 1999, the projected cost of NMD stood at $10. 5 billion between 1999 and 2005.[14] The National Missile Defense Act came into being in 1999. As of that year, the US BMD system included the Patriot PAC-3 ABM (superior in range and accuracy to the hitherto existing PAC-2), the Navy Area Defense System based on hi-tech Aegis-class ships (which are equipped to defend against saturation tactical missile attacks), the Theatre High-Altitude Area Defense System (THAAD) with somewhat dubious capability, Israel's Arrow,[15] and the Medium Extended Air Defense System (MEADS), the latter built in collaboration with Germany and Italy. As of 2001, the NMD/TMD issue keeps growing as a hotly debated topic among nations. Clinton had smartly left the decision to install NMD/TMD in its full-blown version to his successor at the end of his second and final term in office. In early 2001, with the Republican George W. Bush in power, Washington is singing a hard tune. President Bush is more assertive than Clinton. In the election year of 2000, he had declared at the Philadelphia Convention of his party that he wanted full-scale missile defense for both the US and its allies. His administration has been vigorously reiterating the goal of NMD and TMD. The missile defence program is being dubbed 'Son of Star Wars' by the media! The Bush

Administration has even called out for a revision of the ABM Treaty.[16] But Moscow and Beijing have declared their opposition to these US plans. For Russia, the 1972 ABM Treaty remains sacrosanct. In the ratification document on START II, the Duma reserved the right to withdraw from the ABM Treaty and other arms co-control agreements, if the US went ahead with its NMD plan and violated the 1972 treaty. A NATO forum in Munich, in which Russia also participated, was held in February 2001. The Russian security adviser Sergei Ivanov warned that any transgression of that treaty would undo a host of agreements between Moscow and Washington, whichwere based on it. [17] For Beijing, a TMD umbrella extended to Taiwan would be gross interference in China's domestic affairs and constitute an extremely unfriendly act. In fact, Russian leader Vladimir Putin's China summit in mid-July 2000 spawned agreement between the two states that any attempt to install NMD/TMD was highly condemnable, and the two sides were prepared to take counter-measures.[18] Speculations and debates are going on in the USA and among its allies, as well as and Russia, China and others, over the desirability and implications of ballistic missile defense. Is SDI being resurrected from the catacombs of the 1980s? It would be interesting to study whether some of the arguments used against SDI, which we have seen above, are back, and differences, if any, exist between Star Wars and NMD, the son of star wars.

Readings

1. US Arms control & disarmament agency, *arms control update*, november 1987, no. 2.
2. Department of state, bureau of public affairs, *special report: star wars*, pp. 28-42; "battleground in the heavens," pp. 43-65; edward teller, "the case for the strategic defense initiative," pp. 66-75; carl sagan, "the case against sdi," pp. 66-75, *discover*, chicago, september 1985.
3. Wolfgang Schreiber, *Die strategische Verteidigungsinitiative*, Konrad-Adenauer-Stiftung, Forschungsbericht 45,Verlag Ernst Knoth, Melle, 1985.
4. USIA, *SDI. Strategic Defense Initiative. A Chronology. 1983-1988*, April 1988.
5. Feiveson, op. cit.
6. Robert Jastrow, *How to Make Nuclear Weapons Obsolete*, Little, Brown & Co., Boston,1985.
7. Caspar W. Weinberger," U. S. Defense Strategy," *Foreign Affairs*, New York, Vol. 64, No. 4, Spring 1986, pp. 675-697.

Notes

1. The cruise missile is like a slow aircraft. It flies at subsonic speed and low to avoid enemy radar detection. It never goes to space. Its terrain-comparison of TERCOM system enables it to keep to its pre-programmed route and hit its target with great accuracy. It can be launched from the ground, sea, submarine and air. It is far cheaper than a ballistic missile, which has incomparably greater speed and flies partly through space. More in Jyotirmoy Banerjee, *Strategic Studies*, Allied, Calcutta, 1998, pp. 96, 154.

2. *Endgame*, op. cit., see SALT II Treaty text, p. 281.

3. When a missile is flight-tested, it gives out telemetric data (radio signals) on the performance of its various components. So that a rival nation does not eavesdrop on these signals, cryptologists make sure that they are encrypted or coded. But both the US and the USSR have listened to each other's missiles telemetry. It was entirely possible that they could crack the code and read the real message hidden within. So the SALT II Treaty provided that missile telemetry encryption was allowed except where it impeded verification. See Strobe Talbott, *Endgame: The Inside story of SALT II*, Kalyani Publishers, New Delhi, 1979, pp. 194-202, 304.

4. The CIA estimated that the Soviets were going ahead with a plan for an elaborate ABM defense system that could upset both mutual assured destruction or MAD as well as the 1972 ABM Treaty. It alleged that the Krasnoyarsk radar site did not lie within a 150 km. radius of the Soviet capital, which violated the limit set by the treaty. Nor did it point outward, as the treaty permitted for early warning radars. Hence, felt the CIA, it must have the function of ballistic missile defense of large regions of the USSR, along with several other radars, banned by the ABM Treaty. Robert M. Gates (former Deputy Director, CIA), "The Soviets and SDI," USIS, *News Background*, Calcutta, 8 Dec. 1986, p. 3. On alleged Soviet buildup of first-strike capability, see US Dept. of Defense, *Soviet Military Power* (annually 1985-88), Washington.

5. Harold A. Feiveson (ed.), *The Nuclear Turning point: A Blueprint for Deep Cuts and De-Alerting of Nuclear Weapons*, Brookings, Washington, 1999, p. 10; US Arms Control & Disarmament Agency (ACDA), *Threat Control through Arms Control. Report to Congress, 1994*, Washington, 1995, pp. 12-13.

6. *Strategic Digest*, Vol. XXXI, No. 2, Feb. 2001, pp. 187-189.

7. ACDA, *Threat Control.* op. cit., pp. 16-17. See also Graham Allison et al. (eds.), *Cooperative Denuclearization: From Pledges to Deeds*, Harvard University, Cambridge, MA, 1993; Caspar W. Weiberger, "U.S. Defense strategy," *Foreign Affairs*, New York, Vol. 64, No. 4, Spring 1986, pp. 675-697.

8. See *Readings* for extensive SDI literature. Here is a brief resume of SDI experiments accomplished in the 1980s. In June 1984, the Homing Overlay Experiment (HOE) intercepted and destroyed a mock ballistic missile warhead in its mid-course of flight by kinetic energy, i.e., by simply colliding against it at great speed. In September 1985 the Mid-Infrared Advanced Chemical Laser (MIRACL) system used laser to destroy a liquid-fuel missiles's booster. A few days later that month, a low-power, ground-based laser successfully tracked a sounding rocket in space. In the Lawrence Livermore laboratories in California, incidentally, the world's largest laser, which occupies an area bigger than a football field and stands five stories high, produced energy in a single billionth-of-a second burst, which exceeded the combined energy of all the electrical power plants combined in the USA! (Voice of America *Editorial*, 11 April 1986, via USIS, Calcutta). During April-June 1986, and again in May next year, kinetic energy experiments called FLAGE showed that the guidance technologies needed to intercept a warhead in and out of the earth's atmosphere were feasible. In July 1986 came a particle beam experiment that irradiated and destroyed a re-entry warhead with a high-intensity proton beam. Two months later the Delta 180 experiment also clicked. It was able to gather data for characterizing rocket plumes during the boost phase

and study rocket signatures during the close-in phase of a space intercept. This experiment was vital for the development of small space-based interceptors. It involved a satellite carrying the first laser radar ever flown in space, a Maverick air-to-ground missile infrared imaging system and two cameras. The target was intercepted at a closing speed of 6,500 miles per hour. In 1988, a National Test Bed (NTB) was set up to coordinate these and other often far-flung and diverse experiments, test the alternative architectures for a layered defense and its associated battle management and command, control and communication (C^3I). USIA, *SDI*, unnumbered pp. 3, 5-8. See *Readings* on SDI. Not all experiments were successful, however. In one experiment in 1986, a Hawaii-based laser beam, instead of reflecting off special satellite-based mirrors, pointed to the sun!.

9. Ibid.

10. Jastrow, SDI *Readings*, op. cit., pp. 103-4.

11. Sagan, SDI *Readings*, op. cit., pp. 69-70.

12. Ibid., p. 70.

13. Ibid., p. 74.

14. Michael O'Hanlon, "Star Wars Strikes Back. The Phantom Menace or a New Hope?" *Foreign Affairs*, Nov-Dec. 1999, Vol. 78, Issue 6, p. 5 of 10 (USIS Calcutta reprint).

15. *Strategic Digest*, New Delhi, Vol. XXX, No. 12, p. 1724.

16. State Secretary Colin Powell quoted in *Bulletin*, American Center, Calcutta, Mar 2001, p. 1; Bush made a hyperbolic remark to NMD in his inaugural speech on 20 January 2001, text in *Span*, US Embassy, New Delhi, Mar-April 2001, p. 7.

17. Vadim Solovyev, "USA Adopts Flexible stance on NMD," *The Statesman*, Calcutta, 28 Feb. 2001, p. 7.
18. Deutsche Welle TV, 18 July 2000, 10.30 p. m.

7

Germany: Reunification and Big Power Role?

Introduction: The German Problem

The 'German Problem' is back.

In the 19th century, it meant the unification of a number of German kingdoms and lesser entities. Till 1871, when Prussian Junker (landlord) Otto von Bismarck united those kingdoms under one Reich or empire, Germany had remained a mere geographic expression. The Holy Roman Empire of the German Nation, so christened in the 15th century, was neither holy nor an effective centralised entity as we find in later times. In the first half of the 20th century, the Germans belatedly woke up to the fact that other European powers like Britain and France, and even smaller states like Holland and Belgium had already spread their tentacles overseas and acquired lucrative colonies. So Germany also wanted 'a place in the sun', a nice, big and juicy slice of colonies. The result was the German Question, revolving around Germany's future as a big colonial power.[1] The First World War (1914-1918) started when Kaiser Wilhelm II built a mighty navy to challenge the British and wanted to acquire colonies overseas in the classic European imperialist style. He failed. The Second World War (1939-45) broke out when Hitler wanted to stretch the borders of his Third Reich, not overseas, but on the European continent itself, up to the Ural Mountains in the east. But he ended up marrying at the last moment, to the tune of the approaching Russian artillery in Berlin, and immediately committing suicide thereafter with his new wife, Eva Braun, deep inside his underground bunker in April 1945.

In the process of reaching out for power, Germany had to fight two World Wars. Nearly half of the 20th century passed in trying to find a solution to the German Problem, their need for an impressive international role. When the war ended in 1945, Germany lay prostrate and divided, completely at the mercy of the four occupying powers. Moscow generously donated to Poland a sizable portion of German territory, i.e., the provinces of Pomerania, Silesia and East Prussia, which lay east of the Oder-Neisse Line. We have already seen all this in Chapter One. The rest of Germany, as we also noted earlier, was cut up into four zones of occupation. Berlin, the capital, lying deep inside the Soviet zone, was similarly divided into four sectors and had a special four-power occupation status. The ensuing Cold War seemed to permanently freeze the division of Germany into two mutually hostile states, which started functioning from 1949. The German Problem during the second half of the 20th century, therefore, became that of reunification. It seemed an absurd proposition that the two German parts, one tied to US apron strings and the other to Soviet, could ever unite across the River Elbe that divided them. But miracles do take place. The infamous Berlin Wall, erected by the East Germans in 1961, fell in 1989. Germany reunited in 1990.

The German Problem may not be a problem any more. But a big question has turned up instead. What sort of a role is Germany going to play following its reunification, not only in Europe but also in the world? United Germany, one of the largest countries in Europe and an economic giant on the world stage, is now attracting a lot of attention, not only from its nine neighbors (twelve, if you count the overseas ones like the UK, Norway and Sweden) but the rest of the world. In the present chapter, we shall first look at the German Problem in the Cold War era, then the events which mitigated it and ultimately made reunification possible. Next, we shall come to the current scene and probe Germany's current search for a new identity.

Germany and the Cold War

We noted in Chapter One that the three Western zones merged into a trizonia, out of which the Federal Republic of Germany (FRG), popularly also called West Germany, was created. The FRG, with its temporary capital in Bonn, drew up its constitution (the Basic Law) in May 1949 and started functioning from September. The West Germans deliberately chose a small, sleepy town like Bonn to be the capital of the new state because that would be a permanent reminder that the real capital was big Berlin. Someday, in the indefinite future, the Germans dreamed of getting back full independence and unity of all the four zones and re-establishing the old Reich capital. Meanwhile the Soviets were also ready with their Germany. In October, they responded by creating the German Democratic Republic (GDR) in their zone of occupation. The East German capital was allowed to be located in East Berlin, also under Soviet occupation. With Konrad Adenauer, the first Chancellor (Prime Minister) of the FRG, leading the country to join the US-led North Atlantic Treaty alliance (NATO) in 1955 despite Soviet efforts to dissuade him, the division of Germany became irrevocable, or so it seemed for decades thereafter. Moscow quickly set up the Warsaw Pact to counter NATO. The GDR became its frontline member. Given the ongoing Cold War and arms race between the two blocs, the dividing line between the two German states hardened along the Elbe River. The FRG and the GDR became two frontline states of their respective blocs. The NATO and Warsaw Pact faced each other directly on German soil. Any war breaking out between the two pacts, whether conventional or nuclear, would first hit Germany, which as battleground would suffer immediately. The Elbe border became the most heavily guarded in the world, guaranteed by nuclear weapons of both the superpowers. The Cold War fuelled the German Problem, viz., its division. That division in turn fuelled the Cold War.

Adenauer's Christian Democratic Union (CDU, with its Bavarian wing called the Christian Social Union or CSU), a conservative party, ruled in Bonn from 1949 to 1966, with the help of its coalition partner called the Free Democratic Party (FDP), which, as the party of liberals, has always been small. But due to the peculiarity that neither of the big parties, the CDU/CSU or the Social Democratic Party of Germany (SPD), managed to get absolute majority in the elections, the FDP played a crucial role in helping build a coalition government. Historically, the big two had to seek its help to capture the Bundestag or Federal Parliament in Bonn. During 1967-68, the two bigs built a Grand Coalition government but it was replaced in 1969 by an SPD-FDP coalition that lasted into the early 1980s. As we shall see, the exit of the CDU/CSU from power had important implications for Bonn's relations with Moscow and a direct bearing on the situation in Germany. When Adenauer visited Moscow in 1955, he was pained to see two different German flags flying on top of the two German embassies there. The result was the formulation of *the Hallstein Doctrine*. The latter warned all and sundry that if any nation recognized the GDR, the FRG might cut off all relations with it. The doctrine was designed to isolate the communist GDR from the world community, especially the Third World nations emerging from colonial rule. West Germany had the money, thanks to the US Marshall Plan, the economic genius of the FRG's Ludwig Erhard and the German habit of hard work and thoroughness. So fear of the loss of West German economic aid kept the doctrine afloat for about a decade.

It is relevant here to consider *the respective legal* and *political stands* of the two German governments on the German Problem. Bonn maintained that the FRG was a democracy while the GDR was not. It stood to reason, therefore, that the FRG was the sole representative of all Germans, even those east of the Elbe whose voices were stifled by communist dictatorship. Under International Law, Germany was one legal entity. There was no place for two to represent that entity. Based on the reasons stated above, Bonn, not East Berlin, was the real Germany. The GDR naturally differed. It countered Bonn by asserting that Bonn had to recognize postwar realities. These included two German states, not one. The GDR was as much reality as anything that can be real. By denying the postwar situation, i.e., the altered map of Europe, the FRG was being 'revanchist', seeking to undo the results of World War II and 'revise' the map of Europe all over again. And that was dangerous for all peace-loving European states!

Brandt's Ostpolitik I: Reasons

Gradually, voices against the GDR's isolation were raised. It was argued that the type of government, whether democratic or dictatorial, could not be the criterion for its recognition. Democracies were a rather rare species in the world community of states. Also, if states in the Middle East or Southeast Asia, which sometimes suffered coups literally every week, could enjoy recognition under International Law by other states, why not the GDR? After all, East Berlin had no coups and provided solid stability within. Economically, too, it became the most successful among all the Soviet bloc states, enjoying a living standard higher than the USSR itself. This despite the massive reparation that Moscow extracted from it. The allies of West Germany also became keen to develop economic relations with the East European states, the Cold War notwithstanding. With the growing acceptance of the GDR as a reality, chances increased that the Hallstein Doctrine might backfire and isolate the FRG itself. In 1967, with the Social Democrats now for the first time sharing power with the CDU in Bonn, there came attempts at some opening to the East. This was called the Ostpolitik or policy towards the East, meaning the Soviet bloc. Its architect was an SPD leader, former West Berlin mayor and Foreign Minister of the Grand Coalition government, Willy Brandt. During the brief tenure of the Grand Coalition, the latter managed to rope in Bucharest and Prague and exchange trade missions with these Soviet bloc states. The FRG's economic prowess, its finance and hi-tech were obviously the carrots dangling before them. The GDR was most alarmed. It might become too tempting to resist Bonn's allurements for other Warsaw Pact partners, too. The GDR, Poland — another conservative state at the time —, and the USSR then successfully blocked all West German thrusts with the new Ostpolitik. The latter stopped dead in its tracks. It was clear that without Soviet clearance nothing in East Europe would work. But Brandt's chance came again in 1969 when the SPD beat the CDU in the elections. The FDP tilted in favor of the SPD. Brandt became the Chancellor in the new coalition. This time he did not need the clearance of the former senior partner of the Grand Coalition, the CDU, for his Ostpolitik. The CDU/CSU, for the first time, went into the opposition. And Brandt had a clear way to the East.

Ostpolitik II: Further Reasons

In 1969, the Nixon Administration had started pursuing détente with the USSR and opening up China. France, meanwhile, was forging ahead with trade with the East. So why should the FRG lag behind? Brandt's adviser, Egon Bahr, opened a series of talks with the Soviets, especially with the poker-faced Foreign Minister Andrei Gromyko, a typically bland Soviet apparatchik or bureaucrat. GDR super spy Markus Wolf later revealed that GDR intelligence had managed to bug Bahr's private chamber and happily eavesdropped on his talks with the Soviets for a while until the microphones fell silent.[2] This time there was no mistake. Moscow's nod was needed before Bonn would approach other East Europeans to ease relations. Among *Bonn's urgent goals* was to institutionalize *relations with the GDR* and regularize the conditions pertaining to a peculiarly located and divided *Berlin*. Bonn under the SPD wanted the Germans on both sides of the Elbe to get the opportunity to interact with each other so that *the pain of division* (many families were divided due to the Cold War iron curtain running through Germany) *was mitigated*. It also wanted *the transit routes* connecting the FRG with West Berlin freed of harassment by the GDR authorities. Moscow welcomed the Brandt government. Social Democrats, after all, were not that rightist and conservative as the hitherto ruling Christian Democrats. It was also an opportunity to raise concern in Washington by hobnobbing with Bonn, America's faithful partner in Europe.

The Results of Ostpolitik

The results of Ostpolitik this time were entirely satisfactory. The Eastern Policy spawned the Moscow Treaty (12 August 1970). This was the key to all other treaties signed with East Europe. Within months came the Polish Treaty, on 7 December 1970. The Basic Treaty with the GDR, predictably, took time. It was signed not before 21 December 1972. The Czech Treaty followed on 11 December 1973. Meanwhile, on Bonn's prodding, the four occupying powers had come together and signed the Quadripartite (or Four-Power) Berlin Agreement on 3 September 1971. The latter set up specific rules governing West Berlin's transit traffic, i.e., traffic flowing through East German territory to and from West Berlin.

Eyewitness: Vehicles in the Berlin transit traffic were permitted to stop only at predetermined places, including Intershops run by the GDR where one could buy Western luxury items against payment in hard currency. No photo-taking along the Autobahn! As our group of West Germany-sponsored Alexander von Humboldt Scholars arrived in summer 1980 at the FRG's border town of Helmstedt, our guide asked us to pack up our cameras till we hit West Berlin. The German guide was sharp and hawkeyed. He caught a Scholar from the Far East trying to sneak a shot with his mini-camera at an Intershop and made him pack it up! The little incident illustrated how strict the authorities were with the observation of the 1972 Berlin transit agreement.

At the entry point to Berlin from the west, a huge tank mounted on a pedestal pointed its long gun towards the West in a threatening gesture! Innumerable signs along the highway, put up by the GDR, read, "Berlin. Capital of the GDR" in German! It was an obvious attempt to brainwash. By the time the traveler, including many foreign tourists besides the Germans, drove through the transit route and arrived in West Berlin, he would have seen that message a hundred times over and would subconsciously start associating Berlin with the GDR.

A most important provision of the Berlin agreement was that the Soviets henceforth would be held responsible for managing the Berlin transit, no longer the GDR. Moscow, due to its own détente calculations, agreed, overriding the GDR's reluctance to give up the privilege. In fact, the Ostpolitik was partly responsible for a change in the GDR government. Walther Ulbricht, the all-important communist party chief, had to resign in 1971. He was replaced by Erich Honecker, who ruled for the next nineteen years, till the demise of the GDR itself. Ulbricht, with his conservatism, turned out to be an obstacle in the path of Brezhnev's policy of détente with the West, including West Germany, at the turn of the 1970s. So he had to go.

The other results of the Ostpolitik were as follows.[3] The FRG *de facto* recognized Europe's postwar boundaries, much to the relief of the USSR, Poland and Czechoslovakia. But why not *de jure* recognition, which is legally foolproof? As answer to that, FRG negotiator Bahr put forward a disarming argument. Since the four victorious Allied Powers had reserved the right to decide any question pertaining to Germany which was of national or international significance, how could Bonn extend *de jure*, as distinct from *de facto*, recognition to the changed German borders? Gromyko, though generally dour, was expansive at a point during his talks with Bahr. Regarding the future possibility of German reunification, he remarked that while the postwar borders were "inviolable", they were not "unalterable". The Germans could use peaceful means to reach an agreement, he implied, to eliminate the Elbe border dividing the two states. Who could guess that his observation would really come true after two decades!

But Brandt also had to think of the powerful opposition to the agreements at home. It was easy to accuse him of a sellout of German national interest. The CDU/CSU was only too eager to cry treason by the Social Democrats, especially for their acceptance of two German states. So, Brandt submitted a "Letter on German Unity", first to Moscow, which took it, and then to the GDR, which was extremely reluctant to accept it. The letter stated that notwithstanding these Ostpolitik agreements, Bonn reserved the right to continue to attempt to reunify Germany peacefully. Under Soviet pressure, however, the GDR had to swallow the bitter pill and ultimately receive that letter, though reunification would mean the negation of its very existence! That partly explains the delay in signing the Basic Treaty governing the relations between the two states on either side of the Elbe. The West German Constitutional Court based in Karlsruhe ruled that the Elbe was not to be recognized as an international border. It was difficult for Germans to accept the Elbe border dividing the two parts of their country as final and irrevocable.

With Prague, there were difficulties too. These related to the Munich Pact of 1938. Under that agreement, the British, French and Italians happily gave away the Sudentenland, which was part of Czechoslovakia, to Hitler. Ironically enough, the Czechs themselves had not been invited to participate in the Munich talks! Now, under International Law, that agreement remained valid even after the war. Or so felt Bonn. The question which arose in postwar Europe was: did the Munich Pact continue to be valid? If so, then the Germans could in future claim back the Sudentenland. Prague wanted Bonn to declare it invalid *ab initio*, (right from the beginning). But Bonn insisted that the *ab initio* clause would be absurd since three major European powers had signed it, along with Germany, and in peacetime. The delay in signing the Czech Treaty was largely due to that *ab initio* clause. Ultimately, a compromise was struck. The treaty simply declared that the Munich Pact was invalid. The *ab initio* clause was dropped. With that last hurdle removed, the FRG settled down to a more satisfactory working relationship with the Soviet bloc states. The Ostpolitik of Brandt buried the Hallstein Doctrine and removed some of the worst effects produced by Germany's division and the Cold War. The most important aspect of the Ostpolitik was, of course, West Germany's access to fresh and large markets in East Europe for export of goods, know-how and investment. The Ostpolitik subsequently did ease inter-German visits, increasing other links like road and communication networks, including telephone connections between the two parts of Germany.

Reunification: Implecations And Consequences

The reunification of Germany on 3 October 1990 shook Europe. The movement towards reunification was made possible because Gorbachev came to power in the Kremlin in 1985. Winds of real change started blowing with the spread of his liberal and reformist ideas like 'new political thinking', 'glasnost' and 'perestroika'. Many books and articles in many European languages have been written on both Gorbachev's drastically new policies and the German reunification. Horst Teltschik, the national security adviser to the CDU-Chancellor Helmut Kohl, who had taken office a few years earlier than Gorbachev, has recorded a fascinating insider's story in his *329 Tage* (329 Days).[4] Here are the main events which led to one of the greatest events of the 20th century.

In May 1989, Hungary opened its borders. This enabled thousands of GDR Germans to flee to the West via that country and Austria. West German embassies in Prague and Warsaw became overcrowded with refugees from the GDR. The unprecedented openness that started spreading within the Soviet bloc states was the direct result of Gorbachev's new mantras of openness and transformation. Chancellor Kohl, despite his physical bulk, was quick to seize this opportunity. He wasted no time and rushed to Moscow the next month to hold talks with the Soviet leaders. The outcome of the talks was recorded in a Joint Declaration. Among others, the two sides stated that they agreed with the right of people to self-determination. Gorbachev had already asserted "freedom of choice" for East Europe in June and December 1988 and was merely reiterating his thoughts this time. The two leaders became more specific and also stressed the need for holding free elections in the GDR! These two issues were sufficient to indicate that Moscow under Gorbachev was willing to preside over the liquidation of the Soviet empire, so diligently built up by Stalin and at a huge cost. When the socialist bloc leader himself encouraged the people of East Europe to assert their freedom and choose their own governments, it meant upheaval and total transformation of the social, political and economic fabric of the region. And that was what followed.

The exodus from the GDR in the summer and fall of 1989 made its government under communist leader Erich Honecker face a grave dilemma. Honecker was faced with two options, each equally disastrous. The GDR could use its notorious police force, including the Stasi (the secret police, who maintained elaborate files on most East German citizens), to close all borders. That would keep the rest of its 17 million people in. But closing all borders even with its Warsaw Pact neighbors would mean that the GDR would have to isolate itself. The alternative was to follow the opposite path, i.e., the path of reforms inspired by Moscow itself. But that would mean committing political harakiri. The East Germans had long been voting with their feet at the slightest opportunity to escape the workers' paradise. So reforms and freedom to the people would mean a total bottom-up reconstruction of the East German political, economic and social system. Honecker did not get much time to ponder. On 18 October, he was replaced as the General-Secretary of the Socialist Unity Party of Germany (called the SED in German). Several inconsequential successors followed him, beginning with Egon Krenz.

Meanwhile, Kohl announced a ten-point program on German reunification on 28 November 1989, in which he demanded an end to the SED's monopoly power, the right of the East Germans to hold free elections and the ultimate goal of reunification. Three days later, the GDR parliament struck out the provision for monopoly power of the hitherto ruling communists from the GDR constitution. Kohl kept busy negotiating with the four Allied Powers, who still controlled the ultimate German destiny. Kohl and Gorbachev agreed, on 14 February 1990 in Moscow, to begin the so called *'two-plus-four talks'* on German reunification. *Track One* would be the talks between two freely elected German states, i.e., after free elections had taken place in the GDR. They would negotiate the internal aspects of German sovereignty. *Track Two*, scheduled to begin in February itself, would be the talks among the big four, who would determine the external aspects of German sovereignty. Bonn had luck. US president George Bush, the father of the current President, and Soviet leader Gorbachev gave the green light for Track One to go ahead without waiting for progress in Track Two. The British, not unexpectedly, were skeptical. Prime Minister Margaret Thatcher, in fact, openly opposed the idea of German reunification, saying it would make Germany too big and strong again and upset the neat European balance. The French were more forthcoming, though at times they played some delaying tricks too. But when the superpowers backed something, it was bound to succeed. Soviet support was literally bought by Bonn. The Germans, in their innumerable talks with the Russians, were always dangling financial baits, which the impoverished superpower found irresistible.

Things were moving rapidly. It was often difficult for the governments to keep up with the events, which developed a momentum of their own. On 18 March 1990, the first free elections were held in the GDR. The SED's successor party, the PDS, which had meanwhile entered the fray, was eclipsed. It could obtain only 16.6% of the votes. The parties operating successfully in West Germany, the CDU/CSU, the SPD and the FDP, swept the votes and accounted for three-quarters of all the votes cast. Following these elections, the two freely elected German governments sat down for the Track One talks. The West German negotiators agreed with Lothar de Maziere, the new head of the GDR's freely elected coalition government, on a time-table for economic, monetary and social union with effect from 1 July. The month of July saw Soviet-West German summitry in Moscow, Stavropol and Zheleznovodsk, critical to uniting Germany. Although neither German state was a party to Track Two, an understanding with Bonn was desirable. This was reflected in Kohl's talks with Gorbachev in Zheleznovodsk during 14-16 July 1990. They reached agreement here on the future map of united Germany. The expanded Germany would consist of the territories of the Federal Republic and the GDR along with the whole of Berlin. But territories east of the German-Polish border, the Oder-Neisse Line, would remain Polish (and only fractionally Russian, as hitherto, in the northern part of East Prussia, including the city of Kaliningrad, formerly German Koenigsberg).

The following month, on 23 August, the GDR parliament resolved to accede to the Federal Republic on 3 October. On 31 August, the inter-German unification treaty was signed in Berlin. Track One was complete. In less than two weeks, on 12 September, the second track ended too, and a treaty was signed in Moscow on German unification. The 'two-plus-four talks' came to a successful end. On 1-2 October, on the eve of the target date for German reunification, a document suspending the four-power rights in Germany and in Berlin was signed in New York, thereby removing the last hurdle to German reunification and full sovereignty. Next day, on 3 October, the GDR ceased to exist. The Federal Republic expanded instead, to add five more states to the existing eleven, bringing the total to sixteen. Ever since 1990, October 3 is celebrated by the Germans as their Unity Day.[5]

The Price of Reunification

Both Moscow and Bonn had to pay a price for the reunification of Germany. Let us take a look at *Moscow's concessions*. *First*, it was a concession of momentous import that the Russians allowed Germany to unite at all. For nearly half a century, following the end of World War II, the question of Germany's reunification had remained purely academic. As we saw earlier in Chapter One, the Soviets had offered the possibility of reunification way back in the mid-1950's, provided West Germany did not join NATO and remained neutral between the two hostile blocs in Europe. Adenauer had spurned the offer and took the FRG to NATO. Thereupon the Elbe line dividing the two German states hardened. It became not only the inter-German border with a permanent look— the GDR made sure of that— but also the great divide between the West and the East, between their mutually hostile ideologies, and between the formidable military power of NATO and the Warsaw Pact. In fact, West Germany's friends and foes alike were relieved that the division showed no sign of fading. A divided and smaller Germany seemed infinitely preferable to a big one, given its past record. Reunification had turned into a mere pipe dream, with West European friends showing outward sympathy while perhaps sipping champagne at diplomatic parties. However, the speed of the events of 1989 and 1990 took everyone, even the Germans themselves, by surprise. Moscow had been the most conservative of the four occupying powers on the question of reunification. Normally, it was futile even to broach the topic to the GDR. And yet, under Gorbachev, the unbelievable happened. The Soviets did give their nod. The revolution from below spread like wild fire. East Berlin had to succumb.

Second, Moscow okayed the continued membership of united Germany in NATO. This would mean the extension of NATO into the territory of the former GDR, hitherto the frontline state of the Soviet-led Warsaw Pact, which opposed NATO. *Third*, Moscow, unlike in the mid-1950s, did not ask for German neutrality as the price for reunification. *Fourth*, The Kremlin was conscious that it would be losing a most faithful ally and strategic partner, the GDR. Yet it gave the go-ahead to Bonn. *Fifth*, the willingness to sacrifice the GDR was part of a larger picture. The Soviets were consciously undoing their empire and *cordon sanitaire* in East Europe, which Stalin had built up at a huge cost in terms of human lives and property, as we have noted. This in turn would mean conceding defeat to the West, and to the US Containment policy. *Sixth*, Moscow allowed the Track One, inter-German talks to delink from progress in Track Two, a most liberal gesture on its part. It provided encouragement to Bonn to move ahead towards the goal of reunification as fast as possible. *Seventh*, Gorbachev also promised to pull out the 380,000 Soviet troops permanently stationed in the GDR. Helmut Kohl encouraged him to set a deadline. Gorbachev agreed to 1994. Moscow subsequently kept its promise. The Soviet force in the GDR amounted to some 20 divisions and was the largest Soviet force outside Soviet territory, even when compared to the force operating in Afghanistan. *Finally*, Gorbachev's concessions meant the crumbling of Marxism in Europe. This was conceding not only political but also ideological defeat of the once proud bloc of states, which claimed that the future was theirs.

Ironically, their doomsday predictions for capitalism rebounded on them. The domino theory became astonishingly applicable in East Europe, starting with the USSR itself! The Marxist states collapsed like a house of cards. Capitalism not only survived but seemed to flourish ever more!

The FRG paid a heavy price too. First, the former German territories east of the Oder-Neisse Line were given up. That settled the German-Polish border, which reassured Warsaw. After all, World War II had started when Hitler attacked Poland to settle territorial claims. In fact, already in June 1990, the two German parliaments had announced that the Oder-Neisse would constitute Germany's border with Poland. It was also decided by all the parties involved in the two-plus-four talks that there was no need for a separate peace treaty with Germany. The documents emerging from the two-plus-four talks would be sufficient for legal purposes. *Second*, even before reunification, Kohl and his Foreign Minister Genscher promised to cut the future combined armed forces of the two German states by 45%, i.e., nearly half. This was to reassure the neighbors that united Germany would not again be involved in power politics like in the olden days. The reduced troop level would be capped at 370,000. This auto-restriction in turn served as an important input into the talks on Conventional Forces in Europe (CFE). The CFE Treaty, which provided for reduction of conventional forces, was signed on 19 November 1990 in Paris. *Third*, Bonn had to pay a lot of money to the USSR under numerous heads. The annual Soviet GDP growth rate, with a single exception (4% in 1986), had remained below 2% during 1981-88. Moscow's hard currency debt to the West stood at $31.5 billion in 1988.[6] The Soviets pleaded that the large number of Soviet troops returning home had no place to stay. Bonn agreed to extend a loan of 15 billion DM, including an 3 billion interest-free loan, for providing housing to the Soviet armed personnel in the USSR. As of 1991 the FRG had already committed to pay Moscow 75 billion DM credit. *Fourth*, Bonn also had to pay compensation for Soviet projects underway in the GDR, which stood cancelled. *Fifth*, more payment had to be made to Moscow for the military bases and installations that it had abandoned in the GDR. Even Poland appeared with a bill for the transit fee for the Soviet troops. The troops, after all, used Polish roads and rolling stock to go home. However, moving beyond these never-ending payments, we see that the German reunification did serve as a catalyst for East-West détente. It was also the beginning of a new decade, the 1990s, and a brand new era, that of the post-Cold War.

Sixth, the long-term cost to Germany came from numerous refugees and asylum-seekers. Ethnic Germans from Russia, Kazakhstan, Rumania and other parts of Europe rushed in hordes to the new Federal Republic, partly moved by sentiment, partly by economic lure. A large number of non-German refugees from East and Southeast Europe, where communist dictatorships and socio-economic structures were in turmoil, joined them in seeking the good life. After an initial period, when they managed to pour in relatively easily since Germany's asylum laws were quite liberal, Bonn, now Berlin, tightened the screws. But the numerous asylants inside the country already in are often a burden on the German taxpayer. *Finally*, the attempt at transforming a communist command economy into a capitalist market economy represents the largest price that Germany has to continue to pay.

The Experiment: Integrating the East

This is the first time in history that a command economy is being converted to capitalism. The experiment is novel. The world is watching the measures being taken and waiting for the outcome. Textbooks on political theory and economics may have to be re-written. Already in March 1990, the FRG set up a Trust Agency (Treuhandanstalt) to take a close look at the viability of the firms operating in the GDR. It wrote in a report, "The Eastern German economy, once the pride of the communist world, is for sale". (Treuhandanstalt, *The Chance of the 90's: Investing in Eastern Germany*, Berlin, 2. ed., 1 Aug. 1991, p. 4). The Agency retained those firms, which showed profitability and shut down numerous others that were in the red. About 14,000 firms were privatized. The Agency completed its task in December 1994. Bonn meanwhile appealed to governments and private enterprises worldwide to invest in the five new states of the former GDR. Foreign investments have come not only from Germany's close partners like the USA, other West European states and Japan but even from India (six investments came from the latter in mid-1996).

Uplifting the East German economy is turning out to be a difficult task. A lot of re-training of the work force is needed, as well as reprogramming of East German work habits and mindset. This costs money. In the first three years following reunification, Bonn spent 140 billion DM for the eastern states in 1991, 152 billion DM in 1992 and 183 billion DM in 1993. A special Unity Fund had been set up to give these new five a start for the first few years. Then they automatically came under an ongoing program, under which the richer states of West Germany provide funds for the less rich. On an average, the west has provided the east with 150 billion DM each year since reunification. But East German productivity continues to lag behind the west. It is only 50% of the latter's level. East German income is also less, varying between 30% and 90% of West German income depending on the sector of the economy. Unemployment in the east is about double that in the west and hovers around 18%. If one adds those who are 'artificially employed' in state-supported jobs and training schemes, the figure would reach almost 25%. [7] In East Germany about one-fifth of Germany's population produces just one-tenth of the country's overall economic output and less than one-twentieth of its exports. Since Germany's economy is heavily export-oriented, the contribution, or rather the lack of it, of the east is disappointing. This is largely because production in the east is largely oriented to the domestic market. Unlike in the west, information technology, electronics and other investment goods, which are the hallmark of the western part, are missing in the east. The top firms operating in the east deal with food and supplies instead.

Brandenburg, one of the most backward of the five East German states, makes an interesting case study. Its capital Magdeburg shows high unemployment, low wages, and, therefore, people migrating to the west. Business there find competition a tough proposition, and that includes the problem of marketing products.[8] The major problem of the government in Berlin, which has meanwhile again become the capital, is how to remove the gross imbalance between the two parts of the country. Social differences have developed between the 'Ossis' (easterners) and 'Wessis' (westerners) due to their long separation and hence different habits, work culture and mind-sets. There was little love left between the two once the euphoria of reunification died down. On top of that, xenophobic rightwing groups have sprung up, especially in the east, partly due to various kinds of disillusionment with the west and partly due to unemployment. Some of these have hit the media with their anti-foreigner and anti-Jewish activities. Economic disparity and internal cleavage remain two most important problems currently facing united Germany.

NEW ROLE

The parliamentary elections of September 1998 brought back the SPD to power after a decade and half. CDU Chancellor Kohl, who had brought about reunification, was replaced by Gerhard Schroeder, who led a 'red-green' coalition government. In the year 2000, the 'reunification Chancellor' from the CDU got involved in an unsavory slush fund scandal and spoilt the image of both himself and his party. But to return to the 1998 government: the other ruling partners here are the Alliance 90/Greens (the Alliance 90 is a civil rights party from the former GDR now in alliance with the Green Party) and the Party of Democratic Socialism (PDS), consisting of former communists from the east, who now call themselves 'reform communists'. Their main constituency lies in the eastern states.

The German Problem today is the question: which *way will united Germany move*? Its massive economic power, leadership within the European Union (EU), geostrategic situation in the heart of Europe, close economic and other ties with East Europe including Russia, its stated objective to strive for a permanent seat in the UN Security Council, its willingness to participate in military missions, although multilateral so far, outside NATO Europe, and many other factors converge to sharpen that question. Will Germany again play a big power role in the classical political sense? Germany with its 82 million population (including foreigners) is the second most populous state in Europe. The Germans have a long tradition of hard work and efficiency. No wonder that the country ranks third in the world in the size of its economy. Given all these factors, its foreign policy will affect not only its immediate neighbors but also regions afar. The series of questions on its future role, which are being debated in the west, relate to our opening question. Will Germany again pose a threat, if not quite militarily, then economically and politically? Will this central European power adopt an independent path, with all its unpredictable consequences? Will it increasingly move towards East Europe, given its unique geographical, historical and economic ties with the latter? Will Germany pursue some historic vision that others might have reasons to fear? What role will it play in the new European security structure? As Gordon A. Craig has put it, the biggest economic power in Europe is sure to develop political ideas sooner or later, and the question would be whether these are good or bad.

In this context, let us briefly turn to a study made immediately after the Second World War. Wilhelm Roepke's *The German Question* made certain penetrating observations on the Germans, offering a rare in-depth perspective. As he observed, "There is the irrational element that... continually reveals itself in the history of the German soul and is in such strong contrast to the Latin formality and clarity". In his view, this is seen in the German language and other forms of expression. "In his language," Roepke goes on, "the German seems to be untiringly occupied in pushing forward into the uttermost regions of the expressible, and when he has got as far as that he plunges into the sphere of that which can no longer be made adequately comprehensible by words... the sphere of lyricism, of metaphysics, and, as the ultimate stage, of music. Here there lie open for him supreme opportunities, but at the same time the gravest danger". To curb this perceived characteristic of going to extremes, Roepke suggested that, in the political realm, Germany must cease to be *the large unit centrally organized for a common purpose which Bismarck made her*, if she is not again to be a danger to European peace. He prefers neither a big, centralized Germany of the past nor a balkanized Germany, but a genuine confederation.[9] So far, Germany has remained a model of democracy and decentralization. But will united Germany stick to it? Or will it again show a centralizing tendency and 'organization for a common purpose'? If so, to what purpose? Will that purpose be 'good' or 'bad'? The situation at this writing (March 2001) is fluid and still evolving. While it is always hazardous for a social scientist to predict events, we consider here certain factors which will remain constant in the evolution of a future German role and foreign policy.

The Question of Identity

Germans are extremely conscious of their Nazi past, and of their war-mongering image that the Allied Powers projected during the two World Wars. Not least has been Hollywood's contribution to the stereotype image of the stiff German who behaves like a military robot! German sensitivity to the possible reaction of neighbors even gave rise to a school of thought that prefers the term *unification* to *reunification*. It argues that the word *reunification* might rake up the image of old Germany reverting to the pre-World War II conditions. That would only stimulate wrong historical comparisons and damage the chance of starting on a clean slate. As Karl Kaiser observes, a new Germany was created in 1990. It consciously broke with the pre-1945 Germany but was equally consciously linked to the old Federal Republic (West Germany).[10] Such arguments reveal Germany's ongoing search for identity, a result of its history and geography. The country's central location exposes it to the crosswinds of influence from the Slavic East, the Roman West and South, and the Germanic North and Northwest. Germany lies astride the border between the two worlds, those of the stable and prosperous democracies of the West and of the politically and economically uncertain, even partly unstable, East.

United Germany seems unsure of how to relate to power in international relations.[11] This is largely the legacy of two lost World Wars. Contemporary Germany shies away from concepts like 'national interest' and 'power', as if these were necessarily stained by Machiavellianism and could lead to a repeat Third Reich. While other states take armed forces for granted as an attribute of national sovereignty, the Germans today perceive the military in a more negative light. While other powers like Britain, France and Italy do not hide their national interest, Germany rarely shows interest in the concept, even though the speed with which it achieved reunification startled all and sundry. Hans-Peter Schwarz has summed up the situation well. For him, the Germans have made a volte face from power-mania to power-amnesia! Four decades of Allied occupation after World War II significantly contributed to that amnesia. Also, the Germans, like the Japanese, have simultaneously discovered that economic well-being does not depend on possessing overseas colonies. The Germans never had it so good in terms of enjoying a high standard of living as now. So, political power play in the international arena no longer appears very attractive to them. In this they share a remarkable similarity with post-war Japan. Also, as Karl Kaiser comments, "After Hitler a dispassionate attitude to power was impossible".[12] The fact that Germany champions the cause of European unity is partly a result of its uncertainty to shape its foreign and security policy on its own. Berlin seems to fear the 'return of history'. It seems to be as scared of itself, because of its built-in insecurity, as its neighbors potentially fear it. Former Italian Premier Prodi once mused that he would be afraid of a Germany that was afraid of itself! The German Ulysses is thus seeking to tie itself to the European mast in order to withstand the siren call of the past. [13]

Much of Germany's uncertainty regarding its future course in foreign affairs and its identity stems from perceptions and expectations of other European nations and the USA. We have already noted this. To elaborate a bit on this point, voices are heard both inside and outside Germany, which warn against its return to 'normalcy', i.e., traditional Realpolitik behavior. European integration started as a response to a perceived Soviet threat. That threat has disappeared now. The rationale for integration continues, however. An important reason for it is to bind the potential hegemon, Germany, even if 'soft', to a community with commonly accepted rules and norms. On the other hand, Germany's active promotion of European integration also comes under a cloud of suspicion as a camouflaged promotion of hegemony. Further, the West suffers from the latent fear that Germany's close economic and other ties with East Europe, including Russia, could lead to undesirable Germanic influence in the region. Germany could access through business the considerable natural resources of Russia what it failed to achieve by military means. Yet, at the same time, when Berlin asks the EU to share in co-ameliorating East Europe's economic ailments, it is criticized for allegedly using an unfair ploy to pass on problems which are primarily in Germany's own backyard.[14] Indeed, during the heady days leading to reunification, Kohl's adviser Horst Teltschik cautioned his boss that not only the "objective" but also the "subjective" security interests of all European states must be respected. [15]

An additional dimension to united Germany's search for role and identity is provided by its unique east-west cleavage, both external as well as internal. Historically, Germany has been exposed to the pull from the west as well as from the east. This is the 'external' aspect. 'Internal' cleavage means that though the East Germans constitute only 20% of the total population, they could nevertheless swing issues, especially those over which the West Germans are divided. The PDS and Alliance 90 from the east are already in the government in Berlin.[16] A poll in March 2001 showed that less than a third of Germans were 'proud' to be Germans while a large number of youth were indifferent to their nationality (*Der Spiegel*, No. 13, 26. 3. 01,p. 22).

New Militarism?

Critics also claim to smell reviving jingoism in Germany. On 12 July 1994, the Constitutional Court of Germany ruled that the Bundeswehr, the armed forces, could participate in 'out-of-area' (OOA) operations (i.e., outside traditional NATO-Europe) under multilateral aegis like the UN, NATO or the West European Union (WEU). This flexing of military muscle all over again is dangerous, assert critics. Further, they also see big-power ambition in the decision to shift capital again to Berlin (though Berlin won against Bonn by a very thin majority).[17] The German armed forces define as part of their mission the task to keep open free world trade and access to strategic raw materials.[18] Critics would interpret this as the beginning of a new cycle of militarism. Also, the FRG is developing a 53,000-strong crisis-reaction force for quick, long-distance intervention, even though it depends heavily on the USA on matching airlift and sealift capability. This force will increase Berlin's influence within NATO and WEU. A Franco-German Corps is also in place. Critics also point to a number of German military missions in the 1990s. These ranged from mine-sweeping in the Persian Gulf in summer 1991, flying warplanes and surface-to-air missiles (SAMs) to Turkey and UN inspectors to Iraq, naval and air monitoring of embargo on Bosnia and Montenegro, troop deployment in Somalia during 1993-94, continued deployment of 4,000 troops in Bosnia-Herzegovina, and the promise to provide NATO with Tornado warplanes to counter Serbian assaults against Albanians in Kosovo. Germany fully supported the NATO bombing of Kosovo. German troops were also present in the 5-nation Eurokorps mission in Pristina (Kosovo) in early 2000. Over 6,000 of them, partly equipped with tanks, continue their mission as part of the KFOR to help the latter secure Kosovo's mountainous borders with Macedonia. NATO stated, in March 2001, that only Berlin responded positively to its call for extra troops to secure the borders; Washington and London did not.[19] Even though these acts fell short of actual combat, critics see in these the growing role of the German military and, consequently, militarism.

However, there are facts to the contrary, too. During the Yugoslav crisis, the FRG energetically supported the Croats against the Serbs. The UN sanctions relating to Yugoslavia raised domestic political controversy in Germany. An attempt in January 1993 to seek a wider interpretation of the military's defensive role by amending the constitution failed. Also, even though the Rome NATO summit of 1991 had decided to broaden NATO operations by approving of OOA, Germany took three years before it made up its mind to participate. Again, in 1995 the German Foreign Office turned down several UN requests for the Bundeswehr's participation in military missions. As of early 1995, the FRG ranked 56th in the UN's Blue Helmet missions, trailing behind even tiny Switzerland.[20] The FRG also declined that year to enter its armed forces into the Standby Register of the UN's Department of Peacekeeping Operations, even though that entry did not mean an automatic obligation to serve UN military missions. Paradoxically, Germany aspires after a permanent seat of the UN Security Council. A major criterion for getting such a seat is the ability and willingness of the candidate nation to participate in UN peacekeeping operations. Yet, the few missions it has already carried out has raised suspicion in certain quarters of Germany's allegedly growing jingoism. So, the Germans have to be very careful. They have to carry out a well-balanced tightrope walk between, on the one hand, allegations of not facing up to international responsibilities commensurate with their big status and ability, and being too militaristic on the other, between not doing enough and overdoing things! In anticipation of such allegations of jingoism, Germany had agreed, as we have seen, to cut its combined armed forces by nearly half during the reunification talks. Indeed, they have cut the armed forces further from the permissible manpower limit of 370,000 to 340,000.[21] The SPD-led red-green government has also given the axe to the military budget as announced in March 2000.[22]

But more than its military, it is Germany's financial power that creates trepidation and resentment in many countries of Europe. The strong position of the DM is one reason. In the fall of 1993, the British, for example, showed their reservations on the question of seating the European Currency Institute, which preceded the European Central Bank, in Frankfurt, Germany's financial capital. Germany's strong economic and financial position has given rise to many European jokes that are revealing. In Warsaw, the Poles maintain that Germany does not need to conquer Poland, it can simply buy it up. The Czechs observe that the only thing worse than being economically dominated by the Germans is not to be so dominated! And the British maintain in their characteristic wry fashion, "We won the war, but they (the Germans) won the peace!"[23]

Two Schools

A survey of German literature on foreign policy in the 1990s shows two schools of thought on the future path of

Germany. One of them may be dubbed *the special way school*. It maintains that the country should pursue a special and independent path since it has achieved unity and full sovereignty. The old Federal Republic's ties with the west should be revaluated, given the end of the Cold War and thereby the perceived anachronism of some of those ties. This view is popular with the rightwing spectrum, including the extreme right wing of the Union parties (CDU/CSU). These parties are now in the opposition in the new Bundestag, which has shifted from Bonn to the historic Reichstag building in Berlin, refurbished with 300 million DM. A variation of this school is represented by Egon Bahr, former Chancellor Brandt's adviser and by no means a rightist. But Bahr wants his country to shake off its "vassal-like attitude" and develop "sovereignty of thought".[24] As an example, he wants Berlin to oppose the US-led NATO expansion in East Europe. Michael Stuermer also holds the "continuity" of German foreign policy as dated, and wants his country to develop leadership. Karl Kaiser and Hanns W. Maull also seem to suggest that "continuity" will be plodding along the beaten track, given the significant transformation of Germany, Europe and the world. These scholars are also not necessarily rightists. So, they may be said to represent a *variant school*. Some of them would also agree with some of the elements of the second school, which may be called *the continuity school*. This school represents the mainstream of Germany's political groups. It favours the continuation of the country's firm entrenchment in and deepening of western institutions. In its view, the deep-rooted ties with the west are not merely a byproduct of the Cold War but represent the fundamental orientation of Germany's foreign policy. It is only by belonging to the west and sharing in its community of values that a recurrence of unhealthy nationalism can be prevented and the perception of German power-mania altered. It believes in the famous German author Thomas Mann's observation that not a Germanized Europe but a Europeanized Germany is desirable.

There is a latent fear in Europe that if Germany decided to go its *special way*, the Rapallo Treaty of 17 April 1922, spelling out a special understanding with Russia, cannot be ruled out, given Germany's close and very active financial and economic ties with East Europe. Russia is the centerpiece of Berlin's relations with the region. Several agreements in the 1990s have forged these relations with Moscow. The Two-Plus-Four Treaty, a bilateral agreement including a non-aggression clause (November 1991), the Joint Declarations of 1991 and 1992, plans for technical aid by German firms like Siemens and Mannesmann to Russia's power sector, gas, oil and motor industries, etc. are some instances. Germany has been Moscow's leading advocate for the latter's access to the exclusive 'rich men's club' like the G-7 (with Russia, now called the G-8) and other European and international institutions. The bulk of foreign aid to Russia and other Commonwealth of Independent States (CIS states, which had belonged to the former USSR) comes from Germany.[25] The country acts as an honest broker between the European institutions and East Europe. It advocates, for example, greater access of CIS products to EU and OECD markets. One-third of Russia's foreign trade is with EU. Germany occupies the position of Russia's largest trade partner in the west, accounting for 11% of that country's foreign trade as of 1995. Finally, Germany has a program for counseling East and Southeast European states on reforms.

The GDR's old economic ties with the USSR are still alive but ailing, even with generous Hermes credits granted to Russia to promote them. Turbulence in the Russian market, partly created by separatist movements and partly by organized crime, threatened 50,000 export-oriented jobs in Saxony in East Germany in 1998. In a topsy-turvy situation, while unemployment remained high in the latter region, hundreds of thousands of 'guest workers' from Russia, Poland and Ukraine found jobs in the East German state of Mecklenburg-Vorpommern.[26] Economic factors and geographical proximity have shaped the special German relationship with the east. It is no longer a Drang nach Osten (drive to the east) but rather a Zwang nach Osten (compulsion in the East). The expected eastward expansion of the EU worries German farmers. They fear the flooding of the German and other West European markets by cheaper agro-products from the east. At the same time, there is optimism in Germany that the expansion will boost German exports. The German eastward engagement has evoked misgivings in France, among other countries.[72] France found itself overtaken by the shattering events of German reunification and the Soviet collapse that drastically changed the European, and the world, scene. Paris had championed European integration in the 1980s to contain Germany and enhance French influence. It supported the creation of the common currency, the Euro, so as to be rid of the all-pervading Deutsche Mark. But the rapid events of 1989-91 left it in the position of a 'helpless spectator'.

The European Union And Germany

The Treaty on the European Union was signed in the Dutch town of Maastricht on 7 February 1992 and entered into force on 1 November 1993. The EU grew from the original six member states of the European Coal and Steel Community, signed into existence in 1951, to fifteen by 1995. Thirteen more nations, including the three Baltic states of Lithuania, Latvia and Estonia, expressed their desire to join the Union. In March 2001, Switzerland was scheduled to hold a referendum on joining it.[28] The EU has a population of over 370 million and stretches from the Arctic Circle to Portugal, from Ireland to Crete. It is based on three pillars: the European Communities (e.g., those relating to coal and steel, atom, etc.), Common Foreign and Security Policy (CFSP), and Legal and Domestic Policy. The second and third pillars are still incipient.[29] The image of the Union, which has been much hyped, took a severe beating in March 1999, however. The entire European Commission resigned en masse on charges of corruption, fraud and nepotism. The

European Parliament then set up an anti-fraud office, which was also supposed to check financial waste. After all, 5% of the $90 billion EU budget for 1998 remained untraceable![30] But subsequently the Parliament itself turned against the counter-measure.

In France, as well as some other European states, Maastricht seemed like a forced marriage. France voted for it by only a razor-thin majority. As many as 49% voted against it. As it is, united Germany with an expanded population would have a larger representation in the European Parliament. There are at present 99 German members to 87 each for France and Britain; but with the admission of new members from 1 January 2003, all members will have fewer seats except Germany. France and the other large countries will have 72 seats each, as was decided by The EU summit in Nice in December 2000. The European Council, however, has 29 members from each of the large states of Germany, the UK, France and Italy. Yet Germany will carry greater weight than the other large countries like France due to the new rule that a majority vote must also represent at least 62% of the population. This will make Germany the only country that can block a majority decision in combination with two other large countries.[31] The Nice summit also fell in with the German demand that veto power on asylum be maintained. Further, Nice supported a German proposal on an inter-governmental conference for 2004, to deal with various organizational matters. These are some indicators of Berlin's influence within EU. On top of that, future entry of German-tutored East European states into the EU might increase Germany's already leading influence. So, France and Spain, have been trying to divert EU attention to African, Caribbean and Pacific (ACP) states. Many of these 69 ACP states of the Lome Convention are Francophone. Paris and Madrid have also been advocating greater EU relations with Mediterranean states like Cyprus and Malta.[32] For the first time, the Korfu Summit resolutions of 1994 gave higher priority to the latter than Central and East Europe.

Conclusion

Part of Germany's almost missionary zeal for the success of EU is to involve West European institutions to share the burden of East Europe's economic woes and related socio-political instability. As we noted, this multilateral and institutional linkage with East Europe would also absolve Germany from the allegation that it is trying to colonize it. Under these circumstances, a *special way*, especially in liaison with Russia, seems a remote possibility. But much depends on the future shape of Europe and Germany's role in it. *The Atlanticist view of Europe* considers the USA and West Europe as a natural unit, with the Atlantic being merely a kind of Mediterranean that binds the two shores together. Their natural opponents begin with Russia and lie further east. The Western alliance must push its borders to the east to widen the buffer zone with Russia, weakening it whenever convenient. At the core of this alliance are the Anglo-Saxons, the USA and the UK. The rest of Europe is seen as a decentralized mosaic of regions and towns that enjoy wide autonomy within the framework of a continental free-trade zone.

Opposed to this view is *the continental perspective*. Here, the axis of the confederation of Europe runs through the Rhine and Danube basin, connecting the North and the Black Seas. The continental view revives Mackinder's and Haushofer's geopolitics, although in a modified form. In modern Europe, liberals and socialists often tend to be Atlanticists while the far left and the conservative right (including much of the CDU/CSU in Germany and the Gaullists in France till recently) lean towards the continentalists. Germany constitutes the center of gravity of their map. But the heavy Anglo-Saxon influence on Berlin prevents its politicians from embracing the second view whole-heartedly. Russia is interested in the continentalist strategy to defeat the Atlanticists. Even during the days of the USSR, Gorbachev used to talk about "a common European home". Close Russo-German cooperation, therefore, comes under a cloud of suspicion in London and Washington, not to speak of other European capitals. But Chancellor Schroeder replied "no way" to Moscow's plea for debt relief at the G-8 summit in Okinawa in July 2000, even though his country had close ties with Moscow and was its largest creditor. This was partly in order not to be too closely identified with Moscow. The German Chancellor, however, promised to consider rescheduling of the $42 billion debt that Russia has largely inherited from the USSR. The total Russian external debt to the Paris Club, London Club, the IMF, and other international bodies amounts to a whopping $120 billion [33]. Close Russo-German ties can also be seen in the fact that, having supported the NATO bombing of Kosovo, which infuriated Moscow, Germany was able to initiate talks with Russian leaders in early 2000.[34]

The final shape of 'Europe' is yet to emerge as EU grinds its way ahead. German foreign policy at 2000 meanwhile strikes a balance between an inward-looking European and a broad Atlantic policy. In the words of Green Party Foreign Minister Joschka Fischer in the SPD-led Schroeder government, German foreign policy goals are as follows: to complete European integration, to expand and "recalibrate" the transatlantic partnership, develop ties with Russia, bring greater stability in the Balkans and Southeast Europe closer to European integration, strengthen the UN, and promote cooperation with the Third World.[35] But what is the picture at the grass-roots level in Germany? As a CNN TV commentary aptly put it, Germans do not want any more 'history', i.e., revival of earlier romanticism about history, power and ideology, but "want to make a living".[36]

Germany takes quiet pride in being a 'civil power'. This means that, unlike in the past, its power today does not derive from military might and conquest but rather from economic strength, political stability and democracy. But the concept of civil power should not turn out to be a hindrance to united Germany's thinking and acting independently, even though within the framework of continued cooperation with its Western partners. With its civil power, Germany can make, indeed is already making, a significant contribution to tackling diverse problems, not only in Europe but worldwide. Environmental protection, the decision of the red-green government to end all civilian nuclear programs (postwar Germany had abjured nuclear weapons altogether), participation in UN peacekeeping missions and economic cooperation with it all are among the numerous examples. Today's Germany can, and should, continue to move away from the burdensome past legacy of Hitler and forge ahead confidently in the concert of free nations.

Readings

1. Wilhelm Roepke, *The German Question*, George Allen & Unwin, London, 1946.
2. Lawrence L. Whetten, *Germany's Ostpoliti: Relations between the Federal Republic and the Warsaw Pact Countries*, Oxford Univ. Press, London, 1971.
3. Michael Freund, *From Cold War to Ostpolitik: Germany and the New Europe*, Oswald Wolff, London, 1972.
4. Jyotirmoy Banerjee, *GDR and Détente: Divided Germany and East-West Relations*, Europa Union Verlag, Bonn, 1981; "Bonn's Ostpolitik at the Crossroads?," *India Quarterly*, New Delhi, Vol. XXXIX, No. 3, July-Sept. 1983, pp. 233-262; "The Reunification of Germany: The Process and Its Implications," in Arun K. Banerji (ed.), *Integration, Disintegration and World Order*, Allied Publishers, Calcutta, 1995, pp. 119-126; "United Germany's role in the Post-Cold War Era," *International Studies*, New Delhi, Jan-March 2000, Vol. 37, No. 1, pp. 41-59; "United Germany, Divided Russia: Coping with New Conflicts," in Arun K. Banerji (ed.), *Conflict Resolution in the Post-Cold War Era*, Minerva, Calcutta, 2000.
5. *Facts about Germany*, Inter Nationes, Bonn (irregular annual).

6. Hannes Adomeit, "Gorbachev and German Unification," *Problems of Communism*, Washington, July-Aug. 1990, Vol. XXXIX, No. 4, pp. 1-23.

7. Elizabeth Pond, *Beyond the Wall: Germany's Road to Unification*, Brookings, Washington, 1993.

8. Inter Nationes, *On the Path to German Unity. Chronology of Events,* Bonn, 1991.

9. Come Carpentier de Gourdon, "Whither the European Union?" *World Affairs*, New Delhi, Vol. 4, No. 3, July-Sept. 2000, pp. 66-79.

10. *A Community of Fifteen: Key Figures*, ed. 2000, European Commission, Brussels, 2000.

11. EU periodicals, including *Monthly Newsletter*; German perodicals in English: *German News*, New Delhi; *Deutschland* (English ed.), Frankfurt; back issues of *Aussenpolitik* (now defunct).

Notes

1. German history in *Historia Mundi*, Francke Verlag, Bern, 1960,Vols. 9 & 10; John Lord, *Beacon Lights of History*, The Waverly Book Co. Ltd., no date, chapter entitled "Prince Bismarck. The German Empire," pp. 251-314; German Bundestag, *Questions of German History*, Bonn, 1984; *Deutsche Geschichte seit dem Ersten Weltkrieg*, Vol. I, Deutsche Verlags-Anstalt, Stuttgart, 1971.

2. Markus Wolf, *Spionagechef im geheimen Krieg: Erinnerungen*, Econ, Munich, 1998, pp. 245-6.

3. Lawrence L. Whetten, *Germany's Ostpolitik: Relations between the Federal Republic and the Warsaw Pact Countries*, Oxford University Press, London, 1971; Michael Freund, to *From Cold War to Ostpolitik: Germany and the New Europe*, Oswald Wolff, London, 1972; Jyotirmoy Banerjee,"The Bonn-Moscow-East Berlin Triangle," *IDSA Journal*,

New Delhi, Vol. XII, No. 2, Oct-Dec. 1979, pp. 192-207; *GDR and Détente: Divided Germany and East-West Relations*, Europa Union Verlag, Bonn, 1981; "Gas-Pipes and Missiles: Bonn's Ostpolitik at the Crossroads?" *India Quarterly*, New Delhi, Vol. XXXIX, No. 3, July-Sept. 1983, pp. 233-262.

4. Horst Teltschik, *329 Tage*, serialized in *Der Spiegel*, Hamburg, as "Helmut Kohls Weg zur deutschen Einheit," I,"Der Zehn-Punkte Plan," Vol. 45, No. 39, 23 Sept. 1991, pp. 96-125; II, No. 40, 30 Sept. 1991, pp. 118-140; III, No. 41, 7 Oct. 1991, pp. 125-150.

5. Jyotirmoy Banerjee, "The Reunification of Germany: The Process and Its Implications," in Arun K. Banerji (ed.), *Integration, Disintegration and World Order*, Allied, Calcutta, 1995, pp. 119-126.

6. Central Intelligence Agency, *Handbook of Economic Statistics*, 1989, US Govt. Printing Office, Washington, 1989, pp. 59, 70, respectively.

7. "Ten Years of German Unity," Inter Nationes/IN Press, reprinted in *Aajker Germany* (Bengali), German Consulate-General, Calcutta, No. 4, 2000, p. 12.

8. DWTV, 13 Jan. 2001, 10. 15 a. m.

9. US expert on Germany Gordon A. Craig, cited in Hans Arnold, *Deutschlands Groesse: Deutsche Aussenpolitik zwischen Macht und Mangel*, Piper, Munich, July 1995,pp. 98-99.

10. Karl Kaiser, "Das vereinte Deutschland in der internationalen Politik," in Karl Kaiser, Hanns W. Maull(eds.), *Deutschlands neue Aussenpolitik*, Vol. I, Oldenbourg, Munich, 1994, pp. 1-2.

11. Ibid., p. 9.

12. Ibid.

13. Robert O. Keohane et al. (eds.), *After the Cold War*, Cambridge, MA, 1993, p. 389, quoted in Thomas Jeger *et al.* (eds.), *Europa 2020 Szenarien politscher Endwicklung*, Leske & Budrich, Opladen, 1997, p. 10.

14. Hans-Peter Schwarz, "Das deutsche Dilemma," in Kaiser, Maull, op. cit., pp. 95-96.

15. Document 166, Teltschik's memo to Chancellor Kohl, undated but probably of Feb. 1990, entitled "Gesamteuropaeische Sicherheitsarchitektur," in Hans Juergen Kuesters, Daniel Hoffmann(eds.), *Deutsche Einheit: Sonderedition aus den Akten des Bundeskanzleramtes*, 1989/90, Oldenbourg, Munich, 1998, p. 774.

16. See collection of articles on 10 years of German Unity, *Deutschland*, Frankfurt/M., English ed., No. 4, Aug-Sept. 2000, pp. 39-65; *German News*, German Embassy, New Delhi, Vol. XLII, Feb. 2001, pp. 8-9.

17. See Arnold, op. cit.; Caroline Thomas, Klaus-Peter Weiner, "Neuer Interventionismus—die deutsche Aussenpolitik nach der Vereinigung," in Thomas, Weiner(eds.), *Auf dem Weg zur Hegemonialmacht? Die deutsche Aussenpolitik nach der Vereinigung*, Papy Rossa Verlag, Cologne, 1993, p. 151; Wolfram Wette, "Der Wunsch nach Weltmacht," *Die Zeit*, 30 July 1993. See also Francois Heisbourg, "Trittbrettfahrer? Keine europaeische Verteidigung ohne Deutschland," *Internationale Politik*, Vol. 55, No. 4, April 2000, pp. 35-42.

18. Thomas, Weiner, op. cit., p. 152.

19. DWTV, 7 March 2000, 8. 30 p. m; www. dwelle. de, 17. 2. and 25. 3. 2001.

20. Winrich Kuehne, "Multinationale Friedensmissionen und nationale Interessen," in Karl Kaiser, Joachim

Krause(eds.), *Deutschlands neue Aussenpolitik*, Vol. III, Oldenbourg, Munich, 1996, p. 15.

21. Simon Duke, *The New European Security Disorder*, Macmillan, London, 1994, p. 154.

22. DWTV, 15 Mar. 2000, 9.30 p. m.

23. Helmut Hubel, "Das vereinte Deutschland in der internationalen Wahrnehmung," in Hans Suessmuth(ed.), *Deutschlandbilder in Danemark und England, in Frankreich und den Niederlanden*, Nomos, Baden-Baden, 1996, pp. 66, 72.

24. Egon Bahr, *Deutsche Interessen: Streitschrift zu Macht, Sicherheit und Aussenpolitik*, Karl Blessing Verlag, Munich, 1998, blurb, pp. 17-18.

25. Hannes Adomeit, "Russland, Deutschland und die 'neue' Weltordnung," in Gustav Schmidt(ed.), *Ost-West Beziehungen: Konfrontation und Détente*, Vol. II, Universitaetsverlag Dr. N. Brockmeyer, Bochum, 1993, p. 33. See also Jyotirmoy Banerjee, "United Germany, Divided Russia: Coping with New Conflicts," in Arun A. Banerji(ed.), *Conflict Resolution in the Post-Cold War Era*, Minerva, Calcutta, 2000, pp. 185-199; Klaus Kinkel, "Partner im Wandel. Deutsche Aussenpolitik und die GUS-Staaten," *Internationale Politik*, Bonn, Vol. 51, No. 10, Oct. 1996, p. 56; *Internationale Politik*, Bonn, special issue on Germany in Europe, Vol. 54, No. 11, Nov. 1999.

26. DWTV, 15 Feb., 6. 40 p. m., 22 Feb. 2001, 8. 50 p. m.

27. Euro News TV, Bonn, 29 Sept. 1998, 9 p. m. Central European Time (CET).

28. DWTV, 1 March 2001, 10. 15 p. m.

29. Emile Noel, *Die Organe der Europaeischen Gemeingschaft und der Europaeischen Union*, European Commission Office, Luxemburg, 1997, p.

526; *A Community of Fifteen. Key Figures, Edition 2000*, EC Office, Brussels, 2000. Other EU sources include *Monthly Newsletter* of European Commission, Brussels; *German News*, op. cit. (covers EU summit in Nice, in December 2000); *Internationale Politik*, special issues on Europe, Vol. 52, No. 11, Nov. 1997, and Vol. 55, No. 8, Aug. 2000; Ernst Friedrich Jung, "European Policy 40 Years On," and Carlo Masala, "Institutional Reform of the European Union under Debate," in *Aussenpolitik*, Hamburg, (English ed.), Vol. 48, 3/97, pp. 220-227 and pp. 228-236, respectively.

30. DWTV, video clippings of 16 March 1999 beamed on 1 March 2000, 9. 50 p. m.

31. *German News*, op. cit., p. 8; *Deutschland*, No. 1, 2001, Feb-Mar 2001, pp. 20-21.

32. Come Carpentier de Gourdon, "Whither the European Union?" *World Affairs*, New Delhi, Vol. 4, No. 3, July-Sept. 2000, pp. 66-79; Lord Weidenfeld, "Ten Years of German Unity," *Deutschland*, op. cit., p. 56.

33. DWTV, 21 July 2000, 5.50 p. m.

34. DWTv, 24 Mar. 2000, 10 p. m.

35. Joschka Fischer, "Tenth Anniversary of German Unity," *German News*, Vol. XLI, Oct. 2000, p. 7.

36. CNN, Bonn, 15 Oct. 1998, 7.30 p. m. CET.

8

Post-Cold War US Foreign and Security Policy

Foreign Policy Paradigms

What Patrick M. Cronin wrote way back in 1991 remains a good way to look at on the emerging options for US foreign policy.[1] Removing all the surface clutter, there were *four paradigms* which could shape the post-Cold War US foreign policy. *The first* is Fortress America or America First. It represents an isolationist school of thought and is inward-looking. *The second* is the Unipolar Moment. This school is internationalist in outlook but prefers that the US boldly shows its predominance. *The third* is termed by Cronin Comprehensive Globalism. It is totally internationalist and believes in multilateral action. *The fourth*, and the final one, is dubbed Pax Consortis. This school is also internationalist but would prefer the USA to act with other key industrial democracies.

The four schools basically differ on two counts. First, the extent to which the US should pursue nationalist, rather than internationalist, goals; and second, the degree to which the US should act in foreign affairs alone or with others. If with others, how many and who should it count upon?

Patrick Buchanan, a prominent columnist, is the proponent of the Fortress America school.[2] In his view, the US had resisted the temptation of building an empire for a century after Washington's death. But with McKinley's invasion of the Philippines, "we were launched".[3] Writing at the juncture when the Cold War was finishing, he wanted the US to pull out of Europe just like the Soviet troops were about to withdraw from central Europe. For him, the rest of the NATO nations, together populous and each quite prosperous, should look after their own defense. However, the US should retain strong armed forces like the navy to keep overseas trade routes safe, as well as forces in air and space, but save money by cutting down the army, which was no longer needed, either abroad or at home. He strongly felt that the US could not go on carrying the heavy mantle of defense on behalf of wealthy states, "mendicant" states, and "economic corpses of socialism without bleeding to death".[4] But the problem with such an isolationist mentality is that the world would have been radically different without US global engagement after World War II. Also, a sudden withdrawal of US power will contribute to international chaos and encourage regional hegemons (like the USA bugbear Saddam Hussein and others) to step up aggression upon their neighbors.

The second school, the Unipolar Moment, is represented by syndicated columnist Charles Krauthammer.[5] For Krauthammer, who advocates that the US seize the opportunity of being the only leader at the end of the Cold War, the old-fashioned balance of power is likely to emerge. Besides the USA, a doubtful USSR (read Russia), China, Japan and a confederated West Europe will be the other main players in the new global system. These actors will be "bleached" of ideology. Of course, conservatives and neo-conservatives would still like to spread Wilsonian democracy. The liberals like former President Jimmy Carter would dub it "human rights". Call it democracy or human rights, they boil down to the same thing. But Krauthammer prefers to cut through all ideological haze and foresees the emergence of three concentric circles of states. At the center is the leader, the USA, accompanied by its industrial and democratic allies. This is the core circle. The second circle would consist of the now destitute Second World states, which are busy "decommunising". The third circle will consist of the Third World states, "graduates" from which (like South Korea, Brazil, Israel, etc.) may eventually join the center. His bottom line is that the US should take advantage of the unique situation that it is the only Superpower left.[6] But the counter-argument to this line of thinking is that if the US rubs in its leadership role, it may lead to the rise of hostile coalitions of weaker powers and increase international tension. In fact, murmurs of dissatisfaction at the predominance of the USA today are heard in Moscow and Beijing. India's favorite justification for the continuation of the nonaligned movement, which seems to dangle in the air in the absence of the East-West rivalry, is to have a forum for the Third World to assert independence, if only largely in words. Acting predominantly alone might also become financially burdensome to the US, apart from being politically counter-productive. It is preferable to go for genuine partnerships, on the basis of equality with others, instead of providing unilateral security guarantees based on superior-inferior relations.

The third viewpoint, Comprehensive Globalism, can be termed 'new world order idealism', which was still-born in the initial flush of high expectations immediately following the end of the Cold War. Harry B. Hollins and John Mueller are associated with this school. It believes in a brand new world order based on international institutions like the UN, and denies any significant role to the USA as the world leader. But as Cronin points out, collective security is hardly likely to be enhanced in such a scenario. Too many cooks spoil the broth, as is the experience with heterogeneous multilateral agencies. It is too romantic to be any good in practice. Finally comes Pax Consortis. This view places less faith in comprehensive regionalism or globalism, focusing instead on expanding core alliances of the US with West European states and Japan. Peace costs money and other resources like manpower. By means of Pax Consortis, the costs and other burden of keeping or restoring peace can be evenly distributed and provide some relief to the US taxpayer.

Post-Cold War Engagement

Let us take a wider look at what a cross section of US scholars and other experts have so far thought about the post-Cold War scenario and the US role in it.

In Thomas J. McCormick's view, the world system at the turn of the 1990s was "decentering" but "the contours of its recentering" remained murky. One heard a similar note in Owen Harries writing at the beginning of the post-Cold War era. For him, while the "high octane" conditions of the Cold War had disappeared, so had the simplicity of a clearly identifiable enemy (the USSR), allies, fixed strategies, and a sense of a cause and morality (communism was evil). The result: "We are a country without maps," no clear marching orders, and no destination![8] For Zbigniew Brzezinski,[9] the emerging world order will depend on:

(a) the degree of EC integration (synonymous with EU; he calls it EC because EU was yet to be born when he wrote way back in 1991) and its integration with East Europe,

(b) whether a regional security accommodation can emerge in the Far East involving China, Japan, the US, "perhaps" Russia (sic!), and other states, and

(c) whether the US can remain the arbiter of security in the Middle East and set in motion a regional peace process.

The choice of the three regions automatically shows that the USA gives the highest priority to them. After all a large volume of trade is involved with West Europe and the Far East, while Middle Eastern oil is still crucial to the overall prosperity of the West. Both Cronin and Brzezinski, and a host of experts besides, agree that the US is destined to remain the world leader— and the sole superpower. No other state has its military reach, political clout, economic impact and socio-cultural appeal. For Brzezinski (and most scholars in the US) the Buchanan-type Fortress America mentality and isolationism are out. This is the age of modern communications and global economy, in which nations are linked and depend on each other for exchange of goods and services, to a degree unprecedented in recorded history. How can the leading economy, and power, stay out of this massive network that is leapfrogging every day? In Brzezinski's view, the alternatives for the post-Cold War world are: increasing instability in Europe; a Far East destabilized by new power shifts (in the absence of the USSR, the center of gravity there may shift to China or Japan, if the US chooses to pull out too); and a volatile Middle East marked by continuous conflict. Any or all of these would mean damage to, or breakdown of, world order. Or, the emergence of an incipient global security structure is possible, derived from widening and increasingly self-reliant regional cooperation (EU and ASEAN are two good examples), and backed by 'selective and proportionate' US commitments.

Paul H. Nitze, a former prominent US government official, opposes isolationism as "shortsighted".[10] In his opinion, there remain numerous international problems that deeply affect US interests. New problems are also bound to arise. The US, therefore, should contribute to the effective solution of these problems in conjunction with others. He is on the Pax Consortis side, like most US commentators. Gregory D. Foster, a West Point graduate and army officer, who also held faculty positions in the academia, proposes in the same vein his notion of 'progressive engagement'. Unlike Containment, says he, which was a policy to safeguard the status quo, progressive engagement means "active international involvement".[11] He takes that to mean global integration in terms of increasingly shared values, goals and resources, global democracy, global standards of conduct and global demilitarization. Strobe Talbott, arms control expert and President Clinton's Deputy Secretary of State, often engaged in promoting Indo-Pakistani dialogue in recent years, observed in 1996 that "in an increasingly interdependent world Americans have a growing stake in how other countries govern, or misgovern, themselves".[12] He is in favor of "vigorously supporting, promoting, and, when necessary, defending democracy in other countries". Unlike some "self-described realists' insinuations," American values and interests reinforce each other, he concludes. As examples of the US readiness to use the military to defend democracy, he cites the dispatch of 21,000 US troops by President Clinton to Haiti in 1994 as part of a multinational force, which restored an elected leader there who had been deposed by a coup. Other examples are Clinton's encouragement to Moscow in 1996, to hold its first post-Soviet Presidential elections, and the US-led 53,000-strong NATO contingent sent to Bosnia to make elections possible. Throughout the 20th century, says Talbott, the US sent troops abroad with some invocation of democracy and its defense, whether in the two World Wars or during the Cold War. Talbott then determines that, for the first time in history, "a slim but clear majority of the world's population— 54 percent— lives under democracy".[13]

Writing two years later, Talbott's boss, Clinton's Secretary of State Madeleine Albright, determined that the post-Cold War world consisted of four categories of states. These were: "full members" of the international system; those in transition, seeking to participate more fully; the third category consisting of those too weak, poor, or mired in conflict to participate; and, finally, those, which rejected the very rules of the system. The US has to fortify the bonds between the leading nations and help the second and third categories, while repelling the fourth.[14] Not unnaturally for a foreign affairs official, but also probably representing the mainstream American view, Albright was for continued US engagement in the new world order. Joseph S. Nye, Jr. of Harvard University, also shows preference for continued US engagement. The US has both 'hard' power (economic and military ability to buy and coerce) and 'soft' power (the ability to attract through cultural and ideological appeal). In the information age, soft power is becoming more compelling than ever before, says Nye. But scope for the use of hard power remains. For Nye, the US has "two simple reasons for preventing disorder beyond its borders. First, events and actors there can hurt America, and second, the US wants to influence distant governments on a variety of issues like proliferation of weapons of mass destruction, terrorism, drugs, shared resources and the environment. Finally, let us turn to Samuel P. Huntington's theory of the "clash of civilizations". Borrowing concepts of geology, he has discovered various "fault lines" separating the major civilizations of the world. He sees, and foresees, increasing conflicts across these fault lines, a sort of tribal warfare on a global scale. The West, in his view, is declining relatively in influence. Thus, the balance of power among civilizations is shifting. Major groups of people share and fight for a common identity, and they cut across the national boundaries. The West has a major adversary in Islam. So it follows that the leader of the West, the USA, cannot simply shirk the responsibility of protecting Western interests.[15]

This survey of US scholarly literature on *quo vadis*, USA? (Where are you going, USA?) shows that there is a general agreement that the USA must continue to engage in world affairs on a variety of fronts, even though the Cold War is over. One of the most important tasks of US foreign policy is said to be to continue efforts at spreading democracy. This reveals an underlying Puritan zeal, a hallmark of US foreign policy. Only Buchanan and his types, much in the minority, strike a strong note of dissent. We have already seen that. But there is another opinion, this time from a British cousin of the Americans, which also begs to differ from the mainstream and provides an interesting, even amusing, perspective. Peregrine Worsthorne of London's *Sunday Telegraph* tells the Americans to forget their all-too favorite missionary zeal and take a leaf from British experience instead. Britain, *Great* Britain to be exact, used to run a worldwide empire till half a century ago. Look at it today. It has in reality become Little England. Britain has shrunk back to its few miserable isles, its original size. But it lives. Britain, according to Worsthorne, does continue to have a foreign policy, but no *role*. It has no mission to spread particular ideals worldwide. So, in the absence of the USSR, the US does not *have* to find a new role in the sense of a new mission to carry out. It should "resign itself to the same perfectly bearable fate" as the UK![16] Crusade is not a must. And talking about US enthusiasm for spreading democracy, the British commentator wryly remarks that important freedoms in the UK predated democracy, and that democracy is not all that suitable everywhere. It turned out to be a "disaster" for Africa. On the other hand, autocracy has been doing very well indeed in Singapore, far better than the democracy in Kenya! The US should not bother about progress of democracy, or the lack of it, in central and eastern Europe; let the peoples there decide which way they want to go.

However, the mainstream thought in the USA, notwithstanding Buchanan and Worsthorne, is still skewed in favor of continued engagement in world affairs, and with a mission, although there might be differences in details. The missionary zeal of 'waging democracy' throughout the world continues through the Clinton Administration to the current Bush Administration. A White House report dated October 1998 and entitled *A National Security Strategy for a New Century* plainly states that one of the three core national security objectives is "to promote democracy abroad".[17] Following the US elections in 2000, then Secretary of State-designate Colin Powell declared before the powerful Senate Foreign Relations Committee that the new government "stands ready to help any country that wishes to join the democratic world".[18] In his inaugural address of 20 January 2001 President George W. Bush declared that "America remains engaged in the world by history and by choice...(To) all nations, we will speak for the values that gave our nation birth".[19] Besides continued engagement and zeal for spreading democracy, Cronin's Pax Consortis, or the US carrying out its foreign policy in close cooperation with key allies, also seems comfortably ensconced in the White House. This is regardless of the change in its occupancy so far.

Let us now turn to the formidable *US military*. It is formally in charge of the security of not only America but of a large number of allies and friends as well. We wish to examine how the sudden end of the Cold War, which provided its *raison d'etre* or justification, hit the Pentagon.

Security Policy

Michael Klare has put it very aptly. The end of the Cold War "provided an enormous shock for American military leaders.... Without the Soviet threat to guard against, they had no basis on which to develop contingency plans, train troops, design weapons, or test their combat skills".[20] The US military plunged into a severe identity crisis! The US Congress started considering significant cuts in the military budget. The Pentagon found it hard to discover an enemy which would have the stature of the USSR to justify the continuation of large US defense spending. In March 1990, Senator Sam Nunn, Chairman of the Senate Armed Services Committee, warned the military that a "threat blank", i.e., no clearly visible enemy anymore, was intolerable and could lead to severe budget cuts; so the Pentagon might as well hurry and fill in that "blank".[21] But the reality showed that the US was least threatened by external enemies. States with considerable military prowess were either friends or refrained from any overt antagonistic behavior towards the US. And none of them was nearly as powerful as even a weakened Russia. Virtually the whole of the Second World, i.e., former Warsaw Pact states, was running after the West seeking economic and political help! Some even wished to join the NATO, the very pact to which they had been hostile for four decades! The Czech Republic, Hungary and Poland, all former Warsaw Pact states, have already taken the total NATO membership from 16 to 19. The East European countries had been great enemies yesterday but wished any amount of cooperation with the West today. The First World, to be sure, contained a few potential candidates as future adversaries, e.g., Germany and Japan. But it would sound ridiculous and be politically unacceptable to reconfigure US forces with these close allies as enemies in mind. That left the Third World to choose from. Several countries were developing weapons of mass destruction (WMD) like nuclear bombs and ballistic missiles. While not all of them were hostile to the US, a few indeed were. These 'rogues' and 'outlaws' were, in the Pentagon's view, Iraq, Iran, North Korea, Libya and Syria. Seen through the Pentagon's lens, there are other prospective rogues too. These are China, Egypt, India, Pakistan, South Korea, Taiwan and Turkey. These candidate enemies are emerging regional powers. They share hegemonstic ambitions and have a clear weakness for acquiring WMD. While most of these states are friendly to the US, yet 'you can never tell'! The military analysts locked on to their 'worst case scenarios' to include them in their threat perception because of their growing military capabilities and because shifts in international relations do occur. As John D. Holum, a senior State Department arms control and international security official, noted subsequently, "military spending in developing countries has been increasing since 1995". He determined that the military burden such as ratio of military spending to GNP was "too high in many places in the developing world".[22] Third World defense expenditure dropped during 1990-94 but then rose to "a new historic high", to $232 billion in 1997.[23]

The Pentagon zeroed in on 'rogue' states and drew satisfaction from filling Nunn's 'threat blank'. The 'rogue doctrine' was adopted. It received formal endorsement in the Bottom-Up Review following shortly after the collapse of the Berlin Wall (November 1989). The newly discovered threat of low-intensity conflicts (LIC) with 'rogue' states provided the much needed justification of steady military funding at near-Cold War levels. LIC became the new basis for reconfiguring US forces against a new type of threat, which was more diffused than focused. Operation Desert Storm and the Persian Gulf War of 1991 came as a godsend for the Pentagon. The conflict confirmed the new threat perception that it had to conjure up to fill in Nunn's 'threat blank'. The US military was also able to gather experience in waging LIC against Iraq. The 'Rogue Doctrine' now came to replace the Containment Doctrine of the Cold War days. Desert Storm became the perfect model of future regional conflicts for the Pentagon. The question which soon arose was: how many 'Desert Storm Equivalents' (DSEs) should the US military be recrafted to fight at any one time? During 1992-93, some Congress members wanted to limit this number to one and a half. But the Pentagon wanted to set the number at two and was successful in pushing through its goal. The 1998 White House report quoted the above approved two-war preparedness. More recently, the Bush Administration has also indicated that it wants the ability to fight "regional conflicts, which might occur near-simultaneously".[24] To the Pentagon's delight, the US government has been committed to meet the post-Cold War challenges, which besides LIC also include drug-smuggling, terrorism etc., by funding the Revolution in Military Affairs (RMA), or hi-tech gizmos and weaponry. The F-22 Raptor jet fighter, for example, which is being developed, would be far superior to any other fighter that the US Air Force ever flew. Its primary mission is to dominate the sky in any battle. Partly titanium-built, its highly automated cockpit, along with other novel features, would give it abilities like stealth (i.e., zero or low visibility on enemy radar), super-cruise, integrated avionics, agility and lethality to make it a great air-superiority as well as air-to-ground attack fighter.[25] The RMA involves taking advantage of advances in computers, telecom, precision-guided munitions (laser-guided bombs were used in Kosovo by NATO), sensors, and so forth. Cuts in defense spending in the West, as well as new threats like LIC, have given rise to the need of a leaner but qualitatively superior, partly quick-reaction force. At the same time, the US is developing *non-lethal* weapons. For example, microwave projectiles that would melt sensitive components in enemy computers, flash blinding bombs that would temporarily blind sensors, low-frequency acoustic beams, which would hit the inner ear drum and cause discomfort or unconsciousness to enemy troops, and the like. The US Army has a program under development called Soldier Integrated Protection Ensemble (SIPE), which is part of the larger Land Warrior program. SIPE blends advanced sensors, communications, computers, and chemical protection into a head-to-toe outfit.[26] The 1997 Quadrenniel Defense Review (QDR) reflected funding for new technologies, as did the 1998 report.[27]

So, the threat perception of the USA today can be summed up with the three lists drawn up by Wiiliam Perry and Ashton Carter. Hitherto, the 'A list' consisted of the USSR, which posed a threat to the very survival of the USA. The 'B list' consists of serious threats to US interests, such as from North Korea and Iraq, but not to survival. The 'C list' includes important contingencies that indirectly affect US security but do not directly threaten US interests, e.g., Kosovo, Bosnia, Somalia, Rwanda and Haiti.[28] With the A list now removed following the collapse of the USSR, the US national security policy is shifting focus and, among other methods, reconfiguring the armed forces to tackle B and C.

Readings

1. Patrick M. Cronin, "American Global Leadership after the Cold War: From Pax Americana to Pax Consortis," *Strategic Review*, Washington, Summer 1991, pp. 9-21.

2. Zbigniew Brzezinski, "Selective Global Commitment," *Foreign Affairs*, New York, Fall, 1991, pp. 1-20.

3. Michael Klare, *Rogue States and Nuclear Outlaws*, Universal Book Traders, Delhi, 1995.

4. Paul H. Nitze, "America: An Honest Broker," *Foreign Affairs*, New York, Fall, 1990, pp. 1-14.

5. Gregory D. Foster, "America and the World: A Security Agenda for the Twenty-First Century," *Strategic Review*, Washington, Spring 1993, pp. 20-29.

6. Lewis A. Dunn, "Rethinking the Nuclear Equation: The United States and the New Nuclear Powers," *The Washington Quarterly*, Vol. 17, No. 1, 1993, pp. 5-25.

7. Strobe Talbott, "Democracy and the National Interest," *Foreign Affairs*, New York, Nov-Dec. 1996, pp. 47-63.

8. Sam C. Sarkesian, "The U.S. Military Must find its Voice," *Orbis*, Philadelphia, Summer 1998, pp. 423-437.

9. Joseph S. Nye, "Redefining the National Interest," *Foreign Affairs*, July-Aug. 1999, pp. 22-35.

10. Madeleine K. Albright, "The Testing of American Foreign Policy" *Foreign Affairs*, New York, Dec. 1998, American Center Calcutta reprint, pp. 1-9.

11. US Embassy, New Delhi, *Preventing Conflict: Military Engagement in Peacetime*, Dec. 1999 (Collection of articles & statements by US military & political officials).

12. A National Security Strategy for a New Century. A White House document, October 1998," Strategic Digest, New Delhi, Vol. XXIX, No. 4, April 1999, pp. 507-569.

13. Thomas J. McCormick, *America's Half-Century*, Affiliated East-West Press, New Delhi, 1992.

14. Owen Harries (ed.), *America's Purpose. New Visions of U. S. Foreign Policy*, Macmillan India, N. Delhi, 1991.

Notes

1. Patrick M. Cronin, "American Global Leadership after the Cold War: From Pax Americana to Pax Consortis," *Strategic Review*, Washington, Summer, 1991, pp. 9-21. The first and second schools have been listed here individually (notes 2, 5). For the third and fourth schools, see Cronin, pp. 12-14.
2. Patrick Buchanan, "America First—and Second, and Third," in Owen Harries (ed.), *America's Purpose: New Visions of U. S. Foreign Policy*, Macmillan India, 1993, pp. 23-34.
3. Ibid., p. 26.
4. Ibid., pp. 31-32.
5. Charles Krauthammer, "Universal Dominion," in Harries, op. cit., pp. 5-13.
6. Ibid., pp. 6-12.
7. 7. Thomas J. McCormick, *America's Half Century: United States Foreign Policy in the Cold War*, Affiliated East-West Press, New Delhi, 1992, p. 240.
8. Owen Harries, "Introduction," in Harries, op. cit., pp. 1-2.
9. Zbigniew Brzezinski, "Selective Global Commitment," *Foreign Affairs*, New York, Fall 1991, pp. 1-20.
10. Paul H. Nitze, "America: An Honest Broker," *Foreign Affairs*, Fall 1990, p. 12.
11. Gregory D. Foster, "America and the World: A Security Agenda for the Twenty-First Century," *Strategic Review*, Spring 1993, pp. 22-23.
12. Strobe Talbott, "Democracy and the National Interest," *Foreign Affairs*, Nov-Dec. 1996, pp. 48-49.
13. Ibid., p. 50.

14. Madeleine Albright," The Testing of America's Foreign Policy," *Foreign Affairs*, Dec. 1998, pp. 1-2 of USIS reprint, Calcutta.

15. Joseph S. Nye, Jr., "Redefining National Interest," *Foreign Affairs*, July-Aug. 1999, pp. 24-29.

16. Peregrine Worsthorne, "Not Too Much Zeal, Please," in Harries, op. cit., p. 124.

17. Text of the report in *Strategic Digest*, New Delhi, Vol. XXIX, No. 4, April 1999, p. 507.

18. Powell quoted in American Center *Bulletin*, Calcutta, March 2001, p. 1.

19. Text in "Inauguration 2001: President George W. Bush," *Span*, US Embassy, New Delhi, Mar-April 2001, pp. 3-4.

20. Michael Klare, *Rogue States and Nuclear Outlaws*, Universal Book Traders, Delhi, 1995, p. 6.

21. Ibid., p. 14.

22. John D. Holum, "Foreword," *World Military Expenditures and Arms Transfers 1998 (WMEAT 1998)*, US Dept. of State, Washington, April 2000, p. iii.

23. Ibid., p. 1.

24. State Secretary Colin Powell's statement, American Center *Bulletin*, op. cit., p. 1.

25. "F-22 to Counter 21st century Threats," *Aviation Weekly & Space Technology*, 24 July 1995, pp. 38-56; more at *http://www.boeing. com/defence-space/military/f22/*.

26. Judith Gunther et al., "The Future of Warfare," Part I, *Popular Science*, Oct. 1994, pp. 60-69.

27. White House report, op. cit., p. 531.

28. Quoted in Nye, op. cit., p. 26.

9

Nuclear Bomb and Strategy in South Asia

India conducted a nuclear test in May 1974 in Pokhran, about 100 km south of the Pakistani border, in Thar desert of Rajasthan. New Delhi dubbed it a 'peaceful nuclear explosion' (PNE). On 12 May 1995, when a review conference on the Nuclear Nonproliferation Treaty (NPT) was held in New York, India voted against the motion for its indefinite extension, which was nevertheless carried by 178 states. In October-November that year, India might have intended to test a second time but postponed the test under US pressure. The Comprehensive Test Ban Treaty (CTBT), provision for which was contained in Article VI of NPT, started taking shape. A United Nations General Assembly resolution in December 1993 and negotiations at the Conference on Disarmament, which began next month, paved the way for it. CTBT finally opened for signature in September 1996 but India, initially a co-sponsor, declined to sign it on the same grounds of discrimination as NPT. While 158 states showed favor to CTBT in its present form, India was joined by only Libya and Bhutan in opposing it in the UN.

Within two months of the nationalistic BJP-led coalition government coming to power in New Delhi in 1998, India conducted five nuclear tests in Pokhran, three on 11 May, in which it claimed to have included a thermonuclear test, followed by two more on 13 May. Raja Ramanna, the 'father' of India's nuclear bomb, celebrated with wine.[1]

Following the tests, which were no longer branded as PNEs, New Delhi declared a moratorium on more explosive or 'critical' tests. It also issued a 'no first strike' pledge and offered to open CTBT talks. It was hardly surprising that Pakistan followed with its own tests before the month was out, on 28 and 30 May. Perhaps surprising was the alacrity with which it responded to the Indian tests. The most astonishing element was the failure of US intelligence to predict India's action. That made it the butt of jokes in the European media.

The Basics

Let us first understand the basic functioning of the nuclear bomb. The nuclear bomb uses fissile material, either separated plutonium (Pu) or highly enriched uranium (HEU). The source of both Pu and HEU is natural uranium.[2] HEU contains 99.3% of uranium-238 and only 0.7% of uranium-235. U-235 can be enriched to weapons-grade quality. Neutrons are used to bombard and split atoms of chemical elements.[3]

The production of plutonium needs major industrial infrastructure, involving at least a 20-40 megawatt thermal reactor. Inside this reactor, uranium is irradiated and plutonium is produced by neutron capture in uranium-238, which is used as ballast. Metal plutonium (Pu-239) is the result, and with longer processing, heavier isotopes such as Pu-140 and 141.[4] Pu can be recycled as fresh nuclear fuel. The irradiated fuel is transferred to a heavily shielded chemical processing facility where the plutonium is separated from the uranium and transuranic elements. Successful construction and operation of uranium-producing facilities are a complex and demanding task, requiring specialized materials and thousands of workers. A difficult step is the separation process itself. The main separation technology is called PUREX, after plutonium-uranium extraction. It involves dismantling and cutting up the irradiated fuel, dissolving it in hot nitric acid, and then separating the plutonium from the uranium by a method called 'solvent extraction'. Tributyl phosphate diluted in kerosene is the common solvent.[5]

For controlled explosion in a nuclear reactor, moderators like heavy-water or graphite are used. The moderator slows down the neutrons. Heavy-water and graphite-moderated reactors can use natural uranium. Light-water reactors, however, need U-235 enriched to 3%. HEU, in contrast, is U-235 enriched to over 90%. In case of an atom bomb, heavy nuclei of fissile material are split, thereby producing a chain reaction of fission and releasing huge energy. With a thermonuclear or hydrogen bomb, light nuclei are fused together; the fusion releases enormous energy. An H-bomb also requires as initial trigger a small atomic explosion. To build this 2-step H-bomb, therefore, is a more complex phenomenon than splitting an atom.

The peculiarities of a plutonium-based bomb need the implosion method. Here, a subcritical hollow ball, or a stuffed ball with fine holes in it, is turned into a critical state by special explosives operating on its surface. These burst simultaneously and are directed to the ball's center to achieve supercompression. Only with supercompression, and not with simple explosion, are low-yield tactical nuclear arms produced, as well as the initial trigger for an H-bomb explosion.[6]

There are several ways of enriching uranium. Uranium-hexafluoride is used and the ratio of U-235 to U-238 changed. The most common commercial methods for changing that ratio are gaseous diffusion and gas centrifugation. There are other methods too, e.g., aerodynamic techniques, chemical processing, electromagnetic processing, and the new technology of using laser. Let us briefly take a look at gas centrifugation, since this is relevant to the South Asian nuclear scene. In this method, the heavier molecules in a rotating gas veer toward the inside wall of a rotating tube. Induced undercurrent in the gas increases the separation of U-235 from U-238. A gas centrifuge plant is somewhat smaller, and uses far less electricity, than a gaseous diffusion plant. The centrifuges rotate at supersonic speed. So, precision engineering and metallurgy are key to its successful operation. The centrifuge plant needs special items like maraging steel, advanced fibers, high-quality computers, special oils, magnets, aluminum piping, etc.[7]

The Separate Routes of Going Nuclear

As the above discussion shows, there are basically two approaches to acquire nukes.[8] Option A is to obtain plutonium by processing U-238. It is the more complex of the two options and involves perhaps greater risks of failure and lapse of time. Its advantage lies in the scope for using existing civilian nuclear reactors. Mastery over supercompression also opens the El Dorado of hi-tech nukes.

Option B enriches U-235 (which constitutes only 0.7% of natural uranium, as we have seen) to HEU (over 90% enrichment) by elaborate isotope-enrichment processes, without the use of reactors and chemical separation.

India opted for Option A. Pakistan chose B. This was because of the different histories of their nuclear development. The centerpiece of the Indian program includes two Canadian Candu-type heavy water reactors at the Bhabha Atomic Research Center (BARC) as well as a chemical reprocessing plant for plutonium separation in Trombay near Mumbai. The *World Inventory of Plutonium* estimated that India had accumulated almost 300 kg weapons-grade plutonium by the end of 1991.[9] Like most nuclear-ambitious states, India started on the nuclear weapons course via the civilian route, which started in this country in the early 1960s, though nuclear energy research here can be traced back to 1944![10] So as not to overly depend on US-supplied light water reactors (which use lightly-enriched uranium and are commercially the leading type of reactor in the world),[11] New Delhi helped itself to Canadian aid for Candu reactors. With its large pool of trained scientists, India managed to move further from purely civilian nuclear base to nuclear weapons projects. The Department of Atomic Energy (DAE) and the Defense Research and Development Organization (DRDO) organized the Pokhran II tests. While DRDO develops advanced weapons, DAE operates the Atomic Energy Commission (AEC) and BARC. It takes care of designing nukes as well. DRDO weaponizes the nuclear devices.[12]

India was in no particular hurry to produce a bomb, even though China had exploded its first way back in 1964, just two years after unleashing an unambiguous defeat on its neighbor south of the Himalayas. Pokhran ! of 1974 was dubbed a PNE but no one really believed it. Pokhran II of 1998 let the cat out of the bag. The tests removed any lingering cobwebs of doubt about India's ability to build a nuke. Unlike India, Pakistan had to steal and beg nuclear tech abroad to catch up with India. Its stealing operations could be used to write a nail-biting thriller!

Pakistani 'Stealth' Operations

Pakistani scientist Abdul Qadeer Khan, who worked in Europe's civilian nuclear centers in the 1970s, "sneaked out"[13] gas-ultracentrifuge (GUC) secrets from Urenco, a German-British-Dutch consortium. He took the blueprints while working at the enrichment plant at Almelo in Holland[14], then returned home. In 1981 the 'A.Q. Khan Research Laboratories' was set up in Kahuta in Pakistan. The GUC, spinning at supersonic speed, separates weapons-grade U-235 from U-238. The Kahuta GUC was based on Khan's illegal smuggling operation. With nonproliferation measures tightening after Pokhran I, Islamabad set up a circuitous network of hi-tech acquisition. It spread its clandestine tentacles in advanced countries. During 1988-93, a German businessman supplied nuclear-relevant machine parts to a cover agency, declaring them to be related to innocuous textile, sugar or ballpoint pen industries.[15] His converters process uranium into uranium-hexafluoride at the Dera Ghazi Khan center, an important requirement for GUC. Islamabad's clandestine network procured tritium, needed for enhancing explosive power, special steel, etc. for processing combustibles. Even though some of the clandestine deals were detected by the late 1980s, Qadeer Khan and Munir Khan, who headed the Pakistani Atomic Energy Commission, continued to maintain contact with European businessmen.[16] The Pakistani embassy in Paris acted as a conduit for nuclear smuggling. Besides, Libya had supplied 100 tonnes of processed uranium ore obtained from Niger in 1977. Firms in Holland, Germany, Switzerland and Belgium helped out with measuring instruments, hardened ball-bearings, special steel pipes, and vacuum pumps. A Belgian enterprise even helped set up a heavy water plant in Multan in 1980.

Islamabad's illicit nuclear contacts were not confined to Europe alone. A treaty with China on peaceful nuclear cooperation, signed in 1986, opened the gate to a lot of help from the fellow Asian rival of India. Beijing provided aid to Pakistan to set up a plutonium factory in Chasma. Even before the cooperation agreement, it had reportedly supplied know-how of a 25 kiloton nuclear bomb in 1983.[17] In 1986, Pakistan may have already tested on Chinese territory.[18] The CIA's proliferation report of 1997 concluded that China had become the most important source of nuclear know-how for Pakistan.[19] From the 1990s, Kahuta started producing 45-100 kg of U-235 annually, which is enough to produce 3-7 bombs. In 1989, US pressure led the Benazir Bhutto government to stop HEU production, which was probably being produced over the past three years. But it was resumed in winter 1990, following Indo-Pakistani border skirmishes. Former Prime Minister Nawaz

Sharif discontinued it again in 1991, while Pakistan continued to produce lightly enriched uranium. Islamabad is suspected to have broken the ban on uranium enrichment in the late 1990s. One estimate puts its weapons-grade uranium stockpile (excluding the material used in its tests) at 335-400 kg till the end of May 1998. At 20 kg per weapon, Islamabad could make 16-20 nukes.[20]

Nuclear Assets in India and Pakistan

Natural uranium is found in at least three places in India, in the west near Udaipur, in the south near Cuddalore, and in the east-central region near Mirzapur.[21] As of 1979, India's 16 nuclear reactors ranged from those fully operational to others under planning. Ten of these were commercial power plants: two at Tarapur, two in Rajasthan, two under construction in Chennai, two planned and located (Narora I and 2) in Uttar Pradesh, and two more at the planning stage. Besides, there were four operational research reactors and two test reactors under construction or planned, including the experimental fast breeder reactor at Kalpakkam.[22] As of mid-1993, 'suspect' were the plutonium separation plant, operating since the 1950s, and the centrifuge in Trombay as well as the Mysore-based centrifuge, operational since the 1980s.[23] BARC also set up a tritium production plant, which extracts the material from the heavy water irradiated in its Candu power reactors. Tritium is used in a thermonuclear device. BARC has also been producing lithium-6 for about a decade, an ingredient also used in a thermonuclear bomb.

Pakistan's Kahuta centrifuge is known since the 1970s for nuclear weapons-related research just as Trombay's facility. Except for the enrichment of fuel for the two light water reactors at Tarapur, all of India's reactor fuel processing is done at Hyderabad's Nuclear Fuel Complex (NFC) consisting of seven plants, which, inter alia, process uranium ore concentrate and import enriched uranium-hexafluoride into finished fuel assemblies.[24] Newer power reactor fuel reprocessing plants were planned for Tarapur and Chennai by the end 1970s. Besides, India had four heavy water plants in various stages of operation and development and, as noted, two more in the planning stage at that time. Of 16 nuclear centers in Pakistan listed by the Carnegie Endowment, which are operational or in the planning stage, about 11 do not have IAEA safeguards.[25] A Brookings Institution study had already concluded two decades ago that India's nuclear program was, "compared with those in other third world countries, remarkably self-sufficient". Estimates differ but all agree that the general technical manpower base and the nuclear component within the country have increased rapidly over the years since independence".[26]

Ballistic Missiles

Concomitant with R&D on the nuclear bomb, both India and Pakistan have been actively engaged in developing ballistic missiles as the bomb's swiftest and virtually unstoppable carrier. India's program encompasses both civil and military space vehicles. Pakistan's focus is on the military aspect. In July 1980, India launched a satellite using its own rocket.[27]Again in July, three years later, India's Integrated Guided Missile Developing Program (IGMDP) saw the light of day. It spawned two missiles of strategic value, the Prithvi and the Agni. The Prithvi SS-150 can carry a 1000-kg warhead to a distance of 150 km. The SS-250 version can carry a 500-kg warhead to a distance of 250 km. Prithvi was first test-flown from the Sriharikota launch site on 25 February 1988. Bharat Dynamics Ltd. in Hyderabad was to produce about 40-50 Prithvis annually. India's 'heavy rocket regiments' consisting of 12-18 transporter-erector-launchers built by Bharat Earth Movers Ltd. were to be equipped with them.[28]

In February 1989, a year after Prithvi's maiden test-flight, Pakistan testfired its Hatf missile with Chinese help. Hatf I and II have a range of 80 km. and 280 km. respectively, with a 500 kg payload capacity.[29] In 1991, Chinese M-11 missiles (300 km. range) started arriving in Pakistan, thereupon officially discontinued under US pressure. Hatf III, a modified M-11 and with the range of 800 km., was first testfired in July 1997.

However, the real long-range missiles (Intermediate Range Ballistic Missiles or IRBM) are India's solid-fuel Agni and Pakistan's North Korea-supplied liquid-fuel Nadong, named Ghauri.[30] Agni I, with 1000 km. range, was first testfired on 22 May 1989. A second (only partly successful) and third test came on 29 May 1992 and mid-February 1994, respectively. Thereupon, the Agni tests were suspended under US pressure till 11 April 1999, when the fourth testfiring of Agni occurred. This time it was Agni II, which covered 2000 km. from the new launch site at C-4 Inner Wheeler Island on Orissa Coast in eleven minutes.[31] Slightly earlier, in February, there were media reports that India was working on a 8000 km. ICBM based on its Agni and PSLV (Polar Satellite Launch Vehicle) experience, especially the re-entry aspect.[32] A.P.J. Abdul Kalam, scientific advisor to the Indian Government, is the key figure behind India's ballistic missiles.

Meanwhile, on 6 April 1998, Pakistan launched its own IRBM, the Ghauri. A few days later, Islamabad announced that it was going to test a longer-range missile, the Ghaznavi.[33] US sources reported further possible tests of Shaheen I and II with 2000 km. range. Ghauri I has a range of 1,500 km. with a 700 kg. payload capacity.[34] Pakistan's reply to the Agni II test in April 1999 was as swift as its response to the Pokhran II tests a year earlier. On 14 April, it responded by testfiring Ghauri II/Hatf V (about 1,500 km-2,000 km range) from Tilla Jogian, 40 km. from the town of Jhelum. It hit its 'target' near the coastal town of Jiwani in Baluchistan in eight minutes. There were also press reports that Pakistan was preparing to test the 800 km. Shaheen from the Ormara naval base in the Arabian Sea.[35]

Way back in 1997, media reports suggested that the Indian government might double outlay for missiles in the Ninth Five-Year Plan (from Rs. 227 crores in the previous plan period to Rs. 504 crores).[36] There were also reports in 1999 that Pakistan was poised to set up a nuclear command chain.[37] These are sure signs of the newly-acquired nuclear power status of the two rival South Asian neighbors. As of this writing, India's attempt to launch a Geosynchronous Satellite Launch Vehicle (GSLV) was aborted seconds before the blast off in March 2001.

Monitoring Nuclear Tests

There are two approaches to monitoring. One is the International Atomic Energy Agency's (IAEA) safeguards system. As of 1993, it monitored about 900 declared nuclear war facilities in over 50 states.[38] The system includes on-site inspections, materials accounting, containment and surveillance. Any facility in a non-nuclear weapon state that is not safeguarded is a suspect nuclear weapons site.

The other approach is a mix of secret methods, together euphemistically called national technical means of verification. We are already familiar with the term, which is mostly the realm of intelligence agencies comprising intercepted communications, monitoring of exports, high-resolution photography, analysis of publicly available information, and pure espionage. The IAEA is even known to have included lock-pickers in its action team operating in Baghdad.[39] The IAEA also had a program, under the Security Council mandate, to analyze the waterways in Iraq for chemical and radioactive effluent that might be emitted by secret nuclear plants. Dual-use equipment may also be carefully screened. The giveaways of clandestine plutonium production are: the reactor's cooling towers, a large work force, the import of specialized equipment or materials, the high heat generated by an operating reactor, the extensive radiation shielding needed for even a modest plutonium separation facility, and the large amounts of nuclear emissions and waste. But both methods may fail to detect preparations for an explosion, as seen in India's case in May 1998. US satellites and other monitoring assets were successfully hoodwinked, unlike in late 1995 when they had discovered the Narasimha Rao Government's preparation for a test. Also, prior to the 1991 Gulf War, Iraq's clandestine nuclear activites were not fully discovered.

India, reputedly, has the most transparent unsafeguarded plutonium production program among the developing nations. As already seen, it was estimated that India possessed about 300 kg. of separated weapons-grade plutonium by the end of 1991.[40]

A centrifuge plant, on the other hand, gives off few unique signatures, and is hence difficult to detect. Nevertheless, the *World Inventory of Plutonium* estimated that Pakistan's Kahuta uranium enrichment plant produced 120-220 kg. of weapons-grade uranium by the end of 1991.[41]

The IAEA's limitations often lie in its methods. Its safeguards have traditionally looked at the facility, not the country. For instance, the IAEA set the amount of HEU needed by a state to make its first bomb— the 'Significant Quantity' or SQ— at 25 kg. If a reactor did not produce that amount, then it was considered safe. But two reactors in the given country could together produce 25 kg SQ! Also, the latter quantity was set too high. A beginner nuclear weapons-state could probably cross the threshold with less.[42] The IAEA also traditionally kept 'yellow cake' (uranium concentrates) outside the scope of its inspections.

Evaluation of the 1998 Tests

Presently, the CTBT monitoring system is being built worldwide. For example, the German Regional Seismic

Network, among others, registered the 1998 tests in South Asia.[43] According to Dr. Anette Schaper of the Frankfurt Peace Research Institute, an earthquake cannot be confused with seismic monitoring of nuclear tests. A nuclear test takes place at a single point on earth while an earthquake means entire plates of soil moving against each other. However, seismic detection has its own problems. It cannot distinguish if several tests take place at the same time and in proximity of each other. Also, not every explosion can be detected. The minimum detectable yield is 0. 8 kiloton (Kt). Tests below that yield may remain undetected.

The following are Dr. Schaper's findings of the total number of tests in India and Pakistan.[44]

Country	Date	No. of registered seismic	No. of declared explosions	Measured yield (kt or TNT)	Declared yield(Kt)
India	18/5/74	1	1	x	15
India	11/5/98	1	3	25-30	43,12,0.3
India	13/5/01	1	2	x	0.5,0.3
Pakistan	28/5/98	1	5	7-8	12,25,3 sub-kt
Pakistan	30/5/01	1	1	1-3	12

Both Schaper and Rudolf Botzian[45] doubt India's claim that it detonated a hydrogen bomb (the 43 Kt. device). In their view, it was probably a "boosted fission" bomb, involving more engineering than physics. Boosted fission is created by introducing gas into fissile materials. Or, according to Botzian, it was probably a misfired Pu-initial trigger based on supercompression.[46]

International seismographs could register only one explosion on each of the four days of the total number of tests in May 1998 by India and Pakistan, though these countries claimed more, as seen in Schaper's chart. This was probably because, as already stated, some of these tests were conducted near-simultaneously and in close proximity to each other. The two Indian tests on 13 May, which were sub-Kt., and were conducted in Pokhran's sand-dunes, went unregistered.[47] However, Schaper's figure of 25-30 Kt. yield for the declared 43 Kt. test on 11 May by India seems to differ significantly from Botzian's view. The latter maintains that the Indian claim of over 40 Kt. yield was compatible with data from US seismic monitors. On the other hand, Western experts doubt Pakistan's claims regarding both the number and yield of the tests.[48] We should pause here to note that there are, of course, other methods of CTBT monitoring besides seismic. These include radionuclide, infrasonic and hydroacoustic sensors.[49] But these do not concern us at present.

According to Botzian, India's second series of tests aimed at the reliability of triggering mechanisms. At least one test on the first day was a normal Pu bomb, i.e., the 'fat man' type dropped on Nagasaki. New Delhi achieved success in making reliable implosion triggering, and in the development of supercompression for low-yield tactical arms and initial triggering of a hydrogen bomb. It further succeeded in miniaturizing nukes for fitting into carriers like missiles and bombers. But, asserts Botzian, India's claim to go for subcritical tests after 1998 and for computer simulation is doubtful, because the ability to produce a hydrogen bomb without further tests would be dubious.[50] One should remember in this connection that the five acknowledged nuclear powers have test exploded over 2000 bombs[51] in the past five decades, before claiming subcritical and computer simulation capability.

The five Pakistani tests, says Botzian, used uranium, i.e., the 'gun barrel' method. This is simpler than the implosion method, but only 2-3 tests were successful. Their yield was only around 10 Kt. US sources reported that no thermonuclear device was exploded. However, Pakistan claimed that in all the tests thermonuclear boosters were used. Botzian and Albright hold this to be possible.[52] A hydrogen bomb can be exploded in a relatively simple way with initial uranium triggering. Islamabad's aim could have been to make reliable gun barrel triggering, on which future thermonuclear weapons could be based.

As already noted, India has been following option A, which is processing U-238 to separate plutonium. But option B, which is uranium-enrichment in centrifuge, is also within its scope of endeavor. Pakistan also has, in principle, the capacity to go for option A. Both states are headed for Pu bomb by means of supercompression.[53]

The Dilemma of Nuclear Strategy

It is one thing to test a nuclear bomb. It is quite another thing to have it ready and to deploy it or to have an adequate strategy for its possible use. It is now time to examine the last two elements, now that the first one, testing, has in principle been done, if not perfected.

To be sure, Indian analysts have spent considerable effort in visualizing the ideal size of the country's nuclear deterrence, which is specific to Pakistan and China. The BJP-led government set up a National Security Council, a Strategic Planning Group and a National Security Advisory Board (NSAB) in 1998. The latter, established in November, produced a report in the following summer, to which we shall turn later. The Cabinet Committee on National Security is a decision-making body; the NSC merely plays an advisory role and is supposed to develop long-term perspectives. In reality, however, it has hardly met. Let us now turn to the size of the deterrent which our analysts think desirable. K. Subrahmanyam, who headed the NSAB, would be satisfied with 60 warheads; Jasjit Singh, Director of Delhi's defense studies institute, 2-3 dozen; ex-General K. Sundarji 150; Brigadier V. K. Nair 132; ex-Rear Admiral Raja Menon, understandably for a naval officer, would take most of the nukes under water to submarines; Bharat Karnad 328; R. R. Subramanian 425; ex-Lt. General Pran Pahwa 182; Gurmeet Kanwal 200; and C. Raja Mohan would be happy if India rejected nuclear disarmament and retained nukes.[54] One may safely assume somewhat similar views prevailing within the government, among those officials who have hitherto been involved in building up India's nuclear arsenal. The government, however, paid no heed to Bhabani Sen Gupta's advice two decades ago, viz., it would be better for India to settle the doctrinal issues before going nuclear, instead of the other way round.[55] Bureaucracies, whether governmental or those of scientists, often fail to act rationally. Usually, what we find instead is that policy is a resultant, an outcome of friction among several views and acts, and the availability, or lack thereof, of information and opportunities.[56] It is not infrequent in policy-making that an act takes place first, its justification is proffered thereafter as sugar-coating. Something to this effect seems to have taken place in India's case.

Most of India's and Pakistan's tests were with low-yield nukes. New Delhi then forwarded the rationale of 'minimum credible deterrence'. This means nuclear deterrence. It implies the introduction in South Asia of the half-a-century old US-Soviet doctrine of mutual assured destruction or MAD. But the low-yield tests point elsewhere. They jibe with tactical or battlefield use (e.g., nuclear shells fired from special guns) rather than the use against the enemy's 'value' (cities, population, communication, industrial and other centers). So bomb and doctrine do not quite match. "Counter-force', rather than 'counter-value', is both good and bad news. A *counter-force strategy* is meant to target the enemy's military formations and bases. A *counter-value strategy*, on the other hand, will target his people. If the low-yield tests are meant to serve counter-force, then the population will be spared (except 'collateral damage', which is military euphemism for incidental deaths and destruction). This is good news. But the bad news is that temptation will rise to reach for the low-yields sooner than in the case of the big, far more destructive, city-busting bombs.

Here comes our *dilemma number one*, the one with low-yield tactical nukes. Admittedly, even these low-yields would create great collateral damage to civilians on both sides if they were used in densely-populated regions like the Kashmir-Punjab sector. The damage would be less disastrous further south along the Rajasthan-Gujarat border. Whatever may be the opaque intentions on both sides regarding low-yields, the probability of their use in battle rises because their explosive power is smaller and especially if one side is losing heavily in a conventional battle. The temptation for the military-ruled Islamabad will easily become a king-sized one, since India's conventional forces are overwhelmingly superior in numbers. Absence of governmental accountability in a military dictatorship, coupled with inferiority in conventional arms, can produce a psychological chemistry in Islamabad that may result in its use of nuclear weapons in a future war with India. And that scenario would be near- fatal to both.

Nuclear bomb and missile tests have become heavily restricted on both sides, thanks to the various arms control regimes pursued hitherto by the US with evangelical zeal. India itself has declared a moratorium on any more hot tests. US-led sanctions are still hurting India's science and technology agencies like the DRDO, the Indian Space Research Organization (ISRO), BARC, etc. Given these constraints, *the second dilemma* is: how reliable are our missiles and nukes (the same question applies to Pakistan)? To put this *second dilemma*, and danger, in perspective, one should note that it took the leaders in the field, the US and the USSR, a quarter of a century to develop accurate missiles and effective nukes, and they conducted any number of tests. In contrast, India has neither the big military budget nor the freedom to test at will. Western experts estimate that running a command, control and communication(C^3) system to efficiently manage the nukes and their platforms (missiles, aircraft, submarines, etc.) would cost $ 40 billion.[57] Pakistan's economy is bankrupt. And India has at this writing (March 2001) congratulated itself for reaching precious foreign exchange reserves of exactly that amount![58]

Dilemma number three is related to number two. Is our second strike capability, i.e., the ability to retaliate, reliable? Our military planners, who *ipso facto* are great fans of worst-case scenarios, must prepare for the enemy's counterforce strategy. China's formidable nuclear force, with its upgraded Tibet-based CSS-5 missiles pointing to India, is even more worrisome than Pakistan's. You can easily visualize a scenario in which the enemy's primary target would be our nuclear forces rather than our population centers. North American Aerospace Defense Command (NORAD) sources point out that China has the capability to develop anti-satellite satellites (ASAT). These would blind our reconnaissance satellites. The Chinese have been conducting space-based imaging of the earth since 1975, with their FSW (Fanhui Shi Weixing) satellites, partly for national security reasons. This means they are keeping an eye on India's security activities. At least our national security planners must assume that. Further, their Shanghai-based Academy of Spaceflight Technology has resurrected programs involving electronic intelligence (ELINT) satellites. China already has an extensive and robust signals intelligence (SIGINT) program in place. SIGINT and ELINT are various methods of keeping track of what your potential enemy is up to. So India has to take this capability of Beijing into account, as well as its potential ability to tamper with our command, control and communications (C^3). China is also reportedly developing new, solid-fuel land and sea-based ballistic missiles with enhanced accuracy and possibly MIRVs.[59] In a well-coordinated first-strike with such capability, it is possible to cripple the opponent's ability to hit back. To 'harden' our second strike for this eventuality would mean a massive investment in concrete underground missile silos, mobile missiles which are difficult to pinpoint (this would include missile-carrying submarines), underground bunkers and command centers along with a survivable C^3. High-tech and money are the key words here. Does India have enough to spare? Is preparation underway for hardening our second strike? If not, then with all our nuclear forces we (that first person plural includes our western neighbor) will be sitting ducks.

Dilemma, and danger, number four is posed by geography. Indian and Pakistani forward air bases can launch strike aircraft to reach the other side in 20 minutes. Missiles would take a fraction of that time. This is even worse than the US-Soviet situation, where each side had at least 30 minutes for missiles to reach their targets. Washington and Moscow each were left with about 3-4 minutes for threat assessment and decision-making.[60] So, once early warning of an impending missile or aircraft strike is received, there are barely minutes left to react. Here, one should consider that Kargil revealed a dismal lack of coordination among India's various security agencies.[61] It is not hard to imagine a similar situation with our incipient nuclear forces. Lack of quick decision on how to react in a nuclear crisis will simply lead straight to disaster. It is probably with this in mind that the government wants to create the post of Chief of Defense Staff (CDS) as recommended by the Arun Singh committee. If created, the post of the CDS will go to the three branches of the armed forces by turn. The CDS, representing a single point military advice, will report to the Defense Minister and will probably be in charge of our nuclear forces. The government has cleared the post, though Cabinet approval is pending.[62]

Our *fifth dilemma* is also closely knit to the previous one. Even assuming that a single point reaction is available, that New Delhi is ready to respond to an impending nuclear attack, what means are available to make sure that the warning is not false? How many minutes, or is it seconds, are left for threat assessment? It is on record that on several occasions in the past, US radars mistook migrating Siberian birds as hostile missiles.[63] As recently as January 1995, the launch of a US scientific rocket from Norway triggered a false attack warning in Russia.[64] Also, one must consider that the incentive to launch in retaliation will be strong, and that pressure will mount to retaliate in crisis, whether the threat has been properly assessed or not. This is largely because of anxiety to use the second strike assets, so long as they are still intact. It is well known that a nuclear blast over missiles just taking off can vaporize them, so the bombs do not even have to hit the targeted silos physically in order to destroy them. Hence the great temptation to hurry. The same mindset works regarding C^3. The incentive to launch remains strong so long as C^3 is still working. A failed command system which functions like Calcutta telephones will allow our missiles and strike aircraft to be caught napping while they are being taken out. Nobody wants another Pearl Harbor. But lack of time, lack of proper threat assessment and the need to hurry increase the risk of starting a nuclear war, which neither side wants. Here lies the catch.

The *sixth dilemma* relates to the need for a specific nuclear strategy or doctrine. US and Soviet print media have published innumerable books and articles on nuclear strategy and doctrine over the past half-a-century. (A Google search for materials only on the North American Aerospace Defense Command or NORAD came up with 79,300 items!). These have now largely been relegated to the dustbin of history. But India and Pakistan retrieved a piece from there, the half-a-century old MAD or 'mutual assured destruction'. It is simplicity itself. If you hit me with nukes, I am going to do the same service to you. New Delhi's officially proclaimed 'minimum credible deterrence' is but Indian MAD. At a formal gathering in Bonn in summer 1998, the present author asked the Indian President the rationale behind India's bomb. His reply was pure history text book. India, he explained, had been invaded many times in the past, and this must never happen again.[65] There was no hint of strategy, doctrine, or parameters within which nukes could be used. This type of imprecise reply is typical of our political leaders. This is also because no precise doctrine has been developed so far. The 'Indian Nuclear Doctrine' of 17 August 1999, drawn up by the National Security Advisory Board, stands out for its vagueness. It talks mostly in the future tense, admits its vagueness, and relegates the task of detailing nuclear policy and strategy to the future.[66]

Madness

Why is MAD, or minimum credible deterrence, insufficient? This is partly because nukes are dangerous toys to play with. Uncertainty or anxiety about the other side's intentions in a given set of circumstances could lead to a nuclear disaster, which neither side wants. Hence, the need for strategy and doctrine that specify nuclear reaction, or refraining from it, under specified circumstances. Especially needed is a clear delineation of those circumstances that will trigger the use of tactical nukes in the battlefield. Or the use of the heavier, city-busting ones. Nuclear adversaries must communicate to each other their strategy and doctrine. This will enable them to foresee and calculate the results of any hostile action that they may contemplate to undertake.

The Indian government has pledged 'no first use' of nukes. Politically, that sounds pretty. But let us consider the following scenarios. Will India, or can India afford to, stick to its pledge *under all circumstances*?

SCENARIO A: Suppose India is losing heavily in a conventional war with either Pakistan or China, or worse still, against the combined forces of both? Can New Delhi resist the temptation of dropping battlefield nukes to even up? Can Islamabad resist it if losing against India, as already pointed out?

SCENARIO B: The half-a-century of US-Soviet Cold War arms race produced a number of startling scenarios and nuclear doctrines.[67] One of them in their inventory was 'launch-on-warning'. This will be highly relevant in the event that Indian radars detect incoming hostile missiles or bombers or both. Bombers can be shot down, missiles not. What will New Delhi do? Wait till they have actually devastated us ('launch-under-attack'), or let fly our second strike forces at once? If New Delhi waits in order to stick to its pledge of 'no first use', India may suffer unacceptable damage including damage to its retaliatory power. Politically and militarily, that move, or rather its lack despite the knowledge of imminent doom, will be extremely unwise. It may draw the sympathy of the world community, but sympathy is a poor substitute for gross damage to life and property. If, on the other hand, India launches on warning, this will be cutting its pledge too thin. There will remain not even seconds to properly assess the threat under launch-on-warning. India's hair-trigger reaction will undergo the risk of an enormously avoidable spasmodic nuclear war, in case the warning on incoming hostile missiles turns out to be false, something which we have noted earlier. Radar and other sensors are, after all, machines. Like all machines, they can go, and have gone, wrong. Several years ago, a young German student piloted a simple aircraft, hoodwinked Soviet radar and landed in the city of Moscow to prove precisely that even a Superpower defense can be beaten by an amateur. More recently, our air force radars failed to pick up in time the aircraft which dropped illicit arms over Purulia (though subsequently the British and Estonian arms peddlers involved were nabbed). Who knows how many Purulias go unreported for the one that was belatedly detected!

SCENARIO C: Reaching deeper into the superpower inventory, we find a still more dangerous doctrine, 'the doctrine of preemption'. This is the situation where India receives information that the enemy is about to launch. India then launches its own strike to preempt the enemy's first strike. While under normal political circumstances this scenario may seem a bit far-fetched, especially given India's 'no first use', under crisis conditions fact has a tendency to overtake fiction. Again, massive time constraints upon assessing a threat and pondering will pre-dominate.

Kargil and the Bomb

Let us take a break at this point and turn to the limited border 'war' in Kargil. How does the latter fit into the nuclear scheme of things?

In mid-1999, a limited border conflict erupted in the 150-km sector of the Line of Control (LOC) in the Kargil area of Kashmir. India accused Pakistan of infiltrating the 18,000-feet high mountainous terrain by regular troops and violating the LOC-related agreements. Pakistan replied that these were Kashmiri mujahideens or freedom-fighters, over whom it had little control. The Indian media created much uproar; the general tenor in our part of the subcontinent was to belittle the Vajpayee government's Lahore initiative earlier in the year and confirm the lurking image of Pakistan as, after all, ever ready to stab us in the back. No doubt the Pakistanis, in a mirror image of the Indian scenario, were fed with similar sentiments by conservative forces (parts of the media, the mullahs, the armed forces, and others) in their country regarding India.

Islamabad has endeavored to internationalize the Kashmir dispute with India over the decades, despite promises to the contrary under the Shimla Agreement of 1972. The Kargil encounter, which is part of the larger Kashmir problem, throws some interesting light on the burgeoning nuclear issue in the subcontinent. Several months of a literally uphill struggle by the Indian army in Kargil threw into sharp relief the distinct limits to nuclear power and deterrence. This quite apart from reports of the deficiencies posed by bureaucratic infighting, lack of adequate logistics like mountain-warfare equipment for the jawans (including even adequate snow-boots, which at one point had to be rushed in from Switzerland at heavy expense), and prevailing centuries-old primitive modes of supply in the mountains of Kashmir, where not modern army trucks but pack animals are still often the most practical.[68] Reports periodically surfaced on how the army's acquisition, in the past and even after Kargil, has sometimes fallen short of GSQR (General Staff Qualifying Requirements) of the military.[69]

It is remarkable that neither Islamabad nor New Delhi rattled their newly demonstrated nuclear might during the armed conflict. In fact, India showed restraint in militarily response to the Pakistani aggression by severely restricting its air operations against the intruders. It took painstaking care to avoid bombarding supply lines and bases, which kept feeding the infiltrators from the other side of the LOC, so as not to escalate the situation into an all-out air war. Similarly, Pakistan also refrained from escalating in the air. Both sides also maintained restraint in on-land operations. New fronts were not opened on land. The Arabian Sea also remained quiet. The human cost of India's restraint in Kargil, however, was considerable. The Indian army suffered heavier casualties in their attempt to dislodge the enemy from their often well-ensconced niches because it lacked all-out air support.

Part of the reason for this mutual restraint lay, of course, in the domestic shakiness of the two governments. The border hostility also quickly attracted international public attention. But the tacit silence over invoking nukes also underlines the fact thrown up by the preceding discussion, viz., mere detonation of a nuclear device, or launching a long-range missile, does not yet prove a nation's ability to marry the two for actual, and accurate, battlefield use. Theory is not always practice. As Goethe observed in *Faust*, "Grey, dear friend, is all theory; green is the eternal tree of life". Secondly, the bypassing of the nuclear question in the Kargil context also showed, once again, *the limits of nuclear deterrence*. While MAD may have worked, nukes failed to deter the violation of the LOC. This is typical of the post-Cold War threat scenario, that of low-intensity conflict, which also is a major item to ponder in the Western capitals, especially Washington. We have studied this in Chapter Eight.

Kargil pointed to the shape of crises that are increasingly likely to confront nations in the 21st century, i.e., low-intensity conflicts, which lie well below the nuclear threshold, and which can often be very confusing in terms of distinguishing between 'regular', 'mercenary' and 'patriotic' forces. LIC creates a low-level crisis and, hence, renders it nuclear-incompatible and nuclear deterrence irrelevant. The US dilemma in Vietnam during the 1960s and 1970s provides an excellent example of such a situation. Besides the regular North Vietnamese forces, the US had to tackle the Viet Cong guerrillas and their sympathizers, who were difficult to identify. With all its nuclear might, the US, as we saw, thanked its lucky stars when it was able to ultimately quit 'the Nam'. The Soviets faced a similar dilemma in 'managing' the innumerable fiercely independent and hostile mujahideen factions during Moscow's misadventure in Afghanistan in the 1980s. It is clear that nuclear weapons can probably deter only more large-scale, overt, conventional cross-border wars, but they fail in the sort of pin-prick-type, salami-slicing, ticklish low-intensity conflicts, especially when the issue at stake is blurred. Kargil has confirmed all over again that conventional weapons and warfare remain highly relevant, even in the nuclear age. We have seen how Moscow learned that lesson during the Cuban missile crisis of 1962. So, even with its nuclear bombs and missiles, India will have to prepare more for future low-intensity conflicts.

Two days after the release of India's draft nuclear doctrine on 17 August 1999, the Indian and Pakistani envoys to the UN Conference of Disarmament in Geneva debated the nuclear issue in South Asia. Reports on the debate typically revealed that politics, not serious force-posturing, was at its kernel. Pakistani envoy Munir Ahmed denounced the Indian document as reflecting the latter's ambition to create "a huge arsenal" of both conventional and nuclear forces, thereby lowering the nuclear threshold. The Indian envoy, Savitri Kunadi, shot back that conventional arms build-up would in fact raise the threshold. She also used this opportunity to point out that the document in question was a draft for public debate and quipped that Pakistan, which at best had a questionable democracy, was possibly not "familiar" with India's "open transparency program".[70]

What is Needed

Unfortunately, the India-Pakistan debate on the role of nuclear weapons for South Asia's security remains largely confined to one-upmanship debates like the one just depicted. It is high time that both India and Pakistan, and China too, make clear their mutual strategies and doctrines, and the related scenarios. The greater the clarity and communication of each side's thinking, the less the uncertainties, even anxieties, regarding its intentions. All the adversaries must think clearly about likely scenarios of crisis and talk to each other about them. That process in turn will help avert groping in the dark, of over-reacting, of taking wrong decisions in the nuclear age when there is simply no second chance. The nuclear bomb is merciless. Once exploded, it does not permit backtracking, undoing the enormous damage already done. The bomb involves not merely huge direct blast but also longer-term harm like radiation and fallout. The effects of these can last decades. People in Hiroshima and Nagasaki are still paying the price in terms of long-term genetic damage.

A great paradox of the nuclear age is that potential adversaries must talk to each other. This is unlike the pre-nuclear age of history, when political conflicts often led to withdrawal of embassies from the adversary's territory. Nuclear adversaries must keep their lines of communication open at all times. It is little wonder that, following their eyeball-to-eyeball confrontation in October 1962 over the Soviet missiles deployed in Cuba, both Washington and

Moscow hastened to set up the hotline, so that the US and Soviet leaders could directly talk to each other in a future crisis. Bureaucratic procedures, elaborate protocol and red-tape were simply out. After all, 30 minutes were all that each had in the face of a missile launch before attaining an unwilling instant nirvana!

In the South Asian context, India, Pakistan and China too can borrow a leaf from the East-West détente in the past, which took place despite the ongoing Cold War. The 35-nation Helsinki Conference on Security and Cooperation in Europe (CSCE) in 1975 paved the way for more such dialogues in Madrid and elsewhere. There also came the Strategic Arms Limitation Talks (SALT) Treaties (1972,1979), the Intermediate-range Nuclear Force (INF) Treaty (1987), the Strategic Arms Reduction Talks (START) Treaties I & II in the 1990s, a whole range of Confidence-Building Measures (CBMs) and so forth. There is no reason why New Delhi, Islamabad and Beijing cannot hold a meaningful strategic dialogue and reach similar arms control agreements. This could be accomplished with UN help if necessary. The USA and Russia, the two most powerful nuclear states, could also lend a hand. China may retain its long-range missiles as hedge against these two powers but must provide credible guarantee that India-specific missiles will be eliminated. India and Pakistan could follow China in providing similar mutual assurances. These would enormously help worldwide arms control measures like the Nonproliferation Treaty (NPT), the Comprehensive Test Ban Treaty (CTBT), the Fissile Material Cutoff Treaty (FMCT) and the Missile Technology Control Regime (MTCR).

Two Track Dialogue

We said that the need is for a trilateral dialogue. The dialogue should be two-fold. In the first track, it will try to work out a *nuclear code of conduct* to be observed by the parties. This would involve spelling out respective nuclear strategy and doctrine, the parameters within which the concerned states can be expected to act or react with nuclear arms, and the way they will do so. A mutually agreed nuclear code of conduct will go a long way in removing avoidable suspicion and uncertainty regarding the other's intention. In the second track, the dialogue should also aim at the freezing, followed by reduction, of the existing nuclear arsenals. The record of US-Soviet/Russian dialogue, the difficulties and accomplishments are there to guide us. This two-track dialogue must widen and go beyond government bureaucrats to include non-governmental experts from the academia, media and industry. Seminars and conferences held regularly between India, Pakistan and China could provide a valuable supplement to, even perhaps a substitute for, purely government-level talks, which usually involve people with a bureaucratic mindset and tired ideas. K. Subrahmanyam, India's ranking defense expert and security advisor to the BJP-led government, complains of the "callous indifference to national security and laziness" of our governments.[71] What is needed is a fresh outlook and new perspectives on nuclear arms control and even nuclear disarmament in South Asia.

Readings

1. David Albright, "A Proliferation Primer," *The Bulletin of the Atomic Scientists*, June 1993.
2. Jaswant Singh, "Against Nuclear Apartheid," *Foreign Affairs*, New York, Sept-Oct. 1998, pp. 41-52.
3. Gurmeet Kanwal, "India's Nuclear Force Structure" *Strategic Analysis*, New Delhi, Vol. XXIV, No. 6, Sept. 2000,pp. 1039-75.
4. Jyotirmoy Banerjee, "Pokhran II—Fallout and Implications," *World Affairs*, New Delhi, Vol. 3, No. 3, July-Sept. 1999,pp. 23-45.

5. Anindyo J. Majumdar (ed.), *Nuclear India into the New Millennium*, Lancer's Books, New Delhi, 2000.

6. Raju G. C. Thomas, Amit Gupta (eds.), *India's Nuclear Strategy*, Vistar, New Delhi, 2000.

7. Stephen Philip Cohen (ed.), *Nuclear Proliferation in South Asia: The Prospects for Arms Control*, Lancer International, New Delhi,1991.

8. Harold A. Feiveson (ed.), *The Nuclear Turning Point: A Blueprint for Deep Cuts and De-Alerting of Nuclear Weapons*, Brookings, Washington, 1999.

9. "National Security Advisory Board. Indian Nuclear Doctrine," *Strategic Digest*, New Delhi, Vol. XXIX, No. 9,Sept. 1999,pp. 1439-1442.

10. K. Subrahmanyam, "Challenges to Indian Security" *USI Journal*, New Delhi, Vol. CXXX, No. 542, Oct-Dec. 2000, pp. 541-562.

11. "Recommendations of the Kargil Review Committee Report," *Strategic Digest*, New Delhi, Vol. XXX, No. 11,Nov. 2000,pp. 1547-1553.

12. Jyotirmoy Banerjee, *Strategic Studies*, Allied, Calcutta, 1998.

13. Raja Menon, *A Nuclear Strategy for India*, Sage, New Delhi, 2000.

14. Kargil Review Committee. K. Subrahmanyam et al., *From Surprise to Reckoning: The Kargil Review Committee Report*, Sage, New Delhi, 2000.

Notes

1. *Sueddeutsche Zeitung*, Munich, 13 May 1999.

2. In India, natural uranium is found in the west (near Udaipur), southeast (near Cuddalore) and north-central part (near Mirzapur). Map, *Informationen zur*

politischen Bildung: Indien, 4. quarter, 1997, Bonn, pp. II-III. India also has thorium reserves.

3. An isotope is one of two or more forms of an element with difference from each other in weight of atoms. For atomic details, George Gamow, *The Birth and Death of the Sun*, Mentor Books, New York, 1956.

4. Cosmic radiation creates neutrons. They are abundant on the earth's crust.

5. Rudolf Botzian, "die indischen und pakistanischen Nukleartests: Bisherige und kuenftige Wege des 'going nuclear'," in *Nach den Nukleartests in Suedasien: Regionale und globale Auswirkungen*, Stiftung Wissenschaft und Politik, Ebenhausen, Sept. 1998, pp. 79-80, *and David Albright*, "A Proliferation Primer," *The Bulletin of the Atomic Scientists*, June 1993, p. 16. Henceforth, Albright, "Primer".

6. Botzian, ibid., p. 82.

7. Albright, "Primer," op. cit., p. 19.

8. Botzian, op. cit., pp. 81-82.

9. Albright, op. cit., p. 17. Albright's later estimate put that figure at about 370 kg. by the end of 1997, generated by the two BARC (Trombay) reactors. This was equivalent of 74 nukes. David Albright, "The Shots Heard Round the World," *The Bulletin of the Atomic Scientists*, July-Aug. 1998, p. 24. Henceforth, Albright, "The Shots". Only 6 kgs. of plutonium, or 25 kg. of uranium, are needed to run a civilian reactor. Botzian, op. cit., p. 80. The two BARC reactors are the Canada-supplied 40-megawatt cirus and the indigenously built 100-megawatt Dhruva. Of the early 1960s vintage cirus' performance deteriorated and was shut down for renovation at the end of the 20th century. The 1974 nuclear test used cirus-generated plutonium.

10. Joseph A. Yaeger, (ed.), *Non-proliferation and U. S. Foreign Policy*, Brookings, Washington, 1980, p. 95. In 1944, Homi Bhabha obtained private support for a group of nuclear scientists from the Tata Institute of Fundamental Research, Mumbai.

11. General Electric Co. supplied to light-water reactors to India on turnkey basis. Botzian, op. cit., p. 80.

12. Albright, "The Shots," op. cit., p. 21. The US stepped up measures to discourage nuclear proliferation by, inter alia, cutting off its nuclear fuel supply in the 1970s, and pressuring France to withdraw its offer of replacing US supply.

13. "Stole" is the word frequently used about Khan by Western commentators. The scientist is also called an "industrial spy". See Hans Leyendecker, "der Kern der Islamischen Bombe ist deutsch," *Sueddeutsche Zeitung*, 26 May 1998; Gerd von Randow, "With a little help...," *Die Zeit*, 4 June 1998; Christian Hundhausen, "Das nukleare Netz," *Rheinische Merkur*, 5 June 1998; Albright, op. cit., note 12, p. 19. The nuclear test program itself was headed by Pakistan Atomic Energy Commision's key official Sumar Mubarak Mand. Albright, ibid., p. 24. A. Q. Khan is credited with being the father of both Pakistani uranium enrichment program and the Ghauri missile.

14. Yaeger, op. cit., p. 102. The advance German centrifuge prototypes were G-1 and G-2. Hundhausen, op. cit.

15. Leyendecker, op. cit.

16. Ibid.

17. Hundhausen, op. cit.

18. Ibid.

19. Ibid.

20. Johannes Preisinger, *Deutschland und die nukleare Nichtverbreitung*, German Society for Foreign Affairs, Bonn, July 1993, p. 12. The uranium estimate for Pakistan in Albright, "The Shots," op. cit., p. 25.

21. Map, see note 2.

22. Yaeger, op. cit., p. 96.

23. Albright, "Primer," op. cit., p. 17.

24. Yaeger, op. cit., p. 96.

25. Hundhausen, op. cit. The centers are at Wah, 2 PINSTECH centers in Rawalpindi, Isa Khel, 3 centers at Chasma, Chagai, Dera Ghazi Khan, Multan, 2 centers at Karachi, Khusab, Sihala, Kahuta and Golra. Tarwanah is listed as housing a rocket factory while Sargodha as storage for deploying Chinese M-11 missiles.

26. Yaeger, op. cit., p. 96.

27. Kathleen C. Bailey, "Can Missile Proliferation be Reversed?" *Orbis*, Philadelphia, 35(1), Winter 1991, p. 5.

28. *SIPRI Yearbook 1993*, Oxford Univ. Press, 1993, p. 249; Jyotirmoy Banerjee, "Indo-Pakistani Missile Race," in Arun K. Banerji(ed.), *Nonproliferation in a Changing World. India's Policy and Options*, Allied, Calcutta, 1997, pp. 148-163.

29. Botzian, op. cit., p. 87.

30. According to another opinion, however, the Ghauri is really a product of Chinese technology. North Korea, says Jha, denies missile sales to Pakistan and has Scuds with far shorter range than Ghauri. Prem Shankar Jha, "What's Behind the India-Pakistani Arms Race," *International Herald Tribune*, 30-31 May 1998.

31. *Asian Age*, Calcutta, 12 April 1999. Agni II is 20-meter long, 16 tonnes, solid fueled, can carry 1,000 kg. payload.

32. *Asian Age*, 8 Feb. 1999. This report was quickly denied by the government already in mid-October 1994 and a year later the launching of remote-sensing satellite by PSLVs demonstrated that India has successfully developed critical technologies.

33. Jha, op. cit.

34. Botzian, op. cit., p. 88.

35. *Asian Age*, 15 April 1999. The estimated range of various missiles as found in published materials sometimes varies widely.

36. *The Telegraph*, Calcutta, 11 May 1997.

37. *Asian Age*, 12 April 1999.

38. Albright, "Primer," op. cit., p. 14. In the mid-1980s, a Scientific Expert Group of the Geneva-based Conference on Disarmament worked out and tested an International Verification System, which had three components. First, a global network of at least 50 fairly uniformly distributed highly sensitive seismological stations, which belong to host countries but abide by internationally agreed rules. Second, an efficient exchange of data worldwide between participating states and specially established International Data Centers. And third, after receiving and processing data, these Centers transmit them back to participating states for national assessment. Ola Dahlman, "Verification of a Nuclear Test Ban," in Hartwig Spitzer (ed.), *Scientific Aspects of the Verification of Arms Control Treaties*, Hamburg, November 13/14, 1986, Part I, Instt. fuer Friedensforschung und Sicherheitspolitik, Hamburg, Vol. 19, June 1987, p. 26.

39. Albright, ibid., p. 15. Intelligence is subdivided into categories like HUMINT (human intelligence), SIGINT (signals), ELINT (electronic), IMINT (imagery), etc.

40. Ibid., p. 17.

41. Ibid., p. 19.

42. David Fischer, "Consequences of the Iraq Case for Nonproliferation Policy," in David Fischer, et al. (eds.), *Nichtverbreitung von Kernwaffen*, German Society for Foreign Affairs, Bonn, 1991, pp. 30-33.

43. Anette Schaper's presentation at an international seminar on the South Asian nuclear tests held at the German Society for Foreign Affairs (DGAP) in Bonn on 7 September 1998. This author was among the participants.

44. Schaper. The declared yield for Pokhran I (1974) test was reportedly 12 Kt., according to Albright, "The Shots," op. cit., p. 21.

45. Schaper and Botzian, op. cit., p. 85. R. Chidambaram, DAE Secretary and Chairman AEC, reportedly put the smallest explosion on 11 May as 0. 2 Kt. Albright, "The Shots," ibid., p. 21.

46. Botzian, ibid. A hydrogen bomb needs an initial atomis trigger explosion. So it is a two-step (two-explosion) bomb. Senior Indian official R. Chidambaram is quoted as having asserted at a press conference on 17 May 1998 that the 43-Kt. explosion was such a two-step fission-fusion (hydrogen) bomb, having denied that it was a boosted fission weapon. He is further reported to have observed on another occasion that India could have produced even a 200-Kt. thermonuclear weapon but had kept the yield deliberately low because of fear of seismic damage to nearby villages, the nearest ones being 5 Km. from ground zero. David Albright seems to treat the Indian claim to

have exploded a hydrogen bomb more sympathetically than Schaper and Botzian. Albright, "The Shots," op. cit., pp. 23-24.

47. Botzian, op. cit., p. 85. The 8th and 58th Engineer Regiments were to be awarded special appreciation certificates for construction and maintenance of the underground shafts for Pokhran II explosions. Asian Age, 12 Jan. 1999. The three 11 May explosions were said to have taken place in individual shafts, though some accounts said that only two shafts were used. Albright, "The Shots," op. cit., p. 21.

48. Botzian, op. cit., p. 85. The controversy over actual yield as measured by the international network of seismic detectors has created some confusion. Albright, ibid., pp. 22, 24-25.

49. Jyotirmoy Banerjee, *Strategic Studies*, Allied, Calcutta, 1998, p. 145.

50. Botzian, op. cit., p. 86.

51. See Jaswant Singh, "Against Nuclear Apartheid," *Foreign Affairs*, New York, Sept-Oct. 1998, p. 41.

52. Botzian, op. cit., p. 86. Albright, "The Shots," op. cit., p. 25.

53. Botzian, op. cit., pp. 86-87.

54. Gurmeet Kanwal, "India's Nuclear Force Structure," *Strategic Analysis*, New Delhi, Vol. XXIV, No. 6, Sept. 2000, p. 1039-75. Also Kanwal, "A Nuclear Force Structure for India," *The Statesman*, Calcutta, 6 Jan. 2001, p. 6. See also opinion survey by Kanti Bajpai, "The Great Indian Nuclear Debate," in Anindyo J. Majumdar (ed.), *Nuclear India into the New Millennium*, Lancer's, New Delhi, 2000, pp. 47-81.

55. Quoted in Kanwal, "India's...", op. cit., p. 1041.

56. A full analysis in superbly presented Graham T. Allison's classic, *Essence of Decision. Explaining the*

Cuban Missile Crisis, Little, Brown & Co., Boston, 1971. See the three models of decision-making expounded there.

57. NATO expert Lothar Ruehl's observation at a seminar on the South Asian tests attended by the present author, which was held by the German Society for Foreign Affairs in Bonn, 7 Sept. 1998.

58. *The Telegraph*, Calcutta, 7 Jan. 2001, p. 12.

59. *Http://www. fas. org/spp/guide/china/military/sigint/geosigint. html;http://www. fas. org/spp/guide/china/military/imint;_http://www. fasorg/spp/guide/china/comm/fh-1. htm*; US General Accounting Office, *National Security Impact of China's Military Modernization in the Pacific Region*, Washington, 1995,p. 25.

60. "Nuclear Arms Control at a Crossroads," in Harold A. Feiveson (ed.), *The Nuclear Turning Point: A Blueprint for Deep Cuts and De-Alerting of Nuclear Weapons*, Brookings, Washington, 1999, p. 4.

61. "Recommendations of the Kargil Review Committee Report," *Strategic Digest*, New Delhi, Vol. XXX, No. 11, Nov. 2000, pp. 1547-1553.

62. *The Statesman*, Calcutta, 5 Jan., p. 1, 27 March 2001.

63. See Jyotirmoy Banerjee, *Strategic Studies*, Allied, Calcutta, 1998, p. 71.

64. "Nuclear Arms Control...," in Feiveson, op. cit., p. 4.

65. President K. R. Narayanan at Hotel Dreesen in Bonn-Bad Godesberg was delivering a lecture under the auspices of the German Society for Foreign Affairs, where the present author was Alexander von Humboldt Fellow.

66. "National Security Advisory Board. Indian Nuclear Doctrine," *Strategic Digest*, New Delhi, Vol. XXIX,

No. 9, Sept. 1999, pp. 1439-1442. For a discussion of inadequate debate on strategy and many of the toher shortcomings pointed out by the present author, see K. Subrahmanyam, "Challenges to Indian Security," *USI Journal*, New Delhi, Vol. CXXX, No. 542, Oct-Dec. 2000, pp. 541-562.

67. Details in Banerjee, *Strategic Studies*, op. cit., pp. 62-80.

68. Three hundred years ago, Bernier described one of Aurangzeb's massive excursions to Kashmir. In a letter dated 6 March 1664 he reported that even sturdy camels and mules had to be supplanted by elephants to carry the heavy baggage of the Emperor's entourage further uphill since the latter, even though unwieldy, were more sure-footed. Francois Bernier, *Travels in the Moghul Empire: A. D. 1656-1668*, S. Chand & Co., New Delhi, 1972, pp. 388-392. For the present Indian army's deficiencies, Raj Chengappa, Rohit Saran, "Short on Firepower," *India Today*, New Delhi, 26 July 1999, pp. 50-51. The daily cost of maintaining 8,000-10,000 troops on the affected 150 km. LOC would amount to Rs. 10-15 crores for India. *Asian Age*, Calcutta, 20 July, 1999, p. 1.

69. *Asian Age*, 4 Nov. 1999, pp. 1-2; other Indian shortfalls, inter alia, in Raj Chengappa, "Holding the Heights," *India Today*, 16 August 1999, pp. 46-54.

70. *Asian Age*, 20 Aug. 1999, pp. 1-2.

71. Subrahmanyam, "Challenges to...," op. cit., p. 543.

10

The Clinton Visit and Indo-US Relations in the New Millennium

President William Jefferson Clinton's visit to South Asia during 19-26 March 2000 has thrown into sharp relief the changed contours of America's policy towards the subcontinent. Accompanied by a thousand-member team, including "a very large representation" of Congress,[1] and even though closely guarded by security sleuths of both nations, Clinton created an enthusiastic media-hype by exuding warmth and sincerity, the like of which has not been seen in recent memory. Coming twenty-two years after the last US President, Jimmy Carter, had touched down on Indian soil, the Indian response to Clinton's appearance was as if a reincarnated John F. Kennedy had come for the first time. The Indian gerontocracy, the portly parliamentarians, for instance, swooned over him like teenagers over an idol and literally made a mad dash to shake his hand in the Central Hall of the Parliament. Now that the dust has settled, it is time to draw a balance-sheet of Indo-US relations, how Washington perceives the India of the new millennium, what that perception implies for South Asia and beyond, what has been accomplished and what still remains to be done.

Clinton's very itinerary, which set off much speculation long before his arrival, reflected a change in the direction of US foreign policy. Coming at a time when the Indo-Pakistani clash in the formidable mountains of Kashmir was still fresh in memory, New Delhi noted with anticipatory glee that the President's travel itinerary, which definitely focused on India with a 5-day visit, and graced Bangladesh with one, kept Islamabad dangling in mid-air. Smarting from the Kargil crisis, which had caught it slumbering, New Delhi turned officious and tried to dissuade the President from visiting Islamabad at all. The Ministry of External Affairs (MEA), or rather the Prime Minister's Office behind it, apparently forgot in its zeal to tender unsolicited advice that the US President has his own advisers and a mind of his own. While Clinton brushed aside New Delhi's objections, his call on Pakistan's military dictator General Pervez Musharraf turned out to be nothing more than a 5-hour stopover. The Clinton Administration also repeatedly made clear that the visit to Islamabad was not to be construed as endorsement of the dictatorial regime but rather as a way of keeping open a channel of communication. In the perennial Indo-Pakistani rivalry, Pakistan's old ally decidedly tilted more eastward; even Bangladesh merited a day of 'darshan'[2] by the most powerful executive on earth, but not Pakistan.

Indo-US relations at 2000 AD seemed truly new and multifaceted. Three issues stood out as the salient ones: nonproliferation, Kashmir and the related cross-border terrorism, and business.

Non proliferation

A long-standing irritant to Indo-US relations, nonproliferation branches out in two directions, viz. The Comprehensive Test Ban Treaty (CTBT) and the Missile Technology Control Regime (MTCR). There is also the Fissile Material Cutoff Treaty (FMCT). Way back in December 1993, India had cosponsored CTBT but declined to sign the draft when it was opened for signature three years later. Like the larger Nuclear Nonproliferation Treaty (NPT)[3], New Delhi considered the CTBT text as it emerged as discriminatory to nuclear have-nots. External Affairs Minister, Jaswant Singh, articulated India's stand in a *Foreign Affairs* article following the Pokhran 2 nuclear tests in May 1998. According to him, the nuclear haves conducted over 2,000 tests in the past decades but were crying a halt to tests by non-nuclear weapons states, even while they reserved for themselves the right to continue testing in subcritical mode.[4] Washington became highly agitated at Pokhran 2 and Pakistan's Chagai Hills tests. Part of its agitation sprang from the failure of its intelligence to forecast them, unlike three years earlier when India's preparation for test was detected and successfully discouraged, as we already noted. It took eight rounds of talks between Singh and US arms control expert Strobe Talbott for Washington to get over its frustration. The latter subsequently toned down its demand for an "immediate" and "unconditional" signing of CTBT by India,[5] words that sounded like America's demand of "unconditional" surrender by Hitler Germany in the Second World War! Things looked up in New Delhi-Washington relations when Premier A.B. Vajpayee indicated, in December 1999, that India was willing to sign.[6] The Premier added a qualifier, though. The signing needed a "positive atmosphere," meaning that the US should remove its post-Pokhran sanctions imposed on India, particularly on dual-use technology. Indeed, the sanctions imposed under the Enhanced Proliferation Control Initiative were designed to plug loopholes left open in those imposed seven years earlier. Although direct US economic aid to India amounted to a paltry $140 million annually, Washington could still use its influence with international financial institutions like the World Bank and the IMF to arm-twist India.

During his visit to India, Clinton emphasized the need to halt nuclear proliferation but did this rather mellifluously. After all, India had announced that it would forego any more explosive tests while reserving the right to continue computer simulation. New Delhi had also announced a 'no-first-use' policy. Not that America's CTBT record was any better; the Republican-held Senate poured cold water over Clinton's arms control zeal, so much so that the Democratic Administration announced in March 1999 that it would not re-introduce CTBT to the Senate for ratification.[7] In fact, the government in New Delhi can sign yet withhold ratification, or even ratify (if it can master enough votes in Parliament) but block deposition of the instrument. Since the effectiveness of the treaty can be held up at the second and third stages, there is no reason why New Delhi cannot sign.[8]

Besides signaling willingness to hold talks on nonproliferation, New Delhi undertook other steps conciliatory to Washington. A little noticed move was its refusal to sign a Russia-drafted joint statement at the end of former Foreign Minister Yevgeny Primakov's India-visit in December 1999. The draft contained a strong condemnation of US air strikes against Iraq. While it also deplored the US action, New Delhi exercised restraint when it came to condemning the USA. It also let Primakov's flamboyant idea of an Indo-Russian-Chinese geopolitical triangle die a natural death.[9] After all, the all-important Indo-American Memorandum of Understanding of 1984, which the Reagan Administration instituted to give India access to US high tech, was at stake.

The Clinton visit showed that differences on the proliferation question continued to persist. While the Indian leaders reiterated that they were not about to give up 'minimum credible deterrence', Clinton in public statements deftly appealed to India's conscience to decide upon its future nuclear weapons policy". Only India can know if it was more safe after the tests," he observed. Clinton also drew attention to the impact India's tests had on other nations, who were thereby encouraged to keep their options open, but "it is not my place to tell you what to do".[10] Despite India's adamant public stand on CTBT, notwithstanding Vajpayee's softening mentioned before, national security adviser Brajesh Mishra reportedly told foreign newsmen that the government was considering introducing the CTBT issue in the Parliament.[11] US fears that the two South Asian nuclear neighbors may come to exchange dangerous blows are not unfounded. While India, confident of its conventional military superiority has abjured a nuclear first strike, Pakistan has declined to follow suit so as to retain the nuclear option to offset India's edge. This contains the seeds of real danger, more so since geographic proximity will result in only a few minutes time for each side to react to the other's missile attack. Given the incipient command and control system of both, this could spell sure disaster.[12]

We saw in the previous chapter that India's Integrated Guided Missile Development Program (IGMDP), which began in July 1983, has spawned strategic missiles like the short-range Prithvi (150-250 km in range) and the intermediate-range Agni (2,500 km and above). The IGMDP is propelled by the Indian threat perception of Pakistan's Hatf, Ghauri and Ghaznavi missiles, which are reincarnations of China's nuclear-capable M-11 and North Korea's Nadong missiles, as well as that of China's new CSS-5. China is replacing the older CSS-2s. The new CSS-5s are very conveniently located in Tibet just across India's northern border.[13] Unlike Pakistan's, India's nuclear and ballistic missile R&D has largely been the result of indigenous effort. An Indo-Soviet agreement had stipulated the transfer of cryogenic (low temperature) rocket technology to India, which Soviet-successor Russia pledged to carry out. Even though it was meant for India's civilian space agency, the Indian Space research Organization (ISRO), and not the military Defense Research and Development Organization (DRDO), the US messianic zeal against proliferation was aroused. In May 1992, the former Bush Administration clamped down a ban on US exports to both ISRO and its Russian counterpart, GLAVKOSMOS.[14] Washington became anxious that India would use the technology to develop an intercontinental ballistic missile based on its successful tests of the Polar Satellite Launch Vehicle (PSLV), a civilian rocket. The cryogenic transfer also attracted the Missile Technology Control Regime (MTCR), which continues to confine India's rocket-related hi-tech imports within narrow limits. More recently, the Federation of American Scientists timed the release of satellite photos of Pakistani buildup of M-11s in Sargodha on the eve of Clinton's visit to underscore the threat of missile proliferation in South Asia.[15] The timing of the release of a CIA statement on 23 March that it long knew of Chinese delivery of the M-11s to Pakistan but had kept quiet was also intriguing.[16]

Notwithstanding the ongoing irritations over US sanctions related to CTBT and MTCR that have succeeded in slowing down, but not halting, India's strategic R&D,[17] it is a measure of the basic strength of Indo-US relations that Clinton did partially lift the sanctions in November 1998 and again following his visit in March 2000. This partial relaxation shows that the influence of proliferation crusaders like the boss of the former US Arms Control and Disarmament Agency (now merged with the State Department) John D. Hollum, or Gary Milhollin, whose dream is to rid India of all things nuclear, also has limits. Prior to the visit, sanctions affected about 200 Indian enterprises, both government and private, which were named on the Entities List. That US Commerce Department hit-list must have prominently figured in the talks in New Delhi. Since significantly reducing the dreaded blacklist is hooked to progress in nonproliferation, the only hope for India is that its tantalizing economic opening up might act as a moderating influence.

Kashmir and Cross-Border Terrorism

The West has periodically speculated about the potential danger in and over Kashmir.[18] Pakistan, notwithstanding the 'bilaterality' stipulated in the Shimla Agreement of 1972, has consistently played up the issue, especially in international fora. That irritates India, which downplays it. The Pakistani High Commissioner in New Delhi summed up Islamabad's own frustration to CNN. According to him, New Delhi tells the international community that Kashmir is a purely bilateral issue and no third party mediation is needed. But when talking to Islamabad, it asserts that Kashmir is its domestic problem, so Pakistan has no locus standi there!

Clinton's visit was immediately preceded by several speculations on Kashmir by US think tanks, which were carefully leaked to the media and hardly calculated to soothe India's nerves.[19] During the visit itself, terrorists stepped up violence in the valley, including mass murder of civilian Sikhs and raids on a base of the Indian Border Security Force.[20] Clinton told his Indian interlocutors to reopen dialogue with rival Pakistan in the spirit of Lahore.[21] But he had an additional suggestion for General Musharraf, the ruler of Pakistan: Islamabad needed to respect the Line of Control (LOC) in Kashmir.[22] To India's enormous relief and Pakistan's dismay, he repeatedly stated in New Delhi and the Pakistani capital that he was not about to mediate on Kashmir". I have certainly not come to South Asia to mediate," said he.[23]

If Kargil had once again drawn international attention to Kashmir, which was exactly what Pakistan wanted, it also became an important turning point in the US attitude towards India, which had turned hostile over Pokhran in 1998. Pakistani sophistry, distinguishing between mercenaries and freedom-fighter mujahideens infiltrating on the Indian side of the LOC, did not cut ice with Washington. When the outgoing Pakistani Ambassador in Washington, Riaz Khokar, objected to a State Department statement that the Kashmiri mujahideens were "infiltrators from Pakistan," the US government rejected it saying it was confident of its information. At the height of the Kargil crisis in June 1999, Clinton tilted in Prime Minister Vajpayee's favor when the latter resorted to the Indian version of Thomas C. Schelling's 'rocking-the-boat' strategy. He sent a message to Clinton, who was in Geneva at the time, that continued Pakistani armed infiltration across the LOC would force India to drop restraint and strike the supply lines on the other side, thereby escalating the conflict. Clinton thereupon phoned Pakistani ex-Premier Nawaz Sharif and asked for an immediate pullout.[24] He also used his influence with the G-8 nations, who were conferring in Cologne, to condemn the armed infiltration of the LOC. Clinton followed this up by dispatching US Central Command chief General Zinni to Islamabad to talk to Sharif and his military commanders. At stake for Pakistan was an IMF loan, due shortly in July.[25] Washington also got in touch with Beijing and urged restraint on Kargil. Beijing, of course, did not need much urging; encouraging Kashmir's separatism would mean encouraging the same in its own backyard of Tibet and Taiwan. There was also the additional danger of Islamic fundamentalism infecting China's Muslim-majority province of Xinjiang. On 4 July, while America celebrated Independence Day, Clinton grilled Sharif for three hours in Blair House in Washington. The joint statement, which was hammered out agreed that "concrete steps will be taken for the restoration of the LOC".[26] Since the intrusions came from Pakistani territory, both the G-8 statement as well as this one put the onus squarely on Islamabad. Sharif's capitulation to US pressure caused outrage among the right-wingers in his country and may have contributed to his downfall in October 1999. Three days after the Clinton-Sharif talks, The *Washington Times* noted that Pakistan had "tumbled" from its status as a US favorite. The State Department told the daily that Islamabad had played a "provocative role" in Kargil.[27]

On terrorism across the border, the US does not need much hearing from India. America itself is target number one for the elusive millionaire terrorist Osama bin Laden, currently ailing under Taliban protection in Afghanistan. The US has put the latter's name on the FBI's 'most wanted' list. Clinton, in fact, encouraged Musharraf to use his ties with Kabul to tone down cross-border terrorism in Kashmir. Musharraf agreed but pleaded helplessness in achieving results.[28] Pakistan narrowly escaped from being put on the State Department's list of terrorist-sponsor states, even though the Department's global report on terrorism determined Pakistani connivance with infiltrators in Kashmir.

Clinton reiterated the Pakistani connection in New Delhi.[29] Reportedly, the Pentagon and the CIA urged the State Department not to name Pakistan for fear of creating massive resentment in that country and pushing it further into the arms of the radicals.[30] In all probability, Clinton demanded a ban on Harkat-ul-Mujahideen in Islamabad, which was branded as a terrorist organization by his Administration.[31] The Singh-Talbott talks in London in 1999 created a joint counter-terrorism working group, which met in Washington on 8 February in 2000. The US team, headed by Michael Sheehan, the State Department's coordinator for counter-terrorism, and the Indian counterpart headed by Alok Prasad, Joint Secretary in the Ministry of External Affairs, agreed that legal coordination to fight terrorism and bring the hijackers of the Indian Airlines flight IC 814 to justice would be accomplished in April.[32] The US would also lend a sympathetic ear to an upcoming India-sponsored anti-terrorism convention in the UN.

Clinton has clearly laid his cards on the table over Kashmir: no US mediation, unless both sides wanted it, and the need to resume Indo-Pakistani dialogue. The Indian side noticed that for the first time the US delegation did not refer to Kashmir as "disputed territory" and also dropped the idea of involving "the wishes and aspirations" of Kashmiris in any settlement.[33] Immediately after Clinton's departure from Islamabad, Musharraf told a press conference that he was ready to hold talks, "anytime, anywhere, at any level".[34] But when asked if he would pick up the hotline to New Delhi, the military dictator stalled and replied that his Foreign Minster had to make "necessary arrangements" first. The same day, on 26 March, the then India's Minister of State for External Affairs Ajit K. Panja lashed out: "Dialogue with whom?" India, he fumed, was not about to open a dialogue with someone with "blood on his hands". The infiltrations must stop before India agreed to any dialogue.[35] Musharraf, incidentally, was disarming on the question of infiltration in his press conference". Have you seen the mountains?" he asked newsmen pestering him with thorny questions. If India could not stop infiltration with its hundreds of thousands of troops, how could Pakistan with its 60,000 soldiers, he mused.

The issue of Kashmir remained where it was, regularly punctuated with the din of gun- and grenade fire.[36] As Indian Kashmir's parliamentarian Abdullah observed, the average Kashmiri police was still equipped with outdated arms, while the terrorists possessed sophisticated AK-47 automatic rifles and other weapons.[37] So, despite all security measures, the valley remained wide open to terrorist violence. Clinton was blunt on Pakistan's role in this. While in India, he openly stated that, like India, he was concerned at "the way Pakistan is moving," and that he had "understanding" for India's difficulties as a democracy to coexist with "a nondemocratic neighbor".[38] To ABC TV's Peter Jennings, he remarked that "I believe there are elements within the Pakistani government that have supported those who engage in violence in Kashmir".[39]

Pakistan cut a sorry figure in the wake of the visit. The US President's five days in India contrasted sharply with five hours in Pakistan as did the joint Indo-US Vision Statement with Clinton's reading of tutorial to Musharraf's government.[40] His public contention that Pakistan was involved in the LOC infiltrations must have shaken Musharraf, whose reactions during and after Clinton's visit to South Asia were astounding in their naivete. The repeated US disclaimers notwithstanding,[41] Musharraf rejoiced at Clinton's last-minute announcement granting him a few hours of 'darshan' as recognition of his government's legitimacy.[42] When Clinton took away even that illusion, Musharraf's response was equally pathetic. "My legitimacy comes from the people of Pakistan," he declared pompously. "I don't need legitimacy from anyone (else)," said the military dictator.[43] Clinton wanted a time-table for Pakistan's return to democracy, which Musharraf, despite hurried last-minute steps taken to hold local body elections, failed to deliver. The US President also reminded the latter that Islamabad's nuclear program would weigh heavily on its already sick economy.[44] Clinton publicly warned that if it did not meet "the challenges" of restoring democracy and the sanctity of the LOC, then "Pakistan will be even more isolated".[45] The bottom line of his message to Islamabad was that the jihad mindset was poles apart from civilized intercourse among nations. And to rub salt in the would, New Delhi hurried with a formal statement expressing satisfaction with Clinton's tough speech in the Pakistani capital.[46]

Business

A major reason for the vindication of the Indian position on Pakistan and Kashmir was the promise of the large Indian market, which continued to liberalize over the past years. Americans love money. So do Indians, even if there were official pretensions to the contrary till now. Now that India is moving, and pretty fast at that, from the saffron (symbol of renunciation) segment of its national flag to the green segment (the sign of earthly prosperity; also the US dollar is called 'greenback' because of its color!), it is clear that the two nations are rediscovering each other like never before.

India Inc. is the title of an article reprinted from *The Washingtonian* in the *Span* magazine published by New Delhi's American Embassy in early 2000.[47] It asserts that the days when India was regarded as a land of snakecharmers and sitar players were over. Instead, the current image of the country is that of a vibrant economy that is poised to become the fourth largest in the world, or so are reportedly the estimates of the IMF and the World Bank.[48] Clinton himself complimented India as being one of the ten fastest growing economies in the world with almost a third of the world's information technology (IT) experts.[49] Indeed, the oft-heard assertion that the Indians have conquered California's Silicon Valley, where IT industries are concentrated, is not wholly a figment of the imagination. India has the second largest pool of English-speaking scientific manpower, right after the USA. It also has a large middle class, which translates into significant purchasing power. India's software is as much in demand at home as it is abroad, particularly in the USA and in Europe. The Europeans, notably the Germans, are bending backwards to get IT experts from wherever they can, including India, and have started issuing a US-style 'green card' to them so as to short-circuit their own bureaucratic procedures. In fact, the opposition in Berlin raised a battle cry against this liberal policy of the government that read: "Kinder statt Inder!" (i.e., more German children should be given computer education than importing Indians to fill IT jobs). The slogan is actually a compliment to the India of the 21st century. From a mere $300 million in 1985, India's software export has leapfrogged to $4 billion in eight years.[50]

The Clinton visit resulted in $4-5 billion economic and technical cooperation agreements between the two democracies. A major catalyst for the successful conclusion of these agreements has been the non-resident Indians (NRIs) from the USA. In sharp contrast to India's software exports, there stands the $4 billion worth of heroin export from Pakistan's soil, which is yet another source of irritation for its chief destination, the USA. The US Exim Bank has granted a $1 billion loan, denominated in rupees, to India, so as to facilitate export of US goods and services to that country.[51] New Delhi has cut subsidies to natural gas and kerosene in keeping with world trends, lifted curbs on a wide range of import items in conformity with WTO requirements, and has promised to facilitate entry of foreign firms in India's insurance market.

The USA remains India's largest trade partner; 20% of India's exports go there, including 60% of its software exports. The scope for expansion of bilateral trade, be it in electronics, IT or energy, is enormous. The US, like other developed nations, has noted that India has been cutting trade barriers since 1996, is poised to remove quantitative bans on imports by 2003 and change its intellectual property laws by 2005. Its economy remained steady while crisis shook up the so-called tiger economies of neighboring Southeast Asia in 1998. India's average GDP growth rate over the past decade has been an impressive 6.7%. In the coming decades this is expected to go up to 7.8%.[52] Indeed, Clinton's dash on 24 March to Hyderabad, dubbed Cyberabad for its advanced electronics, was a gung-ho homage to modern India's leadership in the cutting edge IT sector. A beaming US President even flaunted his driver's license obtained there from the Internet and predicted India's future as an IT superpower. Among various Indo-US projects that the visit generated is IT major Motorola's upcoming hi-tech school in Hyderabad.[53] The US also sees a lucrative market in India for the US servicing industry.[54]

However, despite all the bonhomie, some of the major sanctions remain in place, especially on dual-use technology, even though some others, for instance those affecting environmental protection, are to be lifted.[55] Also unsolved remained the question of increasing the quota of H-1 visas for technically skilled Indians from 115,000 to 195,000.

In contrast to the overall upbeat Indian scene, its western neighbor has managed to work itself into a corner, both politically and economically. No amount of jihad against 'Hindu' India can wipe out overnight Pakistan's $38 billion external debt (1997-98).[56] With less than 1% of its 140 million paying taxes— and big landowners who control most of the country's wealth pay none at all— Islamabad has to significantly depend on the USA and the international community to access funds to bail itself out.[57] Kargil-type confrontations with India as well as its ambitious nuclear and missile programs cannot be supported by its sputtering economy.

The Bottom Line

The former US President ushered in a new era in relations with the subcontinent with the beginning of the new millennium. The US South Asian policy has undergone a sea change. This is the first time in their 50-year history that Washington and New Delhi have come so close together on a number of fronts that they agreed to call themselves 'strategic partners'. At the same time, Islamabad has receded to the background. As Senator Larry Pressler put it in New Delhi in his inimitable way, " We gotta decide which side we're on".[58] The Clinton visit left India as the clear 'winner'. Clinton publicly chided Pakistan for violence in Kashmir, criticized its volte face from democracy, and delivered a reminder that it could not afford a nuclear arms race.

But Musharraf faces an unenviable dilemma. If he mends his ways to please the US, he will incur the wrath of the fundamentalists and rightwing elements within his army. If he does not, then he will keep steering his country to even greater international isolation. Islamabad's strategic importance as a Cold War partner of Washington has disappeared with the end of the Cold War, the Soviet pullout from Afghanistan, and the collapse of the USSR itself. The danger, not least for India, is that smarting from the US jilting Islamabad may increasingly turn even more to China, India's other strategic rival, Afghanistan and Iran. Indeed, Foreign Minister Jaswant Singh went on record saying he was worried over the turn of events in Pakistan.[59]

On the other hand, US foreign policy is geared to creating "anchors of regional stability and growth," explained former State Secretary Madeleine Albright,[60] and India stands out as the anchor for South Asia. On another occasion, she remarked, "Our goal is a qualitatively different and better relationship with India,"[61] a line of thinking reiterating Clinton's. Clinton flattered New Delhi by expressing his expectation that India was cut out to lead the subcontinent away from nuclear proliferation to improvement in the quality of life. In the South Asian context, this means that education, disease control, environmental protection and clean drinking water should get top priority.[62] He assured Delhi that the US would stand by its side in these matters. It is evident that if, through its foolhardiness, Pakistan draws India into a warlike confrontation over Kashmir, that will unsettle the Indian factor of stability. This in turn will also affect US geopolitical and business interests in the region. It is possible that in addition to viewing India as a stability factor, the US wants India to balance China, which politically is not on the best of terms with Washington at present. We have seen their differences on issues like Taiwan, NMD/TMD, human rights, etc. in previous chapters. The Indo-US Vision Statement[63] assumes importance in this context. It implies that Indo-US political and security cooperation, which will include institutionalized summits and annual Foreign Minister-level talks, will not be confined to South Asia but will have ramifications for regions beyond.

Readings

1. Jaswant Singh, op. cit. Chapter 9.
2. Jairam Ramesh, "Yankee Go Home, But Take Me With You," *Economic and Political Weekly*, Mumbai, Vol. XXXIV, No. 50, pp. 3534-5.
3. Janaji Bhadur Kremmer, "Bill, Buntings, Beginnings," *Outlook*, New Delhi, April 2000.
4. Jyotirmoy Banerjee, "Indo-Russian Rocket Dilemma," *Asia-Pacific Defense Review*, Kuala Lampur, Vol. 5/ 3,Oct. 1993, pp. 29-33.
5. "On High Ground," *India Today*, New Delhi, 28 June 1999, p. 36; "Face-Saving Retreat," 19 July 1999, p. 22; 30 Mar 2000, p. 46.
6. *South Asia Watch*, Jawaharlal Nehru University, New Delhi, Nos. 5-7, May-July 1999.

7. Courtney Rubin, "India Inc.," *The Washingtonian*, reprinted in *Span*, US Embassy, New Delhi, Jan-Feb. 2000,pp. 10-16.

8. Madeleine K. Albright, "The Testing of American Foreign Policy," *Foreign Affairs*, Nov-Dec 1999, op. cit.

Notes

1. Live coverage of Clinton's speech in India's Parliament, Doordarshan (DD) TV, 22 Mar. 2000, 11 a. m.

2. Hindi for rare appearance of God.

3. Article VI of NPT provides for CTBT.

4. Jaswant Singh, "Against Nuclear Apartheid," *Foreign Affairs*, New York, Sept-Oct. 1998, p. 41.

5. *The Telegraph*, Calcutta, 13 Dec. 1998, p. 6.

6. Ibid. China, no doubt encouraged by the USA, played a highly interesting role. It worked hard to change Article XIV of NPT within days of Pokhran 2. The metamorphosed article required all 44 states with nuclear plants, regardless whether these were civilian or military, to sign CTBT and activate it. Singh, op. cit., p. 43.

7. CNN quoting Albright, 14 Mar. 2000, 9 a. m.

8. Detailed analysis in Jairam Ramesh, "Yankee Go Home, But Take Me With You," *Economic & Political Weekly*, Mumbai, Vol. XXXIV, No. 50, pp. 3534-5.

9. *The Telegraph*, 20 Dec. 1998, p. 1.

10. DD, op. cit.

11. Janaki Bahadur Kremmer, "Bill, Buntings, Beginnings," *Outlook*, New Delhi, 3 April 2000, p. 27.

12. A similar scenario in Christopher Chant, Ian Hogg, *The Nuclear War File*, Ebury Press, London, 1983, pp. 64-65.

13. *The Statesman*, Calcutta, 11 July 1997, p. 8.
14. See Jyotirmoy Banerjee, "Indo-Russian Rocket Dilemma," *Asia-Pacific Defence Review*, Kuala Lumpur, Vol. 5/93, Oct. 1993, pp. 29-33.
15. Star World TV, 16 March 2000, 4.45 p. m.
16. Star News TV, 23 Mar. 2000, 10 p. m.
17. An example of sanctions: The US govt. refuses to permit supply of computers to India with capacity exceeding 2,000 MTOPS (million theoretical operations per second) for fear of their military use. While this has hurt, India has developed an indigenous Param computer (eight gigaflops and more capacity) to fill the need and even manage to sell one to Russia. *Asian Age*, Calcutta, 23 Feb. 1998, p. 4.
18. Declassified US Embassy, New Delhi message to State Dept. dated 1 Nov. 1965 on the Kashmir problem, including its Kargil sector, sounds very contemporary. Document No. 00783, copy in Univ. of California-Berkeley, Govt. Docs. Library; Chant & Hogg, op. cit.
19. US- based Kashmir Study Groups paper, "Kashmir—A Way Forward" was circulated in the Kashmir valley calling for a sovereign state. The Brookings Institution and the Council for Foreign Relations also came up with a scenario of a possible Indo-Pakistani war in Kashmir. *Asian Age*, 25 Feb. 2000, p. 1.
20. Star News, 25 Mar. 2000, 1.30 p.m.
21. Reference is to Vajpayee's bus ride to Lahore in early 1999 and the ensuing Indo-Pakistani declaration.
22. Clinton's different 'body language' in India and Pakistan has been much commented upon in the Indian media: "warm" and "easygoing" in India, "tense" and "stern" in Pakistan. Star News, 25 Mar. 2000, p. 9; *Outlook*, op. cit., p. 29.

23. Clinton's speech in Parliament, Doordarshan, op. cit.

24. "On High Ground," *India Today*, New Delhi, 28 June 1999, p. 36.

25. *India Today*, 30 March 2000, p. 46.

26. *South Asia Watch*, South Asian Center for Strategic Studies, Jawaharlal Nehru University, New Delhi, Nos. 5-7, May-July 1999, p. 53. Also, "Face-Saving Retreat," *India Today*, 19 July 1999, p. 22.

27. South Asia Watch, op. cit.

28. Musharraf's news conference, Pakistan TV, 25 March 2000, 8. 45 p. m.

29. "I believe that there are elements within the Pakistani government that have supported those who engage in violence in Kashmir," Clinton's speech in Parliament, *Asian Age*, 23 March 2000, p. 1.

30. *South Asia Watch*, op. cit., p. 7.

31. *India Today*, 20 March 2000, p. 46.

32. *Asian Age*, 24 March 2000, p. 1.

33. "Charming of India," *India Today*, 3 April 2000, p. 38.

34. Musharraf's press conference, op. cit.

35. Panja in Star News, 27 March 2000, 10.15 p. m.

36. Star News reported on 20 March 2000 at 11. 15 a. m. that "Infiltration has increased significantly...". BBC TV report on suicide squads operating in Kashmir, 22 March 2000, 9.45 p. m.

37. Star News, 27 March 2000, 10 p.m.

38. Clinton's speech on 22 March 2000, Star News, 11 a. m.

39. Kremmer, op. cit., p. 26.

40. "The answer to flawed democracy is not to end democracy but to improve it," advised Clinton. Star News, 25 March 2000, 9 p. m.
41. Assistant Secretary of State Karl Inderfurth's interview in Star News, 8 March 2000, 12 noon; State Secretary Madeleine Albright's speech to Asiatic Society (USA) on 14 March 2000 quoted in Star News, 11. 15 a. m. ; Clinton himself on 22 Mar. 2000, op. cit.
42. *Asian Age*, 25 March 2000, p. 4.
43. Musharraf's press conference, op. cit. Parentheses added.
44. Doordarshan, 25 March 2000, 8. 40 p. m.
45. Star News, 25 March 2000, 9 p. m.
46. Ibid.
47. Courtney Rubin, "India Inc.," *The Washingtonian* reprinted in *Span*, US Embassy, New Delhi, Jan-Feb. 2000, pp. 10-16.
48. Stanley A. Weiss in *International Herald Tribune*, quoted in *Asian Age*, 4 Feb. 2000, p. 7.
49. Clinton's 22 March 2000 speech, op. cit.
50. Weiss, op. cit.
51. *Asian Age*, 22 Feb. 2000, p. 14.
52. Doctor Shankar Acharya, Chief Economic Advisor to the Indian govt. on CNN, 24 March 2000, 10 a. m.
53. "Fear of Flying," *Outlook*, op. cit., p. 35.
54. Star News, 16 Feb. 2000, 7. 45 a. m.
55. CNN, 22 March 2000, 9. 30 p. m.
56. *India Today*, 20 March 2000, p. 46.
57. Weiss, op. cit.
58. Pressler's interview, Star News, 21 March 2000, 8. 45 p. m.

59. Singh's interview, Star News, 24 March 2000, 9 p. m.
60. Madeleine K. Albright, "The Testing of American Foreign Policy," op. cit., p. 2.
61. Madeleine K. Albright, "Destination India," *International Herald Tribune*, reprinted in *Asian Age*, 23 March 2000, p. 7.
62. Two months prior to the visit, Karl Inderfurth had set the tone regarding the US recognition of India's leadership role in South Asia. *Asian Age*, 23 Jan. 2000, p. 1.
63. Text in *Asian Age*, 22 March 2000, p. 4.

Index